Beyond

In Partnership with

America Outdoors
American Bird Conservancy
American Hiking Society
American Motorcyclist Association
American Rivers
California Association of Four
    Wheel Drive Clubs, Inc.
Ducks Unlimited
Foundation for North American
    Wild Sheep
The Garden Club of America
International Mountain Bicycling
    Association

The Izaak Walton League of America
National Audubon Society
National Geographic Society
National Wild Turkey Federation
The Nature Conservancy
Pheasants Forever
Quail Unlimited
Rocky Mountain Elk Foundation
Scenic America
Society for American Archaeology
The Society for Historical
    Archaeology
Trout Unlimited

the National Parks

A Recreation Guide
to Public Lands in the West

Edited by Mary E. Tisdale and Bibi Booth

United States Department of the Interior
Bureau of Land Management

SMITHSONIAN INSTITUTION PRESS

Washington and London

Library of Congress Cataloging-in-Publication
Data

Beyond the national parks : a recreation guide to
   public lands in the West / edited by Mary E.
   Tisdale and Bibi Booth.
       p.   cm.
   Includes index.
   ISBN 1-56098-566-6 (pbk. : alk. paper)
   1. Outdoor recreation—West (U.S.)—
Guidebooks. 2. Public lands—West (U.S.)—
Guidebooks. 3. Wilderness areas—West
(U.S.)—Guidebooks. 4. West (U.S.)—Guide-
books. I. Tisdale, Mary E. II. Booth, Bibi.
GV191.42.W47B49   1998
917.804 ' 33—dc21   97-39347

British Library Cataloguing-in-Publication Data
available

Manufactured in the United States of America
05 04 03 02 01 00 99 98   5 4 3 2 1

∞ The paper used in this publication meets the
minimum requirements of the American National
Standard for Information Sciences—Permanence of
Paper for Printed Library Materials ANSI Z39.48-
1984.

For permission to reproduce illustrations appearing
in this book, please correspond directly with the
Bureau of Land Management. The Smithsonian
Institution Press does not retain reproduction rights
for these illustrations individually, or maintain a file
of addresses for photo sources.

PUBLISHER'S NOTE: Every attempt has been made
to verify the accuracy of the information contained
in this guidebook. If you discover errors, please
write to Editor, *Beyond the National Parks*, Bureau
of Land Management, Office of Environmental
Education and Volunteers, 1849 C Street, N.W.
(LS-406), Washington, D.C. 20240.

DESIGN: Janice Wheeler
TYPESETTING AND LAYOUT: Jennifer Kapus
PRODUCTION: Ken Sabol
SEPARATIONS AND PRINTING: World Color Press

Photographic sequence:

(page i) Offering panoramic views of the Black
Mountains, Oatman Road meanders toward its intersection with Historic Route 66 outside Kingman, Arizona. *(Photo by Gordon Warren, Arizona
State Office)*

(page ii-iii) Mountain bikers pause to take in the
spectacular alpine scenery surrounding Kokopelli's
Trail as it enters Utah from Colorado. *(Photo by
Frank Jensen)*

(page iv-v) UPPER LEFT The colors of the setting
sun paint the misty shoreline and rugged cliffs of
California's King Range National Conservation
Area. *(Courtesy BLM)* LOWER LEFT Alaska's
Campbell Tract is an urban oasis prized for its many
recreational opportunities and diverse resident
wildlife. *(Courtesy BLM)* RIGHT Bearing the red
and white standard of "Buffalo Soldier" cavalry-
men, recreational Indian Wars re-enactors lope
along Arizona's rocky Black Canyon Trail. *(Photo by
John Beckett, Beckett & Beckett Photography)*

(page vi-vii) Animal petroglyphs in a Utah canyon
offer a budding archaeologist a glimpse into the
past. *(Courtesy BLM)*

Arizona's sunny San Simon Valley boasts recreational opportunities ranging from hot-water bathing to off-highway vehicle riding. *(Photo by Diane Drobka, Arizona State Office)*

River-runners enjoy Utah's Green River, with Lighthouse Rock towering above. *(Photo by Frank Jensen)*

OPPOSITE **A fisherman helps his daughter reel in a big one at Arizona's Lake Pleasant, a short drive from the Black Canyon Trail.** *(Photo © John Beckett, Beckett & Beckett Photography)*

Contents

Best Bets

Attractions Listed by State

Appendices

   A

   B

A spectacular vista of
brilliant wildflowers, lush
evergreens, and snow-
capped peaks greets
springtime visitors to
Idaho's public lands.
(Courtesy BLM)

A subterranean waterfall cascades over multicolored rock walls in a Utah cave. *(Photo by Jerry Sintz, Utah State Office)*

OPPOSITE Utah's elk, mountain lion, and black bear are irresistible to wildlife-watchers, such as this father-daughter team. *(Courtesy BLM)*

Acknowledgments

Contributing BLM Writers/Editors
Washington, DC, Headquarters:
Richard Brook, Shelly Fischman,
Elizabeth Rieben, Leslie Schwager
Alaska: Danielle Allen, Ed Bovy
Arizona: Bette Arial, Bruce Asbjorn,
Dorothea J. Boothe, Ken Drew, Diane
Drobka, Tom Folks, Mike Henderson,
Susanna Henry, John Herron, Bernadette
Lovato, Jim Mahoney, Dorothy Morgan,
Terry O'Sullivan, Ed Perault, Deborah
Rawhouser, Matt Safford, Deborah
Stevens, Gary Stumpf, Diane Williams
California: Scott Adams, Michael Ayers,
Jonna Badgley, Stan Bales, Rich Burns,
Jim Cooper, Jeff Fontana, Jim Jennings,
Maria Kammerer, Brian Logan, Larry
Mercer, Patrick Mikesell, Meg Pearson,
Carman Prisco, Susan Richey, Doran
Sanchez, John Scull
Colorado: Roger Alexander, Arden An-
derson, LouAnn Jacobson, Wade Johnson,
Chip Marlow, Barb Perkins, Ken Smith
Eastern States: Cathy Applegate, Sunny
Johnson, Sylvia Jordan

Idaho: Bill Boggs, Wade Brown, LuVerne
Grussing, Frank Jenks, Jennifer E. Jones,
Terry Kincaid, Blaine Newman, Larry
Ridenhour, Pete Sozzi, Judi Zuckert
Montana: Ann Boucher
Nevada: Everell (Butch) Hayes, Maxine
Shane, Margaret Wolf, JoLynn Worley
New Mexico: Theresa Herrera
Oregon: Bob Alward, Mark Armstrong,
Rich Bailey, Becky Brown, Earl Burke,
John Craig, Kerry Haller, Tim Haller,
Jonne Hower, Dave Hunsaker, Doug
Huntington, Mel Ingeroi, Larry Johnston,
Lou Jurs, Jeanne Klein, Trish Lindaman,
Max Linn, Fred McDonald, Michael
Noack, Diane Priebe, Bob Ratcliffe, Tom
Sill, Todd Thompson, Fred Tomlins, Dave
Vickstrom, Cathi Wilbanks, Joe Williams,
Utah: Harry Barber, Robin Fehlau,
Sherry Foot, Steve Hedges, Lew Kirkman,
David Moore, Marilyn Peterson, Dennis
Willis
Wyoming: Dave Baker, Krystal Clair,
Mark Goldbach, Ray Hanson, Rod
Sanders, Andy Tenney, Cindy Wertz

The glacial Blue Lakes offer Nevada visitors both recreational opportunities and welcome solitude. *(Courtesy BLM)*

Graphics and Layout
Jennifer Kapus, National Applied Resource Sciences Center, Denver, CO

Preliminary Editing
Robert Woerner, National Business Center, Denver, CO

Technical Support
Jeremy Brodie, Washington, DC, headquarters

Special Thanks to:
- our Partner Organizations, for their dedicated efforts to preserve and foster enjoyment of the public lands
- BLM Director Pat Shea and BLM Director Emeritus Mike Dombeck
- Francis Pandolfi (formerly of BLM), whose enthusiasm for the riches of the public lands sparked the development of this guidebook
- BLM Management, including Gwen Mason, Assistant Director for Communications; Bob Johns, Deputy Assistant Director for Communications; and members of the Executive Leadership Team

Backpackers establish a primitive camp below the layered cliffs of Utah's Grand Staircase-Escalante National Monument.
(Courtesy BLM)

RIGHT **A 66-mile loop road offers visitors stunning Great Basin vistas and opportunities for wildlife encounters at Steens Mountain, Oregon.** *(Photo by Mark Armstrong)*

LEFT Colorado's San Juan Mountains provide a rugged backdrop for bikers pedaling the historic Alpine Loop. *(Courtesy Colorado State Office)*

LOWER LEFT Arizona teens study petroglyphs at Little Black Mountain as part of an academic scholarship competition hosted by BLM. *(Photo by John Beckett, Beckett & Beckett Photography)*

LOWER RIGHT Public lands sites, such as this wall of petroglyphs in Utah, act as open-air classrooms for students of natural and cultural resources. *(Photo by Kelly Rigby, Utah State Office)*

Children sketch prehistoric petroglyphs at an interactive exhibit at Wyoming's National Bighorn Sheep Interpretive Center. *(Courtesy National Bighorn Sheep Interpretive Center)*

Introduction

For Starters

They are the places you know about and the places you never imagined—cacti and canyons, arroyos and outcrops, glacial icefields and frozen tundra, wide-open vistas and solitary hideaways. They are your public lands.

This book offers you a glimpse of these places—lands that are as intriguing and diverse as America itself. Public lands are host to a number of outstanding yet relatively unknown places to hike, camp, fish, hunt, mountain bike, watch wildlife, or just kick back and relax.

The Bureau of Land Management (BLM) is the proud steward of 264 million acres of America's public lands. In celebration of BLM's 50th anniversary, many of our agency's partner organizations have agreed to reveal their favorite spots on the public lands. In addition, BLM employees from across the country have nominated their own "best bets." This book highlights these special places in hopes of sparking your interest in exploring your public lands.

A Little History

Public lands are the remnants of the vast tracts of land that were once known as the public domain. They were originally owned by the federal government and were mostly west of the Appalachians, except for those in Florida. National policy provided for the eventual transfer of many of these lands to private ownership in order to build the nation's economic foundation, encourage settlement of the West, and unite the vast expanses of territory into one nation. Of the original 1.8 bil-

lion acres of public domain, almost two-thirds went to citizens, corporations, and the states. Many of the remaining lands were set aside for national forests, wildlife refuges, and parks and monuments. A large portion of the lands not devoted to these purposes became the public lands managed by the BLM.

BLM: Fifty Years of Land Stewardship

In 1812, Congress established the General Land Office to administer the vast public domain. In 1934, the Taylor Grazing Act established the U.S. Grazing Service to manage the 170 million acres of the public domain that had become public rangelands. On July 16, 1946, President Harry Truman officiated over a marriage of sorts, merging the two agencies to create the Bureau of Land Management.

The new agency had a daunting task—to enforce thousands of laws, many conflicting, while managing over 400 million acres of land in tracts spread mostly throughout 11 western states and Alaska. Congress sorted out these laws and gave the BLM a clear set of marching orders (they called it a "mandate") with the Federal Land Policy and Management Act of 1976. This was welcome news: the BLM was to manage the public lands for the benefit of all Americans, with a policy of multiple use and sustained yield.

These lands generate over $1 billion in revenue for the nation each year while providing such necessities as coal, oil and gas, lumber, wildlife habitat, and grazing lands. The public lands are home to over 3,000 species of wildlife and a wide array of plants, some of which are rare or endangered. The BLM also protects an estimated 4 million archaeological and historic sites—from the campsites of the earliest human inhabitants to the historic "ghost" towns of the Old West.

As more and more people are discovering their public lands, recreation activities are playing a larger role. The BLM manages 2,022 miles of the Wild and Scenic River System, 4,200 miles of National Trails, 174,313 miles of fishable streams, 2,600,000 acres of lakes and reservoirs, and many other sites that offer outstanding recreation opportunities.

Your 264-Million-Acre Backyard

These public lands really do belong to you and to all Americans. As with any backyard, the best way to learn about it and enjoy it is firsthand. Why not get out there and walk on it, smell the air, hear the sounds, touch the earth? Get to know your public lands and develop a personal connection and commitment to these special places. During your visit, be a good steward. Pay attention to rules, such as

A visitor enjoys the serenity of biking through the Glade Run Trail System in New Mexico. *(Photo by Guadalupe Martinez, Farmington District Office)*

packing out trash and not picking flowers and plants, etc.

While the BLM encourages recreational use of public lands, remember that many of these places are wild and undeveloped—which often means no amenities or creature comforts. This book will help you understand what to expect.

The BLM's first and foremost obligation is to maintain and improve the health of the public lands so they will remain productive for current and future generations. Please keep in mind that you can help by following the suggestions in this book as you set out to discover and enjoy America's 264-million-acre backyard!

What This Guide Offers and How To Use It

First we take a thematic approach. Here, in a series of two-page presentations, we introduce our partners, describe their activities of choice, and list their favorite sites—unique and special places on the public lands. Immediately following that, the BLM folks reveal their selections for prime sites. Later in the book, we use a state-by-state format and take a geographic approach (with maps), showcasing these same sites in state groupings. If you're looking for several sites that are close to each other, look here. Since many of the sites offer more than one type of activity, they're also coded with activity and BLM partner icons (on partner-selected sites) to make them easier to use. Information about fees is noted here, too, along with information on accessibility for persons with disabilities.

About the Icons

For your convenience, here's a complete listing of the icons used in the state-by-state section for activities and partners.

Birdwatching

 Boating

 Fishing

 Hiking

 Historical, Archaeological, or Paleontological Attractions

 Horse Packing

 Hunting

 Off-highway Touring

 Plant Viewing

Rafting

 Scenic Drives

 Wild Horse and Burro Viewing

 Wildlife Viewing

 Other (includes such activities as Swimming and Rock Climbing)

AMERICA OUTDOORS

DUCKS UNLIMITED

National Audubon Society

QUAIL UNLIMITED

AMERICAN BIRD CONSERVANCY

FOUNDATION FOR NORTH AMERICAN WILD SHEEP

NATIONAL GEOGRAPHIC SOCIETY

ROCKY MOUNTAIN ELK FOUNDATION

American Hiking Society

The Garden Club of America

NATIONAL WILD TURKEY FEDERATION

SCENIC AMERICA

AMA
AMERICAN MOTORCYCLIST ASSOCIATION

SAA
SOCIETY FOR AMERICAN ARCHAEOLOGY

American Rivers

I·M·B·A
INTERNATIONAL MOUNTAIN BICYCLING ASSOCIATION

The Nature Conservancy

SOCIETY for HISTORICAL ARCHAEOLOGY

CALIFORNIA ASSOCIATION OF 4WD CLUBS INC.

THE IZAAK WALTON LEAGUE 1922-1997

PHEASANTS forever

TROUT UNLIMITED

Want More Information?

This guide pays tribute to the diversity of the public lands and the recreational activities available on them. But it represents just a fraction of the fun and adventures that can be had out there, in your 264-million-acre backyard. We would also like to acknowledge that the partners mentioned in this book represent only a small fraction of the groups that have been working with BLM for many years at the local and national levels to conserve public land resources and provide quality services to the public. If you'd like some more information, we can point you in the right direction. There are state recreation maps and a National Recreation Guide (actually, a detailed nationwide map) for the public lands available from BLM State Offices. Their addresses are listed in Appendix A. More information about individual sites is available through the BLM field office listed with each site description.

Please note that as used in this guide, the term "public lands" refers to those lands managed by the Bureau of Land Management, and information is included for BLM-managed sites only. Since much of this public land is intermingled with additional federal or state land, however, you may wish to check in advance with National and State Forest, Park, and Refuge officials for information on recreational activities on adjacent lands.

Check the back of the book for these appendices. Appendix A provides the addresses, phone numbers, and Internet addresses for each of the BLM State Offices as well as for the BLM headquarters office in Washington, D.C. Contact our State Offices directly to obtain additional information about the sites covered in this book or for specific information about ad-ditional recreational opportunities on the public lands. Appendix B lists the names and addresses of BLM partners that selected sites for this book. Our partners are experts in their fields. Contact them directly to find out more about what they do and what they have to offer.

Planning Ahead

The public lands offer unparalleled opportunities to get "off the beaten path"—but with these adventures come responsibilities. Whatever your choice of activities, please take steps to minimize your impact. (See next section for "Leave No Trace," "Tread Lightly," and other outdoor ethics guidelines.) Many of the attractions in this guide are in very remote areas, and campsites are often undeveloped. In some instances, help may be hundreds of miles away. Many roads require four-wheel-drive vehicles and are treacherous. To ensure a safe and enjoyable trip, please take sensible precautions. Prepare for weather and the hazards associated with certain poisonous plants and animals. Realize that at some point you will become hungry and thirsty, and pack accordingly. Let someone know your itinerary. Pay attention to the advisories included in this book. If you are planning to venture into a backcountry area, become familiar with backcountry rules and carry first-aid supplies and other necessities. When planning your visit, contact the BLM office closest to your destination (see Appendix A for addresses). It also is advisable to obtain detailed maps from BLM and other sources in advance of your trip. Topographic maps are available from the U.S. Geological Survey—please telephone 1-800-HELPMAP for ordering information. A little planning will help make your outing fun **and** safe.

The rugged cliffs of
Arizona's Aravaipa Canyon
are softened by stands of
cottonwood and willow.
*(Photo by Diane Drobka, Safford
Field Office)*

Doing Your Part

While we encourage you to get out and enjoy the lands you own, like any landowner, you have a responsibility to help keep your investment in good shape. Following are guidelines to use while enjoying your favorite outdoor recreational activities. Most of these just require good common sense; some are very specific to the particular activity. Please read over these and use them as a guide while you are out on your public lands. That way, you can play an important role in helping the BLM care for your favorite places on the public lands.

Leave No Trace

Leave No Trace is a national outdoor ethics program that offers these guidelines to minimize your impact. These apply to whatever activity you may choose.

- Choose a route, equipment, and clothing that are appropriate for your goals and outdoor skill level.

- Follow established trails in small groups, and walk single file. Stay off developing, user-created trails to allow those areas time to recover.
- Select off-trail routes that avoid fragile areas, particularly wetlands; unstable slopes; and places covered by shrubs, dense-leafed herbs, or ferns.
- Take rest stops only in areas where your presence will not damage vegetation.
- Camp only in durable areas, preferably in established campsites.
- Learn about animals indigenous to the place you are visiting in order to avoid disturbing them.
- Be fastidious about animal-proof food storage, and clean up leftover scraps. Pack out whatever you pack in, as well as all litter.
- Don't continue to approach animals when they are aware of your presence.
- Leave what you find; allow others a sense of discovery by leaving rocks,

Mesquite and yucca dot the golden sands of Arizona's Hot Well Dunes Recreation Area, a favorite of four-wheel-drive adventurers and connoisseurs of its artesian "hot tubs." (Photo by Diane Drobka, Safford Field Office)

plants, cultural artifacts, and other objects of interest as you found them.

Hiking and Backpacking

In addition to the Leave No Trace Guidelines above, hikers and backpackers should observe the following guidelines:

- When hiking, avoid taking shortcuts across meadows or switchbacks—doing so will prevent severe erosion and trail damage.
- Properly dispose of human waste and waste water. Use established latrines whenever they are available, or dig individual "catholes" at least 200 feet from camp, water, and trails. Cover catholes after use.
- Use fire responsibly. Always carry a gas stove to cook your meals. If a campfire is necessary, use packed-in wood or charcoal, keep the fire small, and always contain it in a fire pan. Burn your fire down to white ash, let it cool completely, and pack out all of the ash.
- Do all washing at least 200 feet from the nearest water source. Use hot water and a minimum amount of soap.

Water and Wilderness

In addition to the above, to minimize your impact in and around rivers, streams, or lakes:

- Select campsites and kitchen sites where river floods will wash away all signs of your stay.
- Avoid camping in the riparian zone—the fragile, green area along the bank of the river. Camp in an established site, on a sand beach, or at least 100 feet from the river.
- All boating parties should carry a portable, reusable waste disposal system that can be flushed out at a proper waste facility.

- Use fire responsibly. See above guidelines.

Wilderness areas are specially designated to preserve places undisturbed by people. In addition to following the guidelines above, to keep wilderness areas pristine:

- Make sure that any campsite you make in a wilderness area is at least 200 feet from trails, lakes, and streams.
- Properly dispose of human waste and waste water. See guidelines above.
- Use fire responsibly. See guidelines above.
- Take along lightweight equipment requiring few pack animals.
- Keep animals 200 feet or more from water sources, and move them frequently.
- Bring food for pack animals to use in

Autumn in Arizona turns the San Pedro River's "ribbon of green" into a golden thread of life, as thousands of neotropical migratory birds follow its corridor south for the winter. *(Photo by Mary Cordano, San Pedro Project Office)*

areas where feed is limited, or where grazing is restricted. This food must be certified weed free.
- Remove or scatter manure, and pack out leftover hay or straw. Hay and straw must be certified weed free.

Hunting and Fishing
While enjoying the sport of fishing, please keep in mind this voluntary Angler's Code: The ethical angler
- supports conservation efforts.
- practices "catch and release" where needed.
- doesn't pollute and properly recycles and disposes of trash.
- doesn't release bait into waters.
- practices safe angling and boating and obeys fishing and boating regulations.
- respects other anglers' and property owners' rights.
- shares fishing knowledge and skills, and promotes ethical sportfishing.

The Hunter's Code of Conduct was created cooperatively and produced by The Izaak Walton League of America. Responsible hunting provides unique challenges and rewards. The future of the sport, however, depends on each hunter's behavior and ethics. The ethical hunter

- respects the environment, wildlands, and property rights.
- shows consideration for non-hunters.
- hunts safely, legally, and only with other ethical hunters.
- supports wildlife and habitat conservation.
- passes on an ethical hunting tradition.
- strives to improve his or her outdoor skills and understanding of wildlife.

Biking and Driving
While touring by bike, car, or off-road vehicle, please refer to the following guidelines.

Mountain Biking
- Ride on open trails only; respect trail and road closures.
- Be sensitive to the dirt beneath you. Even on open (legal) trails, you should not ride on certain soils after a rain.
- Control your bicycle; inattention can cause problems.
- Obey all bicycle speed regulations and recommendations.
- Always yield trail; make known your approach well in advance.
- Never spook wild or domestic animals.

Bicyclists enjoy an easy ride through Fort Ord's verdant maritime environment.
(Photo by Steve Addington, Hollister Resource Area)

- Plan ahead: know your equipment, your ability, and the area in which you are riding, and prepare accordingly.

Back Country Byways (Scenic Drives)
- Obey all signs.
- Know where you are. Use only roads legally accessible to the public. Get maps and information from the BLM before you start.
- Get permission from land owners before walking, hunting, or fishing on private lands.
- Leave gates as you found them — open or closed.
- Avoid any travel that will increase roadway rutting or otherwise damage the land. Don't drive on unpaved roads during storms, and don't create new roads.
- Don't shoot at signs, damage range improvements, or harass livestock.
- Report any vandalism you see to BLM.

Off-Highway Touring
- "Tread Lightly."
- Travel only where permitted.
- Respect the rights of others.
- Educate yourself about the responsible use of off-highway vehicles.

An off-highway driver maneuvers over a rocky section of the Chappie/Shasta Off-Highway Vehicle Recreation Area. *(Photo by Eric J. Lundquist, Esq., American Motorcyclist Association)*

- Avoid using motor vehicles near streams, meadows, or wildlife.
- Drive and travel responsibly.

Visiting Archaeological, Fossil, and Historic Sites
- Treat rock art, historic structures, and archaeological features with respect.
- Avoid moving anything, touching walls, or climbing on the roof or walls of prehistoric or historic structures when walking around a site.

This replica of the John Jarvie General Store in Utah is furnished with late-1800's artifacts and the original safe that figured prominently in a historic robbery and murder on the site. *(Photo by Jerry Sintz, Utah State Office)*

- Enjoy rock art by viewing, sketching, or photographing. Never chalk, trace, or otherwise touch rock art.
- Never build fires in or around archaeological or historic sites.
- Stay on trails that have been built through a site.
- Show respect for the many cultural sites that are of ancestral importance to Native Americans.
- Report looting and vandalism to a BLM ranger or other local authority.

Wildlife

To avoid disturbing wildlife
- Wear natural colors and unscented lotions. Remove glasses that glint.
- Walk softly. Hide your figure behind boulders or vegetation, and try not to throw a shadow.
- Resist the temptation to "save" baby animals—"mom" is usually watching from a safe distance.
- Let animals eat their natural foods.
- Let patience reward you—don't provoke animals into activity.
- Use binoculars or zoom lenses to get a close-up view of animals. Give nests a wide berth.
- Move slowly, smoothly, and steadily, and approach animals in a roundabout way, never directly. Avert your gaze, as animals may interpret a direct stare as a threat.

Wildflower Conservation and Etiquette

Over 15,000 different species of native plants are recognized in the United States and Canada, with new species being discovered each year. To help protect these plants
- "Leave No Trace."
- Please—don't pick the flowers!

Weeds choke out native wildflowers and cause significant ecological damage. Weeds are spreading at an alarming rate on public lands. To help prevent the spread of weeds
- Refrain from picking wildflowers or plants, many of which may actually be invasive weeds. Picking and transporting them can spread their seeds to new areas.
- Check with the local ranger or land manager before starting a back country hike in order to identify the problem weed species in the area. Report any infestations you may come across.
- Clean all camping gear, clothing, and shoes before leaving an area in order to avoid inadvertently taking weed seeds along with you.
- Do not camp in, lead pack animals into, or hike through weed-infested areas.
- Drive only on established roads or trails away from weed-infested areas.
- Carry and use only certified "weed-free" feed for pack animals, beginning four days before entering backcountry areas.

Owls peer from the lava cliffs of Idaho's Snake River Birds of Prey Recreation Area. *(Courtesy BLM)*

The Rogue River, along the Galice-Hellgate Back Country Byway, is one of 20 designated Wild and Scenic Rivers that wind through 767 miles of Oregon countryside. *(Courtesty BLM)*

The fly-fishing aficiona-
dos of Trout Unlimited,
dedicated to fish habitat
restoration and the
re-establishment of native
species, have designated
Wyoming's Green River
one of America's "Great
Trout Streams."
(Photo by Frank Jensoen)

The Partners

The BLM partners that participated in the creation of this guide are private organizations that share common goals with BLM: the enthusiastic appreciation, conservation, and wise use of the irreplaceable treasures of our public lands. These partners have demonstrated their commitment to these objectives through contributions to resource projects or their efforts to educate the public about public lands protection and conservation. Whether the need is close to home or far off in the wilderness, BLM has been blessed with partners that help us care for our public lands.

On the occasion of BLM's 50th anniversary, when the concept for this guidebook was developed, we asked a sampling of our established partner groups to identify public land sites of special significance to their members or of particular importance to their organizational goals or activities. Lush wilderness areas, pristine trout streams, thrilling whitewater, challenging off-highway vehicle trails, intriguing petroglyphs—if they're out there on the public lands, you can bet our partners have taken the trouble to truly know and appreciate these incomparable sites. And while their members certainly enjoy the recreational opportunities afforded by these special areas, our partners are also dedicated to the serious business of focusing public attention on natural and cultural resources and our mutual responsibility for their conservation.

The selections presented in this guidebook are those sites that were determined to be suitable for recreational visitation at this time. In order to protect the fragile resources present at various sites, some partner nominations could not be included here.

With more than 260 million acres of public lands to manage, BLM is grateful for our partners' dedication to the very special treasures within our care.

Feathery cottonwoods
shade a shallow creek deep
within Arizona's Aravaipa
Canyon Wilderness, located
less than 50 miles from
Safford. *(photo by
Robert E. Parker)*

Getaways Close to Home
Picnic Spots Near Urban Areas
Selected by THE NATURE CONSERVANCY

You live in an urban area, yet there are days when heading downtown or going to the mall has zero appeal. What's needed is a little solitude — someplace quiet, where the noises are nature's and where a hike is on a trail, not a sidewalk. Camping would be a welcome option and maybe a little photography to remind yourself that you'd actually been there, done that. And yes, not too far from home. The Nature Conservancy has identified several opportunities for you, and most are located close to big cities. For example, you can travel east of Tucson to the Muleshoe Ranch Cooperative Management Area, where you'll find yourself among 49,000 acres of land offering wonderful wildlife viewing. If you're seeking to escape the hustle and bustle of Los Angeles, journey east to the Big Morongo Canyon, one of the premier birdwatching sites in southern California. Visitors there can also hike the boardwalk to a ridge and view the canyon, or watch the wildflowers shimmer in the breezes along the dry desert wash. These getaways are ideal for the whole family. So what are you waiting for? Pack up your gear, load up the family, and head on out!

About The Nature Conservancy
The Nature Conservancy preserves habitats and species by buying the lands and waters they need to survive. The Conservancy operates the largest private system of nature sanctuaries in the world — more than 1,500 preserves in the United States alone. Some are small parcels, while others cover thousands of acres. All of them safeguard imperiled species of plants and animals. The Conservancy has protected more than 9 million acres of ecologically significant land in the United States, Latin America, the Caribbean, and the Pacific.

Favorite Sites
Big Morongo Canyon (CA)
Cosumnes River Preserve (CA)
Muleshoe Ranch Cooperative
    Management Area (AZ)
San Miguel River Special Management
    Area (CO)
San Pedro Riparian National
    Conservation Area (AZ)
West Eugene Wetlands (OR)

Whitewater rafters
negotiate one of the many
prime western whitewater
rivers, with the help of a
professional guide.
(© Drewelow, Stock Imagery)

Wet and Wild

Outstanding Rivers

Selected by AMERICAN RIVERS

Rivers have long served as the unpaved highways and byways of America. Many are places where you can embark on an exciting fishing excursion hoping to land the big one, watch wildlife in its natural state, or experience a thrilling whitewater rafting ride. Many rivers and segments are jewels that have not yet been discovered. If fishing is what you're after, try Idaho's Lower Salmon River. For those seeking a pleasant float, try canoeing, rafting, or kayaking in Arizona's Gila Box Riparian National Conservation Area. For those in pursuit of the ultimate thrill, Westwater Canyon in Utah offers the "extreme" in whitewater rafting.

About American Rivers

American Rivers is a national conservation organization dedicated to protecting and restoring America's river systems and to fostering a river stewardship ethic. Founded in 1973 to expand the number of rivers protected by the National Wild and Scenic Rivers System, American Rivers has a membership of 20,000 people. Its staff works cooperatively with conservation groups; local citizens and businesses; and various federal, state, and tribal agencies to build coalitions and provide technical support to strengthen local and regional conservation efforts that protect rivers. Along with its conservation efforts, American Rivers promotes public awareness about the importance of healthy rivers and the threats that face them. American Rivers' programs address three key elements of healthy rivers: headwaters, natural flows, and riparian zones.

Favorite Sites

American River Recreation Areas (CA)
Aravaipa Canyon Wilderness (AZ)
Bill Williams River (AZ)
Bruneau - Jarbidge Rivers (ID)
Fortymile National Wild and
 Scenic River (AK)
Gila Box Riparian National
 Conservation Area (AZ)
Lower Salmon River (ID)
Orilla Verde Recreation Area (NM)
Paria Canyon (AZ)
Rogue River Ranch (OR)
Ruby Canyon/Colorado River (CO)
San Pedro Riparian National
 Conservation Area (AZ)
Squirrel River (AK)
Virgin River Canyon
 Recreation Area (AZ)
Westwater Canyon (UT)
Wild Rivers Recreation Area (NM)

A wildlife educator
captivates a young student
at a tidepool along
Washington's rocky coast.
(© 1991 Johanne E. Lotter,
Tom Stack & Assoc.)

Where the Mountains Meet the Sea

Areas to Explore along the Pacific Coast

Selected by the NATIONAL GEOGRAPHIC SOCIETY

Get your feet wet on a black sand beach or stretch your legs on a mountain trail. They're only a few miles apart, but a good portion of that is vertical. The King Range National Conservation Area on the northern Pacific coast is where the mountains meet the sea. The coastline is framed by forested mountains with sharply defined canyons that host roaring creeks and rivers, and a variety of habitats that feature numerous species of birds, reptiles, and mammals. It's tidal pools and mountain tops, beauty and solitude.

About the National Geographic Society

The National Geographic Society was established in 1888 with a singular objective: to increase and diffuse geographic knowledge. Today the Society fulfills that mission through worldwide scientific research and exploration, geography education delivered in the classroom, print and electronic media, and community outreach programs. In 1993, National Geographic launched an unprecedented campaign to gather crucial information on water resources and communicate it to its members and the world.

Favorite Sites

Cape Blanco Lighthouse (OR)
Fort Ord (CA)
King Range National Conservation Area (CA)
New River Area of Critical Environmental Concern (OR)
Point Sal (CA)
Turn Point Island (WA)
Yaquina Head Outstanding Natural Area (OR)

Yaquina Head offers visitors the opportunity to observe wildlife from many habitats: whales and seals in the ocean, terrestrial and marine birds nesting on land, and a wide variety of tidepool life. *(Courtesy BLM)*

Autumn vegetation along
New Mexico's Rio Grande
provides a visual feast for
recreationists and a haven
for diverse animal life.
*(© 1987 Matt Bradley, Tom Stack
& Assoc.)*

Variety in Bloom

Outstanding Plants

Sponsored by THE GARDEN CLUB OF AMERICA

Whether it's a view of the green lush forests of Oregon, the cottonwood and willow oases of the Mojave and Sonoran deserts, or the magnificent display of wildflowers in California's Short Canyon, a detour off the beaten path rewards the adventurous traveler. The Garden Club of America has chosen several areas throughout the West that are visually spectacular visitor destination sites, with regal flora and fauna. "Walk the walk" on the boardwalk in Big Morongo Canyon, a cottonwood/willow oasis in the California desert where lush vegetation (and the critters it attracts) stands in vibrant contrast to the surrounding desert. Or head up to the rarer air and higher elevations of the Mosquito Peaks of Colorado, which support flora of global significance. If there were ever a time to stop and smell the roses . . .

About The Garden Club of America

The Garden Club of America (GCA) is a national organization made up of member clubs that apply their energies and exper-

tise to projects in their communities and the nation. Founded in 1913, GCA has become a recognized leader in the fields of horticulture, conservation, historic preservation, and civic planning. Member clubs are involved in civic endeavors on local, national, and international levels. To further its goals, the GCA works with major organizations such as the World Wildlife Fund, the Smithsonian Institution, and the Center for Plant Conservation. A primary goal of the GCA is the protection of natural resources. GCA has helped to protect endangered plants and their habitats and prevent air, water, and soil pollution, and has taken other initiatives to ensure the health of our land and resources for future generations.

Favorite Sites

Big Morongo Canyon (CA)
Dripping Springs Natural Area (NM)
Fish Slough Area of Critical Environmental Concern (CA)
Fort Ord (CA)
Garden Park Fossil Area (CO)
Mosquito Peaks (CO)
Orilla Verde Recreation Area (NM)
Owens Peak Wilderness Area (Short Canyon) (CA)
Red Hills Area of Critical Environmental Concern (CA)
Rough and Ready Flat Area of Critical Environmental Concern (OR)
Timbered Crater Wilderness Study Area (CA)

Idaho's rivers present boating and hiking enthusiasts with challenging recreational opportunities.
(Photo by Don Smurthwaite, Idaho State Office)

Boots and Paddles
Whitewater Raft Trips and Wilderness Trail Adventures
Selected by AMERICA OUTDOORS

Your muscles ache a bit, but you don't break your stride. The sun is reflecting off the cottonwoods and there's a breeze moving down the canyon. You're part of the picture, indigenous, like the local flora and fauna. Whether you want to put some miles on your hiking boots or test your skills with a paddle, you can find a setting for these adventures among the remote wilderness and whitewater sites suggested by America Outdoors. If a ride on the wild side intrigues you, then check out the volcanic gorge of the Rio Grande River in New Mexico. If rollin' on the river is more your style, try the somewhat calmer waters of the Green River where it flows through the Labyrinth Canyon in Utah, with an eyeful of wildflowers and wildlife as an added attraction. Whatever your tastes or your destination may be, the unique locales selected by America Outdoors will provide you with serenity, adventure, and scenic beauty.

About America Outdoors

America Outdoors is an organization representing over 450 companies that provide outdoor recreation services and equipment. These outfitter companies offer a wide array of outdoor recreation experiences, including whitewater rafting, canoeing, kayaking, horse packing, camping, and fishing. Many of these outdoor trips are conducted by seasoned outfitters and guides. America Outdoors also sponsors an annual National River Cleanup Week each May to encourage member organizations to organize local cleanups of streams, rivers, and lakeshores.

Favorite Sites

Rivers

Bruneau - Jarbidge Rivers (ID)
Dolores River (CO)
Green River (UT)
Merced River Recreation Area (CA)
San Juan River (UT)
Wild Rivers Recreation Area (NM)

Trails

Aravaipa Canyon Wilderness (AZ)
Pacific Crest National Scenic Trail - Owens Peak Segment (CA)
Table Rock Wilderness (OR)
Table Top Wilderness (AZ)

A backpacker is surrounded by wildflowers along the 26-mile Lost Coast National Recreation Trail. *(Photo by Bob Wick, Arcata Resource Area)*

Walk on the Wild Side
Great Hiking Trails
Selected by AMERICAN HIKING SOCIETY

You can listen to the ocean roar as you feel the grainy sand shifting beneath your feet, or lean on a Bristlecone pine for a moment as you prepare to trek up beyond the tree line, with nothing above you but the sky. Strike out for America's great hiking trails and learn something about yourself and your country. American Hiking Society has selected five trails with exceptional recreational, historical, or scenic value. Whether you're inclined to hike up mountains or across flat lands, there's sure to be a great trail waiting for you. So lace up your boots and "take a walk on the wild side"!

About American Hiking Society
American Hiking Society promotes hiking and works to establish, protect, and maintain foot trails in America. In partnership with outdoor organizations, the business community, and public land managers, American Hiking Society is spearheading the effort to establish a national network of trails that will link people and places together so that one day people will be able to walk from their backyards to the backcountry and home again without ever leaving trails. This will ensure that millions of people have places to walk and enjoy the outdoors.

Favorite Sites
Black Canyon Trail (AZ)
King Crest Trail (CA)
Pacific Crest National Scenic Trail – Owens Peak Segment (CA)
Pacific Crest National Scenic Trail – Siskiyou/Cascades Segment (OR)
San Pedro Riparian National Conservation Area (AZ)

Palo verde, prickly pear, and barrel cactus line the Black Canyon Trail northwest of Phoenix, Arizona. *(Photo by David Smith, Arizona State Office)*

Mountain bikers are some of the most ardent recreationists on public lands. (© Bob Winsett, Tom Stack & Assoc.)

Mountain Biking through History

Historic Mountain Bike Trails

Selected by the
INTERNATIONAL MOUNTAIN BICYCLING
ASSOCIATION

Imagine yourself perched atop a metal frame that's connected to two knobby tires while skirting the edge of a canyon, bumping along a dry arroyo trail, or ascending some 4,000 feet above sea level to experience some of America's most remarkable natural and cultural resources. To help you pedal your way through history, the International Mountain Bicycling Association recommends four trails that should whet your appetite.

For a long-distance ride, travel the 70-mile Old Yosemite Valley Railroad route from Merced, California, to Yosemite National Park. If you're a novice rider, or you are limited by time constraints, try Arizona's 8.5-mile Sunshine Loop, just south of the Utah border. Here you'll view magnificent dry washes that rise to colorful buttes featuring 6,000-year-old petroglyphs. So pump up your tires, fill up your water bottles, and strap on your helmet. It's time to go exploring!

About the International Mountain Bicycling Association

The International Mountain Bicycling Association (IMBA) promotes mountain bicycling that is environmentally sound and socially responsible. Over 250 cycling clubs, as well as many individual cyclists, are members. The Association educates mountain cyclists on responsible trail use, and supports trail maintenance and other volunteer projects initiated by its affiliate clubs. It also promotes creative trail management practices that encourage trail use while protecting the environment. IMBA champions a common set of riding ethics called "IMBA Rules of the Trail."

Favorite Sites

Glade Run Trail System (NM)
Kokopelli's Trail (CO)
Merced River Trail (CA)
Sunshine Loop Trail (AZ)

Rugged terrain challenges
motorbike enthusiasts in
California desert off-
highway vehicle areas.

*(©1993 Inga Spence, Tom Stack
& Assoc.)*

Of Trails and Treads
Off-highway Trails for Motorcyclists
Selected by the
AMERICAN MOTORCYCLIST ASSOCIATION

Steel and chrome, earth and sky, wind and water. Your bike vibrates and the landscape beckons with greens and browns and blues. The trail looms ahead. You grip the handlebars in anticipation of the ride ahead and savor the moment. From the cactus and canyons of the Johnson Valley Off-Highway Vehicle Recreation Area to the geysers of the Red Elephant Mine (not to worry—no "Pachyderm Crossing" signs!), you can stop and smell the cypresses or glide by historic gold mines. Enjoy!

About the American Motorcyclist Association

The American Motorcyclist Association (AMA) is a non-profit organization with 210,000 members and more than 1,400 affiliated clubs. Since 1924, the Associa-tion has worked with various government agencies and private organizations to pursue, promote, and protect the interests of motorcyclists. Many members enjoy the recreational opportunities found on BLM trails and Back Country Byways. The Association sponsors programs and contests encouraging motorcyclist involvement in charitable work and community service, including partnering with agencies to enhance the public lands experience. AMA advocates responsible use of public lands by promoting safe riding techniques, rules on motorcycling noise and equipment, and the promotion of "Tread Lightly!" low-impact principles and education.

Favorite Sites

Chappie/Shasta Off-Highway Vehicle
   Recreation Area (CA)
Cow Mountain Recreation Area (CA)
Johnson Valley Off-Highway Vehicle
   Recreation Area (CA)
Red Elephant Mine Trail (CA)

A motorcyclist negotiates a Johnson Valley off-highway vehicle trail across the arid, rocky terrain typical of many southern California deserts. *(Photo by Doran Sanchez, California Desert District)*

In four-wheel-drive
vehicles, modern-day
pioneers explore one of the
California desert's less-
traveled historic roads.
*(Photo by Doran Sanchez,
California Desert District)*

In Gear

Off-Highway Trails for Four-Wheel-Drive Vehicles

Selected by the
CALIFORNIA ASSOCIATION OF
FOUR WHEEL DRIVE CLUBS, INC.

Once traversed by people on horseback, today's off-highway trails are now places where you can feel the thrill and excitement of driving over rocky terrain, through rivers, and up and down steep inclines. From California's rugged desert to the bizarre landscape of the Clear Creek Area near Hollister, California, the California Association of Four Wheel Drive Clubs, Inc., has identified several trails where you're sure to be challenged and guaranteed to witness spectacular vistas. For example, if you're inclined to test your limits and those of your vehicle, try the Aftershock, Sledgehammer, and Jackhammer Trails at the Johnson Valley Off-Highway Vehicle Recreation Area in Southern California. If you'd rather absorb scenery than bumps, try the Volcanic Tablelands in California for a breathtaking view of the White Mountains and the Sierra Nevada Range.

About the California Association of Four Wheel Drive Clubs, Inc.

The California Association of Four Wheel Drive Clubs, Inc. (CA4WDC) promotes the responsible use of public lands by developing programs and projects to teach conservation, education, and safety to its members and the general public. The Association is committed to the betterment of vehicle-oriented outdoor recreation, and works closely with other trail organizations and agencies to identify, designate, and maintain quality driving opportunities on public lands. CA4WDC encourages members (clubs, individuals, and businesses) to complete volunteer projects to help the BLM achieve healthy, sustainable ecosystems.

Favorite Sites

Bradshaw Trail (CA)
Johnson Valley Off-Highway Vehicle
Recreation Area (CA)
Molina Ghost Run Trail (CA)
Volcanic Tablelands (CA)

A desert tortoise moves leisurely through California desert wildflowers.
(© John Gerlach, Tom Stack & Assoc.)

Picture This
Scenic Byways with Outstanding Photo Opportunities
Selected by SCENIC AMERICA

Whether it's a Sunday drive or a family vacation you're after, make sure to pack your camera, because you're about to embark on an unlimited outdoor adventure as you traverse any one of our nation's Back Country Byways. Depending on the Byway you choose, you may see wildlife, such as moose, elk, antelope, wild burros, ducks, geese, and swans; ancient petroglyphs and fossil areas; rivers; unusual geologic formations; and historic mining areas and ghost towns. If you're looking for Byways with the most outstanding photo opportunities, then Scenic America has some recommendations for you. For a trip back through time, saddle up your vehicle and hop on the Pony Express Trail. Time's a-wastin'—you have mail to deliver. And beware, saddle sores are compliments of the ride! For a spectacular view of the desert, take a drive on the Red Rock Canyon Byway. Here you'll see plants, animals, and geologic features unique to the Mojave Desert. If you're lucky, you might catch a glimpse of a burro or two, or maybe even a bighorn sheep.

About Scenic America

Scenic America is a network of thousands of Americans dedicated to conserving their scenic resources by fighting visual pollution and promoting visual quality. Through a program of education, advocacy, and direct assistance, Scenic America helps communities around the nation conserve their urban parkways, rural and scenic roadways, and unique characteristics. Scenic America played a leading role in the creation of the National Scenic Byways Program. Today, members support government policies that preserve critical resources, and help citizens develop plans to conserve scenic areas along roadways and in their communities.

Favorite Sites

Alpine Loop (CO)
Black Hills Back Country Byway (AZ)
Galice - Hellgate Back Country
   Byway (OR)
Garnet Range (MT)
Gold Belt Scenic Byway (CO)
Graves Creek to Marial Back Country
   Byway (OR)
Pony Express National Historic Trail (UT)
Red Rock Canyon National Conservation
   Area (NV)

ADVENTURES IN THE PAST . . .

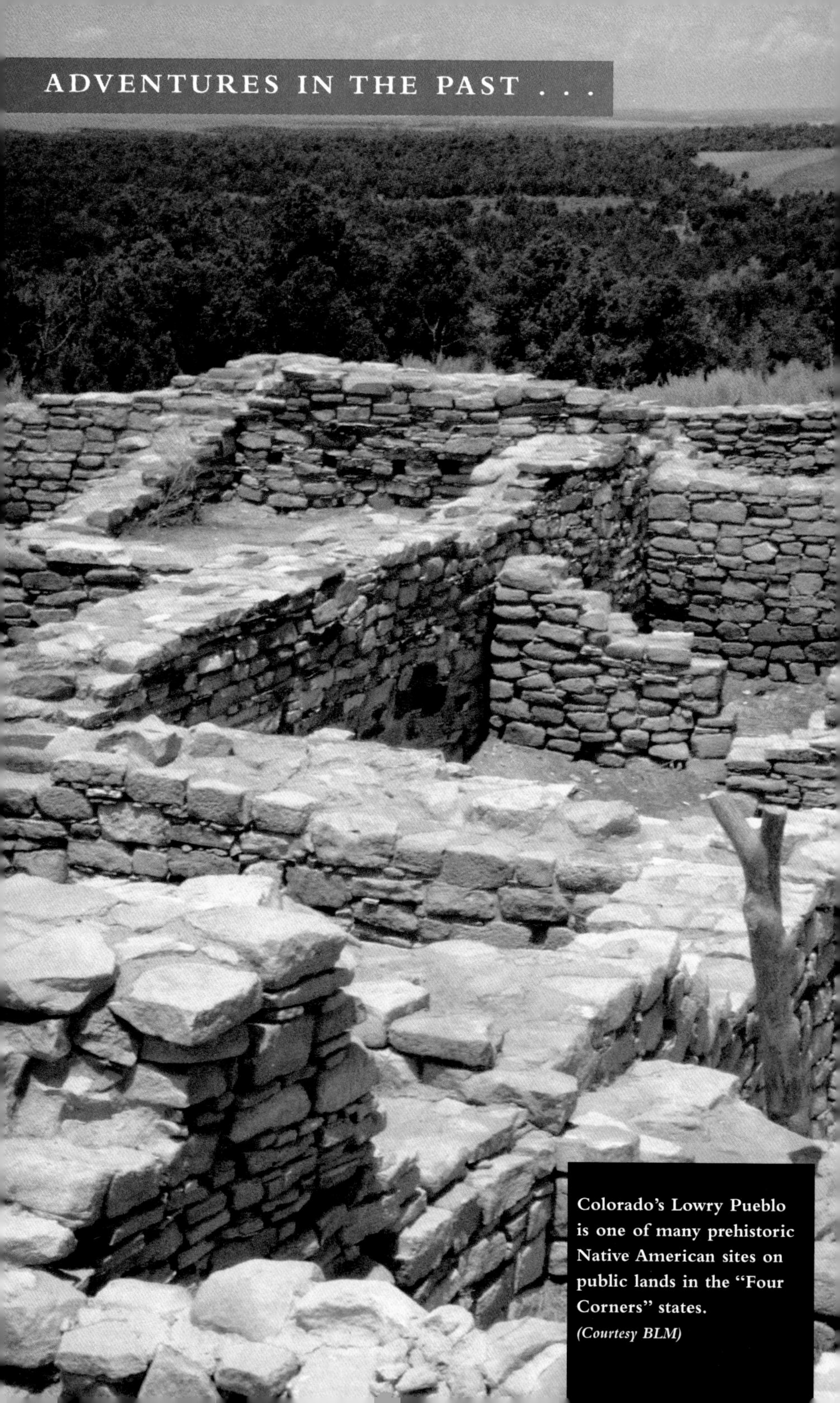

Colorado's Lowry Pueblo is one of many prehistoric Native American sites on public lands in the "Four Corners" states. *(Courtesy BLM)*

Adventures Through Prehistory
Outstanding Archaeological Sites
Selected by the
SOCIETY FOR AMERICAN ARCHAEOLOGY

Reach back though the mists of time and connect with the past. Archaeologists have woven the threads together and sifted through the clues at a number of diverse and unique archaeological sites on the public lands. Stand on a windswept limestone outcrop north of the Arctic Circle, the site of a prehistoric Eskimo hunting camp in the spectacular Brooks Range, America's northernmost mountains. Scan the horizon for caribou and Dall sheep the way the ancients did 4,000 years ago. You might prefer to walk through the ruined village of an ancient people in the canyonlands of the Southwest. Caves and caches. Pueblos and petroglyphs. Rock shelters. Go back to where it all began.

About the Society for American Archaeology
The Society for American Archaeology (SAA) is an international organization dedicated to the research, interpretation, and protection of the archaeological heritage of the Americas. Since its inception in 1934, SAA has worked to stimulate interest in American archaeology, promoted the conservation of archaeological resources, encouraged public access and appreciation of archaeology, opposed looting and the sale of looted archaeological materials, and been a focal point for individuals and organizations interested in the archaeology of the Americas.

Favorite Sites
Baker Caves (ID)
Casamero Chacoan Outlier (NM)
Grimes Point/Hidden Cave Archaeological Site (NV)
Lowry Ruins National Historic Landmark (CO)
Macks Canyon Site (OR)
Mosquito Lake (AK)
Mule Canyon Ruin (UT)
Murray Springs Clovis Site (AZ)

A puzzling petroglyph is one of many prehistoric artifacts at Colorado's Lowry Ruins. *(Courtesy BLM)*

Ruts carved by pioneer wagons traveling the Oregon Trail are still visible throughout Idaho. *(Photo by Don Smurthwaite, Idaho State Office)*

Travels Through Time
Outstanding Historical Sites
Selected by
THE SOCIETY FOR HISTORICAL ARCHAEOLOGY

From a long-silent army outpost on the Yukon River in Alaska to an abandoned settlement in Utah's Green River Valley where the ghosts of Butch Cassidy and Sundance play cards for eternity, public lands play host to history. An outstanding and diverse array of historic, archaeological, and documentary resources provide evidence of the genesis and development of our nation's heritage. Put your ear to the wind at Bonneville Point and hear the voices of emigrants as you stand astride the Oregon Trail. Peer through the coastal mists at the lighthouse at Punta Gorda, a lovely sentinel on a beautiful but treacherous coast. Or imagine yourself in the moccasins of Captain William Clark as he strides up to Pompeys Pillar, Montana, in July 1806 to inscribe his name in the ledger of our nation's history.

About The Society for Historical Archaeology
The Society for Historical Archaeology is the largest scholarly group concerned with the archaeology of the modern world. The main focus of the Society is the era since the beginning of European exploration. The Society promotes scholarly research and the dissemination of knowledge concerning historical archaeology. The Society also is specifically concerned with the identification, excavation, interpretation, and conservation of sites and materials both on land and underwater. By examining the physical and documentary record of these sites, historical archaeologists attempt to discover the fabric of everyday life in the past and seek to understand the broader historical development of their own and other societies.

Favorite Sites
Bonneville Point Section of the Oregon Trail (ID)
Calamity Camp Mining Site (CO)
Folsom Farm Site (WA)
Fort Egbert (AK)
General Land Office Records Project (VA)
John Jarvie Historic Site (UT)
Lake Valley Historic Site (NM)
Oregon National Historic Trail Corridor Sites (WY)
Pompeys Pillar (MT)
Presidio Santa Cruz de Terrenate (AZ)
Punta Gorda Lighthouse (CA)
Rhyolite Historic Area (NV)
Rogue River Ranch (OR)

A mallard drake swoops in for a slippery landing on an ice covered Minnesota pond. *(© Thomas Kitchen, Tom Stack & Assoc.)*

Webbed Feet
Waterfowl and Wetlands
Selected by DUCKS UNLIMITED

Hundreds of millions of beautiful ducks, geese, and swans grace the wetlands and marshes along migratory flyways throughout the nation. From the Cosumnes River Preserve in northern California to the north-slope wetlands and lakes of Alaska, Ducks Unlimited has selected several excellent sites for waterfowl hunting and viewing on the public lands. A site for the very adventurous is the Gulkana River Basin, where the fishing is great in the summer and where hundreds of thousands of scaup, loons, and other waterfowl migrate through. Twenty-five percent of the world's trumpeter swans are also thought to nest here. In California, make tracks to the Cosumnes River Preserve, home to over 200 species of birds, from waterfowl to hawks and cranes, on 6,700 acres of wetlands. Of course, that's only a hint of the spectacular wildlife to be found where wetlands exist, so don't forget your wading boots, camera, and adventurous spirit.

About Ducks Unlimited

Ducks Unlimited (DU) is the largest private, non-profit, wetlands conservation organization in the world. Since 1937, DU has pioneered North American waterfowl conservation by raising funds throughout the United States to fulfill the needs of waterfowl by protecting, enhancing, restoring, and managing important wetlands and associated uplands. DU projects provide havens for hundreds of other wetland species in addition to ducks, geese, and swans. To date, DU has raised nearly $1 billion to help conserve over 7 million acres of habitat. Over 580,000 members continue the DU conservation effort today.

Favorite Sites

Cosumnes River Preserve (CA)
Gulkana National Wild and Scenic River (AK)

Evening falls at Desolation Canyon, one of Utah's most isolated environments. *(Photo by Kelly Rigby, Utah State Office)*

Wilderness Passages
Pack-In Areas for Big Game Hunting
Selected by
THE IZAAK WALTON LEAGUE OF AMERICA

"The sweetest hunts are stolen. To steal a hunt, one must either go far into the wilderness where no one has been or else find some undiscovered place under everybody's nose."

— Aldo Leopold,
A Sand County Almanac

If you're yearning to steal away, take the advice of The Izaak Walton League. They've come up with several wild places on the public lands where only the hardiest dare to travel. Raft the Green River into Desolation Canyon, past magnificent petroglyph panels in Canyonlands National Park, Utah, to hunting areas for mule deer, chukar partridge, and blue grouse on public lands. Or travel by horseback into the Kingston Range Wilderness of California to pursue the elusive desert bighorn sheep as well as mule deer and a variety of upland game birds. These and other exciting escapades await those most adventurous of hunters who are finding it harder and harder to locate untamed wilderness in their own backyards.

About The Izaak Walton League of America

A concern for the conservation and responsible use of natural resources is the common goal that binds the 50,000 members of The Izaak Walton League. Members promote conservation through hands-on, local conservation action, such as monitoring and restoring streams, planting trees, maintaining trails, and teaching people about safe, ethical hunting through hunter education courses. In addition, members educate the general public, as well as local, state, and national policymakers, about conservation and outdoor recreation issues. They also oppose policies and practices that threaten public lands, pollute the environment, or destroy natural resources.

Favorite Sites
Desolation and Gray Canyons (UT)
Kingston Range Wilderness (CA)

A bighorn sheep peers from a craggy outcropping in the California mountains.
(Photo by Bill Templeton, Riverside District Office)

Wetlands throughout western and northern Alaska provide critical nesting habitat for millions of migratory water birds. *(Photo by Bruce Seppi, Anchorage District Office)*

Flights of Fancy
Important Bird Areas
Selected by the
NATIONAL AUDUBON SOCIETY and
the AMERICAN BIRD CONSERVANCY

Whether you have a weakness for webbed feet or your interests tend towards talons, the public lands present an array of birdwatching opportunities that made Audubon himself smile. Located throughout the western United States and Alaska, these birdwatching sites can be found in a variety of latitudes and altitudes, from coastal marshes to shortgrass prairies, with stops at oases and river gorges in between — habitats uniquely suited to the needs of birds and interesting to visit. Pack parkas or desert boots, as appropriate — jackets and ties are most assuredly optional! Site access ranges from the exotic to the commonplace. You may need to fly in with a seaplane or float in on a raft. Sometimes, it's as easy as stepping out of your vehicle. Birdwatching sites on public lands offer unique and diverse opportunities to watch gaggles, flocks, and pairs as they nest, migrate, breed, or just hang out.

About the
National Audubon Society
For more than a century, the National Audubon Society has acted to prevent the extinction of birds that were at one time threatened by slaughter associated with the plume trade. Today, birds as well as other wildlife and their habitats are the primary focus. National Audubon has over 550,000 members and 520 chapters nationwide working to support its mission.

About the
American Bird Conservancy
The American Bird Conservancy (ABC) is a not-for-profit organization dedicated to the conservation of wild birds and their habitats throughout the Americas. ABC's guiding principles in developing programs are to encourage public participation and to develop partnerships for more efficient conservation. Programs cover every aspect of bird conservation, from research and education to policy and land protection.

Favorite Sites
Big Morongo Canyon (CA)
Cosumnes River Preserve (CA)
Jawbone/Butterbredt Area of Critical Environmental Concern (CA)
Kuskokwim Bay - Carter Spit (AK)
New River Area of Critical Environmental Concern (OR)
San Pedro Riparian National Conservation Area (AZ)
Snake River Birds of Prey National Conservation Area (ID)
South Phillips County (MT)
Yaquina Head Outstanding Natural Area (OR)

A startled ring-necked pheasant emerges from grassy cover in an eastern Colorado field.
(© 1992 Wendy Shalit/Bob Rozinski, Tom Stack & Assoc.)

Winging It
Pheasant, Turkey, and Quail Viewing and Hunting Areas

Selected by the NATIONAL WILD TURKEY FEDERATION, PHEASANTS FOREVER, and QUAIL UNLIMITED

"The hope of hearing quail is worth half a dozen risings-in-the-dark."
— Aldo Leopold,
A Sand County Almanac

Nature's bounty is exemplified by the myriad upland game birds that inhabit the plains, deserts, and forests of North America. Quail Unlimited, the National Wild Turkey Federation, and Pheasants Forever have collectively chosen several outstanding places on the public lands where they have worked to ensure that the habitat will support healthy populations of turkey, pheasant, and quail, as well as other upland game birds such as prairie chicken, chukar, and grouse. Whether you enjoy tracking these elusive creatures for sport, watching their colorful strut, or simply listening to their beguiling songs, these places are sure to help you set your sights on some of America's most loved upland game species.

About the Sponsors

National Wild Turkey Federation works for the conservation of the wild turkey and the preservation of the turkey hunting tradition. Conservation programs are funded through the Wild Turkey Super Fund, which pools monies raised by local chapters and individual, government, and corporate sponsors. The Federation is working to restore wild turkeys to unoccupied habitat in the United States by the year 2000. Typical projects include log-road seeding, in-state "trap and transfer" for wild turkey restoration, and education of private landowners on turkey management concepts.

Pheasants Forever is dedicated to the protection and habitat enhancement of upland game birds and other wildlife species in North America. The organization works to improve wildlife habitat, increase public awareness and education, and help establish sound land management policies to benefit ranchers, farmers, and wildlife alike. Since its inception in 1982, Pheasants Forever has been involved in a variety of habitat projects, including fencing riparian areas, planting winter cover, building guzzlers, renovating nesting cover, and acquiring critical habitat.

Quail Unlimited is a national conservation organization dedicated to the preservation and re-establishment of crucial wildlife habitat vitally needed to sustain healthy populations of quail and other upland bird species. Quail Unlimited is involved in developing and maintaining water sources for wildlife, as well as protecting and rehabilitating riparian habitats, assisting wildlife agencies in monitoring quail populations, and planting trees and shrubs. The organization also works to obtain and distribute free seed to landowners, farmers, and hunting clubs for planting food strips around the edges of fields and food plots.

Favorite Sites

National Wild Turkey Federation
Cache Creek (CA)
Fort Meade Recreation Area (SD)
Fort Stanton (NM)
Green River (UT)
Laguna Seca Mesa (NM)
Mt. Trumbull (AZ)
Upper Missouri National Wild and Scenic River and Missouri River Breaks (MT)
Woolsey Ranch Rio Grande Turkey Viewing Area (UT)

Quail Unlimited
Caliente Mountains (CA)
Juniper Flats (CA)
Panoche/Tumey Hills (CA)
San Simon Valley (AZ)

Pheasants Forever
Bruneau - Jarbidge Rivers (ID)
Channeled Scablands (WA)

A magnificent bull elk performs a "lip curl," part of a mating ritual during the fall rutting season in Wyoming. *(© G.C. Kelley, Tom Stack & Associates)*

Of Racks and Hooves

Elk Viewing Areas

Selected by the ROCKY MOUNTAIN ELK FOUNDATION

The bugling of elk has been likened to the beautiful and haunting bagpipe melodies native to the Scottish highlands. These stately creatures define the mountainous regions of the western United States, where they migrate between mountaintop and valley floor throughout the year. Because elk range through expansive and varied territories, efforts to restore elk habitat result in immeasurable benefits to a variety of other wildlife, fish, and plant species. The Rocky Mountain Elk Foundation has carefully selected places on the public lands where elk can be found—even as you fish the wild mountain streams or take in the beautiful vistas typical of the habitat that elk tend to prefer. From the Book Cliffs in eastern Utah to Oregon's Dean Creek Elk Viewing Area, the Rocky Mountain Elk Foundation will surely help you get "up close and personal" with one of North America's largest and most regal wild animal species.

About the Rocky Mountain Elk Foundation

The Rocky Mountain Elk Foundation's mission is to ensure the future of elk, as well as other wildlife and their habitats. The Elk Foundation educates its members and the public about habitat conservation, the value of hunting, hunting ethics, and wildlife management. To promote conservation efforts, the Foundation supports management-related research, elk transplants to areas of suitable habitat, habitat acquisitions, habitat improvement projects, and conservation education.

Favorite Sites

Book Cliffs Area (UT)
Cache Creek (CA)
Dean Creek Elk Viewing Area (OR)

The Book Cliffs offer lush habitat for thriving herds of elk and Utah's largest population of black bear. *(Photo by Jerry Sintz, Utah State Office)*

On the Fly

Great Trout Streams

Selected by TROUT UNLIMITED

Wild trout have captured the hearts and imaginations of many Americans, from the reserved and reverent Native American nations of the Pacific Northwest to the boundlessly enthusiastic anglers standing in streams everywhere. Where once millions of native trout inhabited the clear, cool mountain streams of North America, in far too many areas their numbers have now declined. Continuing the great American tradition of sportsmen leading major conservation efforts, Trout Unlimited has included in its selections several outstanding opportunities for you to join other outdoor enthusiasts in stream and aquatic habitat restoration work on the public lands. So take the bait, roll up your sleeves, and pour a little sweat into these projects to improve some of America's wildest and most beautiful rivers and streams.

About Trout Unlimited

Trout Unlimited (TU) is a 95,000-member organization whose mission is to conserve, protect, and restore coldwater fisheries and their watersheds throughout North America. TU accomplishes its mission through habitat restoration and protection, conservation education, research, and advocacy at the state and national levels. Trout Unlimited is in the forefront of partnering with federal land-managing agencies and other conservation organizations to restore habitats on public lands. Among these partnership programs is the "Bring Back the Natives" program with the BLM and the U.S. Forest Service, which has restored native fish habitats in more than 50 watersheds throughout 17 states.

Favorite Sites

Green River (WY)
Gulkana National Wild and Scenic
    River (AK)
Lower Blackfoot River (MT)
Lower Deschutes River (OR)

This Rocky Mountain bighorn sheep's natural camouflage allows him to blend perfectly with his Wyoming surroundings. *(Courtesy National Bighorn Sheep Interpretive Center)*

Wild and Free
Watchable Wildlife

Selected by the
FOUNDATION FOR NORTH AMERICAN WILD SHEEP

Hot, dry canyonlands or alpine cliffs. They are some of the most spectacular and rugged places in North America, and they're also home to mountain sheep. The Foundation for North American Wild Sheep recommends several such areas on the public lands where the chances of spotting a Rocky Mountain, California, Dall, or desert bighorn sheep are excellent. Preferring to hug mountainsides or narrow cliffs and canyons, these wild sheep may draw you into a few adventures, so be sure to wear sturdy hiking boots and other survival gear. Also remember to take a pair of binoculars along, because these magnificent animals blend easily into their craggy, high-altitude surroundings, big horns and all!

About the Foundation for North American Wild Sheep

The Foundation for North American Wild Sheep is an organization dedicated to the welfare of wild sheep and their continued presence in their native habitats. Organized in 1976 by a group of conservation-minded sheep hunters and other sportsmen, the Foundation is working to increase populations of indigenous wild sheep in North America and fund programs for professional management of these populations. Through cooperative efforts with federal and non-federal entities, the Foundation has been able to restore healthy wild sheep populations to much of their former range.

Favorite Sites

Aravaipa Canyon Wilderness (AZ)
Arkansas Headwaters Recreation
  Area (CO)
Big Morongo Canyon (CA)
Big Sheep Creek (MT)
Dall Sheep Viewing Area/Dalton
  Highway (AK)
Owyhee National Wild and Scenic
  River/Owyhee Canyonlands (OR)
Owyhee Canyonlands and Little Jacks
  Creek (ID)
Red Rock Canyon National Conservation
  Area (NV)
San Juan River (UT)
Steens Mountain, East Rim
  Overlook (OR)

A dog-musher urges his team toward the finish line during a competitive mushing event in Alaska's White Mountains. *(Photo by Ed Bovy, Alaska State Office)*

Best Bets

Sites Selected by
BUREAU OF LAND MANAGEMENT EMPLOYEES

BLM employees take pride in being stewards of the public lands that they manage. And some of our charges really shine in the eyes of our employees as well as those of the public. Tried and true, these sites have seldom been known to disappoint. When we say it's a "Best Bet," you can be sure it isn't much of a gamble that you'll enjoy gliding through Alaska by dog sled or snowmobile, or by going door to door (cabin to cabin) on skis. Chances are, you'll be a winner. A spin down Arizona's Route 66 isn't like a spin on the roulette wheel —here, the odds are with you. And if you decide instead to relax by enjoying the sparkling waters of Idaho's Coeur d'Alene, the game's rigged in your favor. For a different type of sport, view the grizzly bears, bighorn sheep, and other wildlife along the banks of the Lower Blackfoot River in Montana. So if you're wondering if you'll enjoy a visit to these special sites on the public lands, relax — wherever you go, you'll find yourself in the winner's circle.

Favorite Sites

Aguirre Spring Campground (NM)

America's Outdoors, Center for Conservation, Recreation and Resources (WI)

Anasazi Heritage Center (CO)

Betty's Kitchen National Recreation Trail (AZ)

Black Rock Desert Playa (NV)

Black River Special Management Area (NM)

Campbell Tract (AK)

Canyon Pintado National Historic District (CO)

Cleveland-Lloyd Dinosaur Quarry (UT)

Coeur D'Alene Lake Special Recreation Management Area (ID)

Diamond Craters Outstanding Natural Area (OR)

East Fork, Salmon River Canyon (ID)

Eastern United States Wild Horse and Burro Adoption/Holding Facility (TN)

Ely Elk Viewing Area (NV)

Empire-Cienega Resource Conservation Area (AZ)

Gooseberry Scenic Interpretive Site and Hiking Trail (WY)

Grand Staircase-Escalante National Monument (UT)

Guadalupe Back Country Byway (NM)

Hell's Half Acre Lava Flow (ID)

Iditarod National Historic Trail (AK)

Indian Creek Recreation Area (NV)

Lake Abert and Abert Rim (OR)

Lake Vermilion Public Islands (MN)

Little Black Mountain Petroglyph Site (AZ)

Little Rocky Mountains (MT)

Little Vulcan Mountain (WA)

Marietta Wild Burro Range (NV)

Milner Historic/Recreation Area (ID)

Mt. Trumbull Schoolhouse (AZ)

Muddy Mountain Environmental Education Area (WY)

National Bighorn Sheep Interpretive Center and Whiskey Mountain Bighorn Sheep Area (WY)

National Historic Oregon Trail Interpretive Center (OR)

North Algodones Dunes Wilderness (CA)

North Fork Virgin River Merriam's Turkey Viewing Area (UT)

North Platte River and Seminoe Reservoir (WY)

North Umpqua Wild and Scenic River Corridor (OR)

North Wildhorse Recreation Area (NV)

Organ Mountains (NM)

Parker Strip Recreation Area (AZ)

Pine Forest Recreation Area (NV)

Rabbit Valley Trail Through Time (CO)

Red Gulch/Alkali Back Country Byway (WY)

Route 66 Historic Back Country Byway (AZ)

Row River Trail (OR)

Schnell Ranch Recreation Area (ND)

Shotgun Creek Recreation Site (OR)

South Fork Owhyee River/Owhyee River Canyon (NV)

South Fork Snake River Special Recreation Management Area (ID)

South Pass Historic Mining District (WY)

Three Rivers Petroglyph Site (NM)

Trona Pinnacles (CA)

University of Alaska Museum (AK)

Valley of Fires Recreation Area (NM)

Vermilion Cliffs (AZ)

Walker Lake Recreation Area (NV)

White Mountains National Recreation Area (AK)

Yakima River Canyon (WA)

Recreational dog-mushers use one of a network of BLM cabins as "home base" in the pristine White Mountains National Recreation Area northeast of Fairbanks, Alaska. *(Photo by Susan Steinacher, Northern District Office)*

Alaska

The Aleuts named their majestic and beautiful home-
land "Alyeska" or Alaska, meaning the "Great Land."
Among the breathtaking scenes that define Alaska are
frozen deserts, majestic mountain ranges, and even
lush rain forests. Public lands scattered throughout
Alaska contain unusual features such as the limestone
formations of the White Mountains National Recreation Area, portions of the famous Iditarod National
Historic Trail, expansive glaciers, and long-abandoned
historic towns.

The 90 million acres of public lands in Alaska represent about 25 percent of the land area in the state.
Most of these public lands are remote and can only be
reached by aircraft. However, the Denali and Dalton
highways offer extensive scenic drives through public
lands. The BLM maintains campgrounds just off the
road system near Glennallen. The popular White
Mountains National Recreation Area offers extensive
winter trails and public recreation cabins. The most
accessible and perhaps the most visited recreation area
is Campbell Tract, a 730-acre natural area located in
Anchorage.

Summer is the most popular season for visitors. But
the colder months are attracting more and more folks
each year. The 1,000-mile-long Iditarod sled dog race
held each March attracts thousands of spectators. Having reached its heyday during a 1910 gold rush, the
trail today provides the route for the famous sled dog
race. In addition to dogsledding, the growing list of
popular cold weather recreational activities on the public lands in Alaska includes skiing, ski joring (your dog
pulls you on cross-country skiis), and snowmobiling.

The weather in Alaska is something to consider.
Visitors should bring appropriate clothing and gear,
but most of all—they'll need a sense of adventure to
explore the wonders of this Great Land.

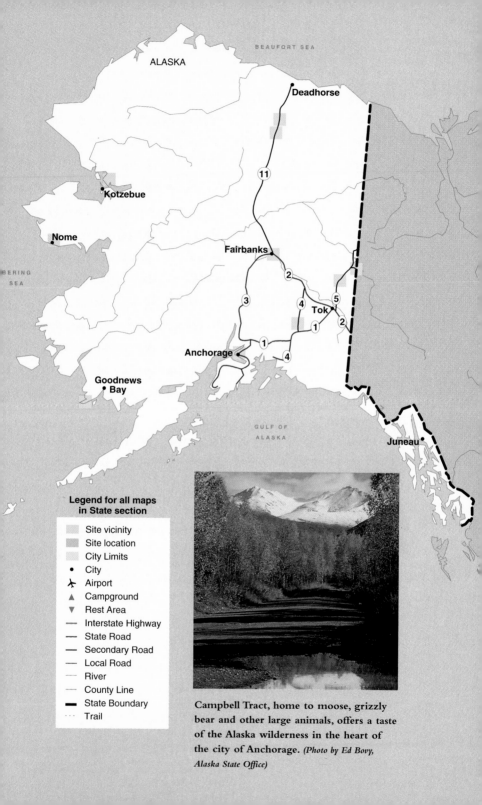

BEAUFORT SEA

ALASKA

Deadhorse

⑪

Kotzebue

Nome

BERING
SEA

Fairbanks

② ⑤

③ ④ Tok

① ②

①

Anchorage ④

Goodnews
Bay

GULF OF
ALASKA

Juneau

**Legend for all maps
in State section**

Site vicinity
Site location
City Limits
• City
✈ Airport
▲ Campground
▼ Rest Area
— Interstate Highway
— State Road
— Secondary Road
— Local Road
— River
— County Line
— State Boundary
⋯ Trail

Campbell Tract, home to moose, grizzly
bear and other large animals, offers a taste
of the Alaska wilderness in the heart of
the city of Anchorage. *(Photo by Ed Bovy,
Alaska State Office)*

Campbell Tract

Location
In east Anchorage, Alaska

Description
The Campbell Tract is a 730-acre natural area used mostly by urban recreationists seeking a piece of Alaska wilderness in the heart of the city. The tract is a BLM administrative site with office buildings and a restricted-use airstrip. Surrounding the administrative complex are forested lands containing shrubs, grasses, forbs, mosses, fungi, and lichens. The tract is home to moose, black bear, wolf, and brown bear. Other animals that visitors may encounter include lynx, coyote, fox, porcupine, and squirrels. Campbell Creek meanders through the property and provides spawning and rearing habitat for rainbow trout, Dolly Varden, and king and silver salmon. BLM operates its Campbell Creek Science Center here.

Mailing Address
BLM – Anchorage District Office
6881 Abbott Loop Road
Anchorage, AK 99507

Phone Number   Fax Number
(907) 267-1246   (907) 267-1267

Sixth-graders visiting BLM's Campbell Creek Science Center pan for gold at one of six learning stations set up for spring Outdoor Week classes, an annual event. *(Photo by Ed Bovy, Alaska State Office)*

Directions

In Anchorage, travel south on Lake Otis Parkway to East 68th Avenue and follow the road until it turns into Abbott Loop Road. The Campbell Tract facility sign will direct you to the tract.

Visitor Activities

Walking, jogging, horseback riding, skiing, dog-mushing, and skijoring.

Permits, Fees, Limitations

No fees. The area is restricted to non-motorized recreational use.

Accessibility

None

Camping and Lodging

Camping is not encouraged; however, non-profit organizations may obtain special recreation use permits for overnight use.

Food and Supplies

Food and supplies are available in Anchorage.

First Aid

Hospitals and clinics are nearby.

Additional Information

The Campbell Tract is BLM's most visited and accessible site in Alaska. Because of its location, it is a favorite getaway for urban dwellers seeking year-round recreational opportunities.

Sponsor

Activity Codes

 - walking, jogging, horseback riding, skiing, dog-mushing, skijoring

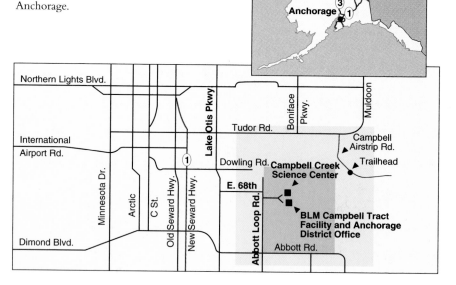

Dall Sheep Viewing Area/ Dalton Highway

Location
65 miles north of Coldfoot, Alaska

Description
Crossing the Brooks Range is one of the true motoring adventures available in North America. One of the best places to see Dall sheep in Alaska is on the rocky slopes of Atigun Pass (mile 240, elevation 4,739 feet) along Dalton Highway. This is the highest point in the Alaska road system. The sheep may also be seen between the pass and Galbraith Lake (mile 275), as well as on Slope Mountain (miles 297-301). Also watch for arctic foxes, muskoxen (particularly north of Slope Mountain), caribou, peregrine falcons, golden eagles, and rough-legged hawks.

Mailing Address
BLM - Northern District Office
1150 University Avenue
Fairbanks, AK 99709

Phone Number
(907) 474-2302 [In summer (June-August), visitors may also call BLM at the Coldfoot Interagency Visitor Center, Tel.: (907) 678-5209.]

Fax Number
(907) 474-2280

Directions
From Fairbanks, drive north about 11 miles on Steese Highway to Fox, then drive north about 76 miles on Elliott Highway to its intersection with Dalton Highway. From there, it is 56 miles northwest on Dalton Highway to Yukon Crossing, then an additional 144 miles northwest to Coldfoot. Check your gas supply

before proceeding, as there are no services until the end of the highway at Deadhorse (mile 414).

Visitor Activities
Birdwatching, hiking, scenic drives, wildlife viewing, and photography.

Permits, Fees, Limitations
No fees are required for non-commercial visits.

Accessibility
None

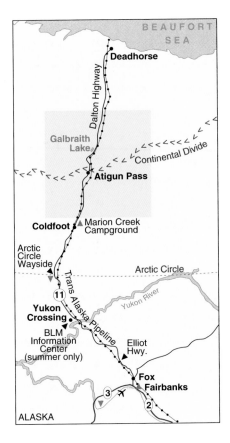

Camping and Lodging

A motel and privately managed campground are located at Coldfoot. There is a public campground (managed by BLM with no hookups) at Marion Creek, 5 miles north of Coldfoot. Camping is also available in Wiseman.

Food and Supplies

Supplies are available in Fairbanks, Coldfoot, and Deadhorse.

First Aid

This site is an extremely isolated area, and visitors must be self-sufficient. The Coldfoot Interagency Visitor Center can summon help by telephone in summer only. The nearest hospital is in Fairbanks.

Additional Information

The best time to drive the highway is between late May and mid-September. Stop at the BLM visitor information stations at Yukon Crossing and Coldfoot for information and obtain a copy of *Birds Along the Dalton Highway* or *Riches from the Earth:*

A Geologic Tour Along the Dalton Highway. Remember that the Dalton Highway is primarily an industrial highway: slow down and pull over to allow high-speed trucks to pass and to minimize the chances of windshield damage from flying rocks. Highway services are limited to Yukon Crossing, Coldfoot, and Deadhorse, so be sure your vehicle is in good working order before attempting this trip.

Sponsoring Partner

WILD SHEEP

Activity Codes

 - photography

Fort Egbert

Location

In the town of Eagle, Alaska

Description

The Fort is a former Yukon River U.S. Army post, which was established in 1899 to bring law and order to the Fortymile country during the Klondike gold rush. After the boom, an Army Signal Corps was established here to operate a telegraphy and wireless station until about 1925. Currently, BLM manages 5 restored structures in cooperation with the local Eagle

Historical Society. Exhibits and tours are available in the summer. An interpretive trail on the Fort grounds provides access to the ruins of other structures. Fort Egbert National Historic Landmark includes the Fort as well as structures in the adjacent community of Eagle.

Mailing Address

BLM - Northern District Office
1150 University Avenue
Fairbanks, AK 99709

Phone Number
(907) 474-2302

Fax Number
(907) 474-2280

Directions

From Tok, travel east 12 miles on State Highway 2 to Taylor Highway. Take Taylor Highway 160 miles northeast to its end in the settlement of Eagle. Visitors coming from Dawson City, Yukon Territory (Canada), can connect with the Taylor Highway at Jack Wade Junction by way of the Top of the World Highway.

Visitor Activities

Hiking and photography. Free guided historical tours are conducted from June to early September.

Permits, Fees, Limitations

None

Accessibility

Several historical buildings can be entered and toured by wheelchair on their lower levels. Upper floors of the old buildings are not wheelchair-accessible.

Camping and Lodging

BLM manages a 16-site, no-fee campground near the fort; campsites are available on a first-come, first-served basis. A motel and cabins are available in the adjacent town of Eagle, within walking distance of the fort.

Food and Supplies

Eagle has both a general store and a cafe.

First Aid

This area is extremely isolated. Limited first aid is available in Eagle from volunteer emergency medical technicians and a local nurse. The nearest hospital is more than an 8-hour drive away, in Fairbanks. Weather permitting, evacuation by plane may be available from an airstrip near Eagle.

Additional Information

Summer access is via the Taylor Highway; for the last 60 miles, it is a narrow, winding road unsuitable for large motor homes or trailers. Plan to visit between May and mid-September, as this road is snowed-in during the winter months.

Sponsoring Partner

SOCIETY for HISTORICAL ARCHAEOLOGY

Activity Codes

 – photography

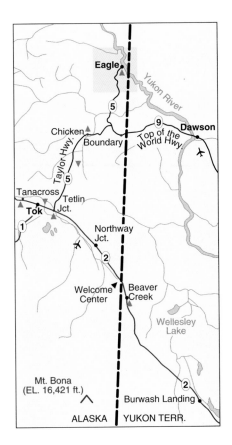

Fortymile National Wild and Scenic River

Location
60 miles northeast of Tok, Alaska

Description
Fortymile River is an extensive network of creeks and rivers in east-central Alaska, 392 miles of which have been given a National Wild and Scenic or Recreational River designation. Boaters have many choices for recreational trips through deep, winding canyons lined by forests of birch, spruce and aspen. Remnants of past mining operations dot the river banks as mementos of the area's rich mining history.

Mailing Address
BLM - Northern District Office
1150 University Avenue
Fairbanks, AK 99709

Phone Number
(907) 474-2302

Fax Number
(907) 474-2280

Directions
Begin your trip at the BLM office in Tok (on East First Street, Tel.: (907) 883-5121), where you can obtain the latest information on river conditions and advice on trip options. Proceed east from Tok 12 miles on State Highway 2 to Taylor Highway and then to a selected drop-off point, such as the South Fork Bridge Wayside or Fortymile Bridge. Air taxi shuttles to remote drop-off and take-out points can also be arranged in Tok or Fairbanks.

Visitor Activities
Photography, boating, birdwatching, historical sites, and fishing.

Permits, Fees, Limitations
No fees for non-commercial use.

Accessibility
None

Camping and Lodging
Camping is available at BLM campgrounds at the Walker Fork (mile 82, Taylor Highway) and West Fork (mile 49, Taylor Highway). The nearest lodging is available in Tok and in Eagle (mile 160, Taylor Highway).

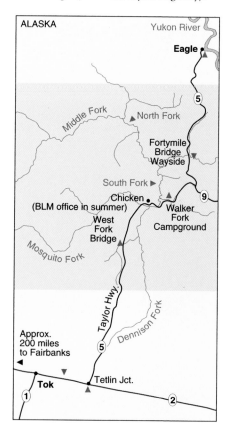

Near eastern Alaska's border with Canada, Gold Rush-era mine remnants dot the banks of the Fortymile River, which boasts challenging rapids with such colorful names as "The Kink" and "Deadman's Riffle." *(Photo by William Robertson (retired), Northern District Office)*

Food and Supplies

Groceries and other supplies can be obtained in Fairbanks, Delta Junction, and Tok.

First Aid

Travelers must be prepared to be self-sufficient; the nearest hospital is in Fairbanks, which could be up to a day's travel once you reach the road. Limited first aid is available in Eagle and Tok.

Additional Information

Be sure to obtain U.S. Geological Survey topographic maps, let someone know your travel itinerary, and bring clothes suitable for all types of weather. River travel is through remote areas where rescue would be both difficult and time-consuming. There are active mining operations (suction dredging) along several portions of the river. (Please respect private property.)

River trips take 3 to 10 days, depending on the trip option selected. River travelers must be capable of dealing with difficult river conditions in a wilderness setting. Contact BLM for detailed information on trip options, as there are many levels of difficulty (rapids vary from Class II to Class V), depending on the trip segment selected.

Sponsoring Partner

Activity Codes

 – photography

Gulkana National Wild and Scenic River

Location
60 miles north of Glennallen, Alaska

Description
The Gulkana is one of the 5 most used rivers in Alaska, primarily because of its easy access at the put-in and take-out points. The river is known for its recreational values, including excellent sport fishing, particularly for chinook (king) salmon during late June and early July. The Gulkana also contains sockeye salmon, grayling, and rainbow trout, as well as the northernmost population of steelhead trout in North America.

The main stem of the river (between Paxson and Sourdough) receives the heaviest use in July and August, particularly on weekends. Other, more remote areas (Middle Fork and West Fork) receive less use; wilderness trips of up to 14 days are possible, and visitors see few, if any, people. Expect to view nesting bald eagles and harlequin ducks along the Gulkana riparian corridor. There are a significant number of small lakes and wetlands surrounding the Gulkana, which provide important habitat for numerous species of waterfowl, such as trumpeter swans, mallards and pintails.

The upper river (approximately 181 river miles) has been designated a National Wild and Scenic River, and is managed by BLM. Another 40 river miles flow through privately-owned lands on the lower section of the river.

Mailing Address
BLM - Glennallen District Office
P.O. Box 147
Glennallen, AK 99588

Phone Number
(907) 822-3217

Fax Number
(907) 822-3120

Directions
From Glennallen, drive northeast about 15 miles on State Highway 1 (Glenn

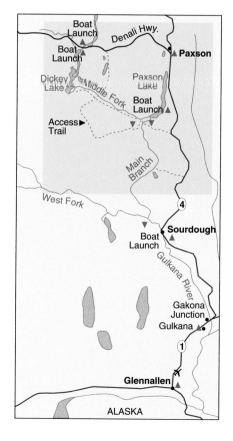

Highway) to State Highway 4 (Richardson Highway). Travel about 20 miles north on Highway 4 to Sourdough Campground. Continue north for an additional 25 miles to the put-in at Paxson Lake Campground.

Visitor Activities

Summer activities include fishing, boating, rafting, hiking, wildlife viewing, hunting, and birdwatching.

Permits, Fees, Limitations

There are no user fees for traveling on the river; however, campgrounds located at the beginning and end of the National Wild River corridor charge fees. Stays at these campgrounds or anywhere within the National Wild River corridor are limited to 2 weeks at any site.

Accessibility

Toilets at both Paxson Lake Campground boat launch and Sourdough Creek Campground are wheelchair-accessible. Sourdough Creek Campground features accessible trails and fishing ramps.

Camping and Lodging

There are numerous undeveloped campsites for boaters along the Gulkana National Wild River. Paxson Lake Campground (mile 175, Richardson Highway) offers 20 pull-in, 20 tent, and 10 walk-in sites, has water and a dump station, and is open from mid-May to early October. There are both drive-in and walk-in fees. Sourdough Creek Campground (mile 147.5, Richardson Highway) has 42 campsites and is open from mid-May to early October. Several roadhouses and lodges may also be found along Richardson Highway.

Food and Supplies

Limited food and supplies are available at roadhouses and lodges along Richardson Highway. A larger selection of food and supplies may be found in Glennallen and in Delta Junction (mile 266, Richardson Highway). A complete selection of food and supplies may be found in Anchorage (250 miles south) and Fairbanks (220 miles north).

First Aid

No first aid is available anywhere along the Gulkana National Wild River. Limited medical facilities are available at the Cross Roads Medical Center in Glennallen.

Additional Information

Floating from Paxson Lake to Sourdough Creek Campground takes 3-4 days to travel 50 miles of Class I, II, III, and IV rapids, including one portage. Call BLM to learn the water conditions before beginning your trip. Be prepared for any kind of weather; it can rain or snow at any time during the summer. Restroom facilities on the river are limited to a few pit toilets. While the frozen river is used for winter travel to some extent, primary river use takes place between river break-up in late May or early June, and freeze-up in late September or early October.

Sponsoring Partners

DUCKS UNLIMITED

Activity Codes

Iditarod National Historic Trail

Location

The Iditarod National Historic Trail begins at sea level at the Alaska port town of Seward and follows narrow valleys through the Kenai and Chugach Mountains to the Knik Arm. From sea level at Knik, the Trail makes a slow climb across the Susitna River Valley and the Skwentna and Happy Rivers to Rainy Pass (approximately 3,350 feet) in the Alaska Range. The Trail descends through the Kuskokwim River Valley to McGrath, then crosses into the Yukon River drainage to the village of Kaltag. The Trail follows the low, broad Unalakleet River Valley, reaching an elevation of 600 feet, and passes through the Kaltag Mountains. From Unalakleet, the Trail is generally at sea level and skirts Norton Sound to reach its end at the coastal town of Nome.

Description

The Iditarod National Historic Trail is a network of 2,037 miles of trails once used by ancient Alaska Natives and early 20th-century prospectors. The vegetation varies from coastal Sitka spruce to the alpine tundra of the Chugach Mountains and Alaska Range. Wildlife is plentiful and includes moose, caribou, black bear, brown bear, lynx, beaver, otter, marten, bald eagle, and all types of waterfowl. Fish species include salmon, steelhead, Dolly Varden, trout, and arctic graying. The Iditarod received its Historic Trail designation from Congress in 1978 for its historic importance. The Trail is the route for the Iditarod Trail Sled Dog Race.

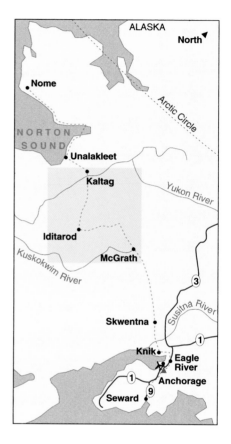

Mailing Address
BLM - Anchorage District Office
Iditarod National Historic Trail Coordinator
6881 Abbott Loop Road
Anchorage, AK 99507

Phone Number   Fax Number
(907) 267-1246   (907) 267-1267

Directions
See "Location" information.

Visitor Activities
Snowmobiling, dog-mushing, and hiking.

Permits, Fees, Limitations
Activities of a commercial or competitive nature require special-use recreation permits.

Accessibility
In the town of Seward, a few miles of the Trail are paved, which could allow wheelchair access.

Camping and Lodging
During the summer, camping is encouraged only for the hardiest sportsmen because of severe terrain (tundra, mountains, river crossings) and harsh conditions (mosquitoes, etc.). Commercial lodging can be found in Seward, Girdwood, Eagle River, McGrath, Unalakleet, and Nome.

Food and Supplies
Same sources as for "Camping and Lodging."

First Aid
Limited medical care can be obtained where lodging is found. Seward and Nome have hospitals.

Sponsor

Activity Codes
 - snowmobiling, dog-mushing

Maintenance crews repair a BLM cabin along the Iditarod National Historic Trail, which commemorates the Alaska Gold Rush as well as the 1923 dogteam deliveries of diphtheria serum to Nome. *(Photo by Ed Bovy, Alaska State Office)*

Kuskokwim Bay - Carter Spit

Location
120 miles south of Bethel, Alaska

Description
The Carter Spit site includes 4 spits and the intertidal mudflats within Kuskokwim Bay and north of Goodnews Bay, on the southwest coast of Alaska. In the spring and fall, this area serves as an important site for migrating waterfowl, such as the northern pintail, greater scaup, green-winged teal, black scoter, Hudsonian godwit, bristle-thighed curlew, and Steller's eider. More than 120 species were observed during a recent fall migration.

Mailing Address
BLM - Anchorage District Office
6881 Abbott Loop Road
Anchorage, AK 99507

Phone Number   Fax Number
(907) 267-1246   (907) 267-1267

Directions
Travel by commercial jet from Anchorage to Bethel. Then travel by charter boat or float plane from Bethel to the site, approximately 120 miles south. (Charters should be arranged with private plane or boat operators well in advance of arriving in Bethel. Contact the Alaska Division of Tourism in Juneau [Tel.: (907) 465-2010] for assistance in obtaining charters.) There is no scheduled service to the Spit, and the availability of charter transportation is limited during certain times of the year. Expect to pay more than $1,000 for a plane charter.

Visitor Activities
Birdwatching, hiking, and floating.

Permits, Fees, Limitations
None

Accessibility
None

Camping and Lodging
There are no developed camping areas in this remote setting. The nearest lodging is in Bethel.

Food and Supplies
Food and supplies are available in Bethel.

First Aid
No first aid is available on-site. This area is extremely isolated; visitors must be self-sufficient for medical problems or emergencies. The nearest hospital is in Bethel.

Additional Information
Weather is unpredictable, and storms can blow in off the Bering Sea with little warning. Spring and fall weather can be cool and moist, typical of maritime areas. No facilities or services of any kind are present, so visitors must be fully prepared for all contingencies. Tides subject the bays to rapid, extreme fluctuations of water levels, revealing extensive mudflats that can trap unwary visitors walking on them; consult tide tables and plan your activities accordingly. Be prepared for extremely wet conditions. There are no trails. This trip is recommended only for the most thoroughly prepared individuals.

Sponsoring Partner

National Audubon Society

AMERICAN BIRD CONSERVANCY

Activity Codes

BLM employees negotiate the tidal mudflats of western Alaska's remote Kuskokwim River, a vital staging area for huge populations of migrant waterfowl and shorebirds. *(Photo by Bruce Seppi, Anchorage District Office)*

Mosquito Lake

Location
This archaeological site is located in the Atigun River Valley along the north flank of the Brooks Range, about 97 miles north of Coldfoot, Alaska, and 110 miles north of the Arctic Circle.

Description
The area has been occupied intermittently during the past 4,000 years by the ancestors of the modern Nunamiut Eskimos. The site was probably a hunting ground for caribou and Dall sheep, and is significant in that it represents one of the earliest and best documented inland sites used by Eskimos. Data obtained from the site have provided important information regarding the vast differences between the Eskimos' maritime and terrestrial lifestyles, and insights into their stone-manufacturing processes.

Mailing Address
BLM - Northern District Office
1150 University Avenue
Fairbanks, AK 99709

Phone Number   Fax Number
(907) 474-2302   (907) 474-2280

Directions
From Coldfoot (mile 175), drive north on Dalton Highway for about 97 miles. Look for an interpretive sign near Galbraith Lake, mile 272.

Visitor Activities
Sightseeing, archaeological site, and photography.

Permits, Fees, Limitations
None

Accessibility
Visitors can view the general area of the site from the road. There are no wheelchair-accessible facilities.

Camping and Lodging
The nearest campground is Marion Creek, at mile 180 on Dalton Highway. There is a nightly fee, and sites are available on a first-come, first-served basis. Indoor accommodations are available in Coldfoot.

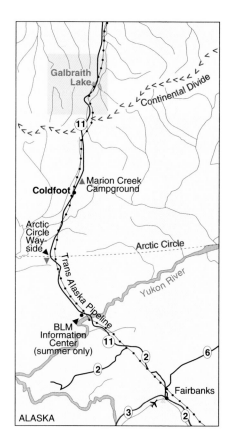

Food and Supplies
Coldfoot has a small store, a restaurant, and a service station.

First Aid
Limited first aid is available in Coldfoot (which also has an airstrip). The nearest hospital is in Fairbanks, about 350 miles south.

Additional Information
Dalton Highway is a long, gravel road used by heavy trucks headed for the oil field at Prudhoe Bay. Weather can change quickly, and the road may be either dusty and dry, or wet and slippery. Travel to this area is recommended only during the months of May through early September. Atigun Pass can receive its first snowfall of the winter in August. Vehicles must be in excellent working order. Windshield damage from flying gravel is a distinct possibility. Gasoline is available at Yukon Crossing (milepost 56), Coldfoot (mile 175) and Deadhorse (mile 414).

Sponsoring Partner

SAA
SOCIETY FOR AMERICAN ARCHAEOLOGY

Activity Codes

 - photography

Squirrel River

Location
30 miles northeast of Kotzebue, Alaska

Description
The Squirrel River begins in the Baird Mountains, north of the Arctic Circle in northwestern Alaska. All but the upper reaches of the river are a Class 1 float. Sport fishing, particularly for grayling, is excellent. Northern pike, pink salmon, and chum salmon are also plentiful.

Mailing Address
BLM - Northern District Office
1150 University Avenue
Fairbanks, AK 99709

Phone Number   Fax Number
(907) 474-2302   (907) 474-2280

Directions
Fly by commercial jet from Anchorage to Kotzebue, then travel by charter float plane for drop-off at the headwaters. Make reservations in advance, if possible. Contact the Alaska Division of Tourism in Juneau [Tel.: (907) 465-2010] for assistance in obtaining a float-plane charter.

Visitor Activities
Floating, fishing, photography, and wildlife observation.

Permits, Fees, Limitations
No fees for non-commercial groups.

Accessibility
None

Camping and Lodging
Camping is strictly primitive on public lands. Lodging is available in Kotzebue.

Food and Supplies
Groceries and other supplies are best obtained in Anchorage before the start of

your trip; however, a good selection is also available in Kotzebue.

First Aid
No first aid is available in this remote, wilderness setting. The nearest hospital is in Kotzebue.

Additional Information
The best time to visit is between June and early September. Visitors must be fully prepared to face all types of weather and emergencies in a remote part of the state.

Sponsoring Partner

Activity Codes

 photography

University of Alaska Museum

Location
The site is located in Fairbanks, Alaska.

Description
This museum curates, studies, and exhibits fossil collections from the public lands administered by BLM in Alaska. The museum collection includes more than 1,000 bones from at least 6 varieties of dinosaurs from the Late Cretaceous Period (65 to 72 million years ago). Pleistocene (10-thousand-year-old to 2-million-year-old) fossils include mammoths, saber tooth tigers, bison, mastodons, camels and many other fauna.

Mailing Addresses
University of Alaska Museum
907 Yukon Drive
Fairbanks, AK 99775

BLM - Northern District Office
1150 University Avenue
Fairbanks, AK 99709

Phone Numbers
Museum: (907) 474-7505;
BLM: (907) 474-2302

Fax Numbers
Museum: (907) 474-5469;
BLM: (907) 474-2280

Directions
Drive to the University of Alaska campus
on the west side of Fairbanks and follow
the signs to the museum on Yukon Drive.

Visitor Activities
Guided museum tours can be arranged
through the museum.

Permits, Fees, Limitations
Admission is charged for entry into the
museum.

Accessibility
The main viewing area is wheelchair-accessible.

Camping and Lodging
Numerous campgrounds, motels, hotels
and bed-and-breakfast establishments are
located in the Fairbanks area.

Food and Supplies
These items can be readily obtained in
Fairbanks.

First Aid
There is a hospital in Fairbanks.

Additional Information
The museum is open year-round, but
hours vary with the season.

Sponsor

Activity Codes

 - dinosaur fossils

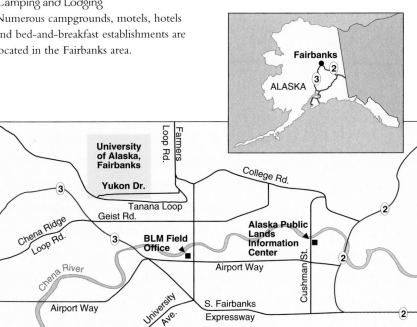

White Mountains National Recreation Area

Location
60 miles northwest of Fairbanks, Alaska

Description
This 1-million-acre area is used primarily from February to April, when dog-mushers, snowmobilers, and skiers come to take advantage of the winter solitude and northern lights. BLM maintains 9 winter cabins, which are connected by a network of more than 300 miles of groomed winter trails. Much of the area is too wet to hike through in the summer, but Beaver Creek National Wild River and several short trails offer opportunities for adventure.

Mailing Addresses
BLM - Northern District Office
1150 University Avenue
Fairbanks, AK 99709

Alaska Public Lands Information Center
250 Cushman Street, Suite 102A
Fairbanks, AK 99701

Phone Numbers
BLM: (907) 474-2302
Alaska PLI Center: (907) 456-0527

Fax Numbers
BLM: (907) 474-2280
Alaska PLI Center: (907) 456-0514

Directions
Begin your trip at the BLM office or the Alaska Public Lands Information Center (an interagency office) in Fairbanks, where you can obtain detailed directions, as well as the latest information on trail and weather conditions. Most summer hiking occurs along the Summit Trail at mile 28,

Elliott Highway. Winter access is at mile 28 as well as mile 57, Elliott Highway. BLM is also developing a new access point off U.S. Creek Road, mile 57, Steese Highway.

Visitor Activities
Summer: Hiking, photography, wildlife observation, river floating, and fishing. Winter: Dog-mushing, snowmobiling, and cross-country skiing.

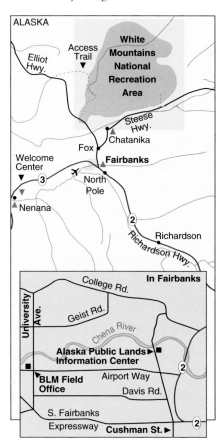

Permits, Fees, Limitations

BLM public recreation cabins are available by reservation only; there is a use fee charged per group per night. Contact BLM well in advance of your trip. Weekend dates in March and April are the first to fill up.

Accessibility

None

Camping and Lodging

Cripple Creek Campground is located at mile 60, Steese Highway. Lodging is available in Fairbanks.

Food and Supplies

Food and supplies are available in Fairbanks.

First Aid

Visitors should carry their own first-aid kits, as no help is available in this wilderness setting. The nearest hospital is in Fairbanks.

Additional Information

Winter use is most popular on weekends, February through April, when moderating temperatures and longer days make travel easier. Visitation is not encouraged from October through January, when temperatures occasionally reach -65°F and there are less than 5 hours of daylight per day. Winter trails are maintained on an infrequent basis, so U.S. Geological Survey topographic maps and good route-finding abilities are necessities. Visitors should also have at least a basic knowledge of winter survival skills. BLM's Nome Creek Project is expected to be ready in 1998; this area will provide improved summer access to Nome Creek and include new campgrounds, hiking access points, gold-panning opportunities and day-use areas. Contact BLM for further information.

Sponsor

U.S. DEPARTMENT OF THE INTERIOR
BUREAU OF LAND MANAGEMENT

Activity Codes

Summer:

 – photography

Winter:

 – snowmobiling, cross-country skiing, dog-mushing

Colorado Creek Cabin offers cozy shelter to intrepid travelers in BLM's White Mountains National Recreation Area.
(Photo by Dave Vickery, National Interagency Fire Center)

A dazzling spring carpet of yellow poppies and other Arizona wildflowers is the welcome result of several consecutive years of abundant autumn rains. *(Photo by Gary Curtis (private, non-commercial); photo donated to Safford Field Office)*

Arizona

Arizona's public lands stretch across more than 14 million acres, mostly in the northwestern corner and the central western corridor of the state. Included are four spectacular deserts, the Chihuahuan, Sonoran, Mojave, and Great Basin. In addition to desert habitats, public lands include pinyon-juniper and ponderosa pine forests as well as small amounts of wetland and riparian (streamside) habitat.

These lands provide opportunities for a wide range of recreational activities, including hiking, biking, rock hounding, hunting, nature study, camping, off-highway vehicle exploration, and, yes, even water sports. They boast developed campgrounds, long-term visitor areas, and commercial recreational facilities that are easily accessible to visitors of all ages and abilities.

Some of the nation's oldest and best preserved prehistoric and historic sites are found on Arizona's public lands. These include rock art up to 6,000 years old, remnants of a Spanish military fort, a historic working cattle ranch and schoolhouse, and Indian dwellings over 1,000 years old.

Visitors to the public lands in Arizona can explore Wilderness Areas, two Riparian National Conservation Areas and numerous recreational facilities. The Colorado River and Lake Havasu are popular year-round destinations, drawing visitors from California, Nevada, Arizona, and beyond.

Another popular attraction is the San Pedro Riparian National Conservation Area, spanning over 50,000 acres of public land in Cochise County, Arizona. Its unique wetland areas are home to hundreds of bird species and other wildlife species. For those with a nostalgic bent, there is the Route 66 Historic Back Country Byway, where travelers can brave hairpin curves and steep grades on one of the last and best preserved segments of the original U.S. 66—one of America's first transcontinental highways.

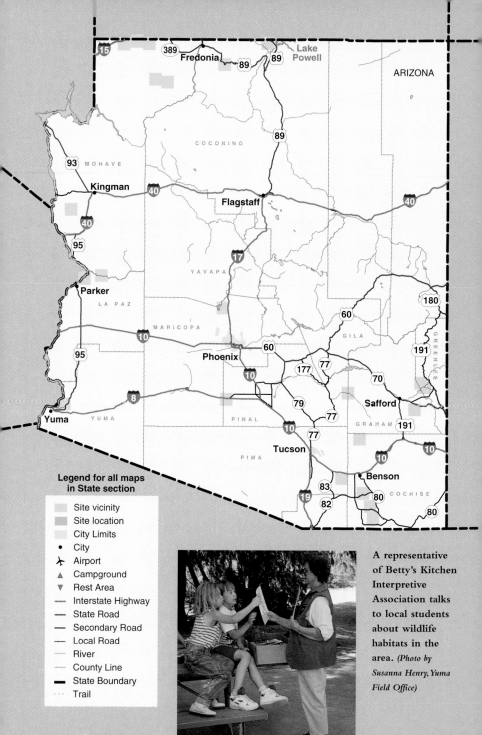

15
389 Fredonia 89 89 Lake Powell

ARIZONA

93 MOHAVE

COCONINO

89

Kingman 40

Flagstaff 40

40

95

17

YAVAPA

Parker

LA PAZ

180

MARICOPA

60

191

10

Phoenix 60

177 77

79 77 70

8 77 Safford

Yuma YUMA PINAL 10 191

GRAHAM

Tucson 10 10

PIMA 10

GILA

GREENLEE

COCHISE

Benson 80

Legend for all maps in State section

- Site vicinity
- Site location
- City Limits
- • City
- ✈ Airport
- ▲ Campground
- ▼ Rest Area
- — Interstate Highway
- — State Road
- — Secondary Road
- — Local Road
- — River
- — County Line
- — State Boundary
- ··· Trail

A representative of Betty's Kitchen Interpretive Association talks to local students about wildlife habitats in the area. *(Photo by Susanna Henry, Yuma Field Office)*

Aravaipa Canyon Wilderness

Location
23 miles southeast of Winkelman, Arizona

Description
The perennial waters of Aravaipa Creek have carved a scenic canyon through the Sonoran Desert at the northern end of the Galiuro Mountains in southeastern Arizona. Saguaro cactus dot the canyon slopes, and a mixed-broadleaf riparian forest lines the canyon slopes at the creek. The canyon, 1,000 feet deep in places, is home to desert bighorn sheep, javelinas, coati mundis, ringtail cats, and other interesting wildlife. The creek is home to 7 species of native fish, and over 200 species of birds live among the cottonwoods, sycamores, willows, ash, and other riparian species in the canyon. Aravaipa Canyon is 11 miles long, and elevations range from 3,000 feet at the eastern trailhead to 2,650 feet at the western trailhead. Nine major side canyons feed into Aravaipa.

Mailing Address
BLM - Safford Field Office
711 14th Avenue
Safford, AZ 85546

Phone Number   Fax Number
(520) 348-4400   (520) 348-4450

Directions
(To east trailhead) From Safford, travel 13 miles west on State Highway 70 to the Aravaipa/Klondyke Road. Turn left, and follow the Aravaipa/Klondyke Road 32 miles to Klondyke, where there is a BLM Ranger Station. From Klondyke, continue on the Aravaipa Road for 10 miles.

Visitor Activities
Hiking, backpacking, wildlife viewing, horseback riding, sightseeing, nature study, photography, and hunting.

Permits, Fees. Limitations
An entry permit is required, and may be reserved up to 13 weeks in advance of entry date. Use is limited to 50 people per day: 30 entering from the west trailhead, and 20 entering from the east trailhead. Call the BLM's Safford Office for more information.

Accessibility
None

Camping and Lodging
Fourmile Canyon Campground is a year-round area located in Klondyke, 0.75 mile southwest of Fourmile Canyon Road. This is a 10-unit campground with tables, grills, toilets, water, and trash cans, but no hook-ups. Daily fees are charged. Camping also is permitted on adjacent public lands with no facilities. Lodging is available in Klondyke.

Food and Supplies
Food and supplies are available in Klondyke, Safford and Winkelman.

First Aid
No first aid is available on-site. The hospital nearest to the east end is in Safford. The nearest medical facilities to the west end are in Kearny, 33 miles northwest on State Highway 177 and San Manuel, 30 miles southwest on State Highway 77.

Additional Information
Hiking in the canyon is considered to be moderately difficult, and numerous calf- and knee-deep stream crossings are required. The wilderness is open year-round, but spring and fall are the best times in which to hike. Summer can be quite hot, and winter is chilly.

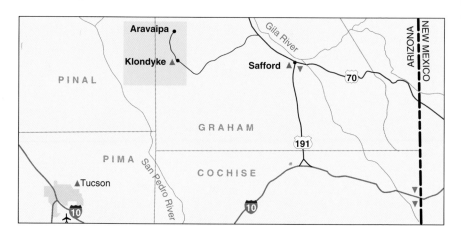

Sponsoring Partners

WILD SHEEP

AMERICA
OUTDOORS

American Rivers

Activity Codes

 - sightseeing, nature study,
photography, backpacking

Betty's Kitchen
National Recreation Trail

Location
17 miles southwest of Yuma, Arizona

Phone Number
(520) 317-3200

Fax Number
(520) 317-3250

Description
Betty's Kitchen and Interpretive Area is a lush, shady spot along the Lower Colorado River, with a picnic area, 0.5-mile interpretive trail, and fishing pier. Betty's Kitchen is enjoyed by many for wildlife observation, picnicking and fishing throughout the year. The Betty's Kitchen Protective Association assists BLM with the management of the site.

Mailing Address
BLM - Yuma Field Office
2555 Gila Ridge Road
Yuma, AZ 85365

Directions
From Yuma, take State Highway 95 (16th Street) east 5 miles to Avenue 7E. Turn north on Avenue 7E, following it 9 miles to a point just past Laguna Dam. Turn left at the sign for Betty's Kitchen Wildlife and Interpretive Area.

Visitor Activities
Fishing, picnicking, wildlife viewing, birdwatching, plant viewing, and interpretive tours.

Permits, Fees, Limitations
No fees. The site is for day use only.

Accessibility

There are fully-accessible vault toilets, picnic facilities, a fishing pier, walking bridge, and interpretive trail.

Camping and Lodging

Free camping is available at nearby Mittry Lake Wildlife Area. Camping for a nightly fee is available at BLM's Squaw Lake Campground, approximately 15 miles north on State Highway 95. A variety of motels and hotels are available in Yuma.

Food and Supplies

No food or supplies are available on-site. Restaurants and food stores are located in Yuma.

First Aid

There is no first aid available on-site. The nearest hospital is located in Yuma. There is also a medical facility at the Yuma Proving Grounds, 9 miles further up the gravel road past the Mittry Lake Wildlife Area.

Additional Information

Betty's Kitchen is best visited during the spring, winter, and fall. Daily summer

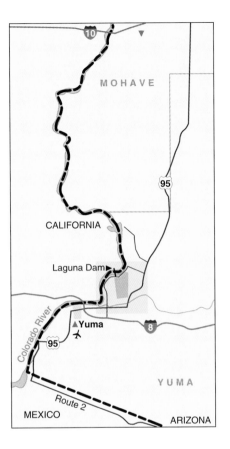

Plentiful drainage from the Lower Colorado River makes Betty's Kitchen an inviting refuge for a variety of desert wildlife. *(Photo by David Smith ©, Arizona State Office)*

temperature highs are usually 100° to 118°F. Although mosquitoes are generally not present, they occur periodically, so insect repellent is recommended. Most anglers fish for bluegill, channel catfish, and flathead catfish, although largemouth bass can also be caught at Betty's Kitchen. The best time of year for birdwatching is during the spring migration (April and May). Tours may be arranged through Betty's Kitchen Protective Association [Tel.: (520) 627-2773].

Sponsor

Activity Codes

 - interpretive tours, picnicking

Bill Williams River

Location
17 miles south of Lake Havasu City, Arizona

Description
Six state and federal agencies have worked together since 1992 to manage the Bill Williams River's outstanding riparian, wildlife, recreational, and fisheries resources. Recreationists will find opportunities for many activities in a unique setting. The Swansea Ghost Town site is also nearby.

Mailing Address
BLM - Lake Havasu Field Office
2610 Sweetwater Avenue
Lake Havasu City, AZ 86406

Phone Number   Fax Number
(520) 505-1200   (520) 505-1208

Directions
From Interstate 40, take State Highway 95 south approximately 37 miles to where the Bill Williams River flows into the Colorado River at Lake Havasu. The marshy delta created at the confluence can be viewed from several Highway 95 turnouts.

To get to the Swansea Ghost Town site: Continue south on Highway 95 approximately 20 miles from the Bill Williams River bridge to Parker, and turn east onto Highway 72 for approximately 2 miles. Then turn onto Shea Road for 28 miles (11 miles on paved road and the next 17 miles on graded road) to reach the Swansea Ghost Town site. From the town site, the river can be accessed by following a four-wheel-drive vehicle road for 3.5 miles. The final 50 yards are closed to motorized vehicles, and you must walk to the river. This part of the river is within the Swansea Wilderness.

Visitor Activities
Scenic drives, sightseeing, birdwatching, plant viewing, rafting, wildlife viewing, historic site, and hiking.

Permits, Fees, Limitations
None

Accessibility
None

Camping and Lodging
No developed camping or lodging facilities are available at the river. Tent sites are available at Swansea Ghost Town site. Full-service hotel accommodations and recreational vehicle parks are available in Lake Havasu City and Parker.

Food and Supplies
Food and supplies can be purchased in Lake Havasu City and Parker.

First Aid
Emergency services are provided by the La Paz County Sheriff and Fire Department. The nearest hospital is located in Parker.

Additional Information
Low rainfall, mild winters, and hot summers are the norm. Because of high summer temperatures, fall through spring is the best time to visit. Access from the Swansea Ghost Town site to the river is limited to four-wheel-drive vehicles and hikers.

Sponsoring Partner

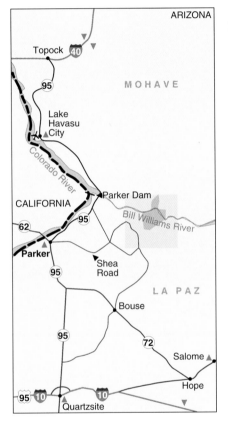

Activity Codes

- sightseeing

Black Canyon Trail

Location
3 miles west of New River, Arizona

Description
For 100 years, the Black Canyon Trail was used by Arizona ranchers to drive livestock from the Phoenix area north toward Flagstaff. From the south, the trail passes through the lower Sonoran Desert, skirts the Perry Mesa National Archaeological District, and culminates near the eastern slopes of the Bradshaw Mountains. Plant life is typical of the Sonoran desert and chaparral woodlands. Many species of animals can be found along the trail, including mule deer, javelinas, bobcats, quail, hummingbirds, and Gila monsters. When completed, the Black Canyon Trail will be more than 70 miles long and will provide fall, winter, and spring recreational opportunities.

Mailing Address
BLM - Phoenix Field Office
2015 West Deer Valley Road
Phoenix, AZ 85027

Phone Number
(602) 580-5500

Fax Number
(602) 580-5580

Directions
From Interstate 17 in the Phoenix area, take the New River exit. Proceed west 3 miles to the end of the paved road. Before the road becomes gravel, turn right into the Emery Henderson/Black Canyon Trailhead. The Black Canyon Trail begins at the north end of the parking lot.

Visitor Activities
Picnicking, hiking, wildflower viewing, plant viewing, birdwatching, horseback riding, and mountain biking.

Permits, Fees, Limitations
No fees. Commercial recreation operators using or crossing BLM land require a Special Recreation Permit, available from BLM.

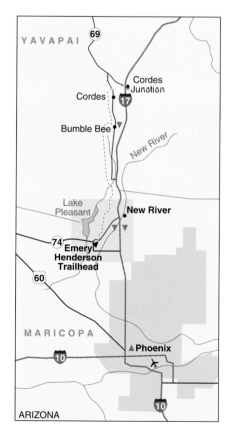

Accessibility

The Emery Henderson/Black Canyon Trailhead and associated facilities are wheelchair-accessible. The facilities include hitching posts, picnic ramadas, an information kiosk and composting toilets. The Black Canyon Trail is a rugged and rough single- and two-track trail, and is not recommended for wheelchairs.

Camping and Lodging

Camping and lodging facilities are not available on-site.

Food and Supplies

Food, water, and supplies are not available on-site. They may be purchased in New River, Black Canyon City, and Cordes Junction, all along Interstate 17 within 20 miles of the site.

First Aid

No first aid is available on-site. The nearest hospital is in Phoenix, 20 miles south of New River.

Additional Information

The Black Canyon Trail is marked and open for most of the distance from New River (elevation 1,500 feet) to State Highway 69 (elevation 4,500 feet), over 40 miles north. The trail incorporates rugged old roads and a newly-constructed, single-track trail. Because of extreme summer temperatures, the Black Canyon Trail is NOT recommended for recreational use during the summer months.

Sponsoring Partner

American Hiking Society

Activity Codes

- mountain biking, picnicking, horseback riding

Black Hills Back Country Byway

Location

18 miles west of Safford, Arizona

Description

The Black Hills Back Country Byway offers 21 miles of back country driving adventure through the northern end of the Peloncillo Mountains in southeastern Arizona. Along the Byway are sweeping views of the Black Hills, Gila Mountains, Mount Graham, and the Gila River Valley. Major attractions seen from the Byway include the Gila Box Riparian National Conservation Area (NCA) along the Gila River, the Phelps Dodge Copper Mine at Morenci, a Civilian Conservation Corps work camp, over 100 erosion-control structures, and a historic prison labor camp. Side trips off the Byway provide access to the Gila River and spectacular overlooks of the Gila River Canyon within the NCA.

Mailing Address

BLM - Safford Field Office
711 14th Avenue
Safford, AZ 85546

Phone Number	Fax Number
(520) 348-4400	(520) 348-4450

The Black Hills Back Country Byway traverses the Gila Box Riparian National Conservation Area via the historic Old Safford Bridge. *(Photo by Diane Drobka, Safford Field Office)*

Directions

To reach the south end: From Safford, travel 10 miles on State Highway 70 to its junction with State Highway 191. Turn left onto Highway 191 and continue 8 miles to the southern end of the Byway (milepost 139). To reach the northern end: From Clifton, travel 4 miles south on Highway 191 to the end of the Byway (milepost 160) and turn right.

Visitor Activities

Scenic driving, sightseeing, hiking, environmental education, mountain biking, wildlife viewing, birdwatching, plant viewing, picnicking, historic site, hunting, and fishing.

Permits, Fees, Limitations

None

Accessibility

The entrance kiosks at each end of the Byway, the Canyon Overlook Picnic Area, and the Phelps Dodge interpretive exhibit are all wheelchair-accessible.

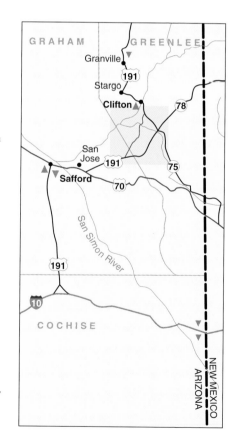

Camping and Lodging

No-fee camping is permitted at the Old Bridge Picnic Area at Gila River; the only facilities are tables and grills. Camping also is permitted on adjacent public lands; there are no facilities. Camping is limited to 14 consecutive days in any one location. Lodging is available in Clifton, Morenci, and Safford.

Food and Supplies

Food and supplies are available in Clifton, Morenci, and Safford.

First Aid

No first aid is available on-site. The nearest hospitals are in Morenci and Safford.

Additional Information

The Byway road is narrow and winding, with occasional steep grades and tight turns. Much of the road is maintained, but a high-clearance or four-wheel-drive vehi-cle is recommended. A 4-mile section near the middle of the Byway can be rough and impassible during the rainy/snowy season. A brochure (free) and an interpretive travel tape (for sale) are available from BLM. Elevation ranges from 3,800 to 5,500 feet.

Sponsoring Partner

SCENIC AMERICA

Activity Codes

  - mountain biking, interpretive exhibit, sightseeing, environmental education, picnicking

Empire-Cienega Resource Conservation Area

Location

45 miles southeast of Tucson

Description

This 45,000-acre conservation area of outstanding high desert, rolling grasslands, woodlands, and riparian zones contains abundant wildlife, including pronghorn antelope and 200 species of birds. A historic working cattle ranch, complete with enchanting old headquarters, now operates under an innovative rangeland management style unique to the area.

Mailing Address

BLM - Tucson Field Office
12661 E. Broadway Blvd.
Tucson, AZ 85748

Phone Number

(520) 722-4289

Fax Number

(520) 751-0948

Directions

From Tucson, drive south on Interstate 10 to exit 281, and drive south on State Highway 83. Near milepost 40, turn east into the ranch entrance.

Visitor Activities

Wildlife viewing, birdwatching, hiking, historic site, hunting, and scenic drives.

Permits, Fees, Limitations

None

Accessibility

Some of the rooms at the cattle ranch headquarters are wheelchair-accessible through the front breezeway entrance.

Camping and Lodging

Primitive camping is allowed on existing sites only. Camping may not exceed 14 consecutive days. Camp at least 0.25 mile from cattle and wildlife water holes. Bring your own water and firewood. The nearest lodging is available in Sonoita, 5 miles south on Highway 83, and in Patagonia. Campfires are allowed except during periods of extreme fire danger. Only dead and downed wood may be used. Use existing fire rings.

Food and Supplies

A gas station and a variety of restaurants and carryouts are located in the town of Sonoita.

First Aid

First aid is available at the Santa Cruz Sheriff's office in Sonoita. The nearest hospitals are located in Sierra Vista and Tucson, approximately 30 miles north.

Additional Information

There is no trash pick-up service at this site; take trash out with you. Leave gates as you find them to keep cattle in the correct pasture. There are no facilities. All roads are dirt.

Sponsor

Activity Codes

Public participants enjoy a guided walk along Cienega Creek at the Empire-Cienega Resource Conservation Area.
(Photo by Diane Drobka, Safford Field Office)

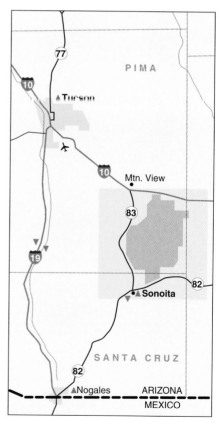

Gila Box Riparian National Conservation Area

Location
20 miles northeast of Safford, Arizona

Description
Twenty-three miles of the Gila River and 15 miles of Bonita Creek are included in this special Natural Conservation Area, which was designated by Congress. The Gila River Canyon section, known as the Gila Box, is composed of patchy mesquite woodlands, mature cottonwoods, sandy beaches, and grand buff-colored cliffs. Canoeing, kayaking, and rafting enthusiasts take advantage of the spring run-off to enjoy an easy to moderately-difficult floating adventure down the Gila. Many people also float the river in inflatable kayaks during the low water of the summer. Lower water also affords hikers the opportunity to safely enjoy the scenic canyon. Bonita Creek, popular for birdwatching, hiking, and picnicking, is lined with large cottonwoods, sycamores, and willows. Cliff dwellings, historic homesteads, Rocky Mountain bighorn sheep, and over 200 species of birds are found along the scenic canyon. The perennial creek and riparian (streamside) vegetation community make this a cool year-round desert oasis.

Mailing Address
BLM – Safford Field Office
711 14th Avenue
Safford, AZ 85546

Phone Number	Fax Number
(520) 348-4400	(520) 348-4450

A variety of vegetation—from cotton-woods to mesquite—adorns Gila Box, complemented by sandy beaches and dusky cliffs. *(Photo © David Smith, Arizona State Office)*

Directions
To reach the west side: From Safford, travel 5 miles east on State Highway 70 to Solomon. At Solomon, turn left on the Sanchez Road and follow the road to the end of the pavement. From there, follow the signs to Bonita Creek and the lower end of the Gila Box.

To reach the east side: From Safford, take Highway 70 east 10 miles to its junction with State Highway 191. Turn left and follow Highway 191 about 29 miles to milepost 160, which is 4 miles south of Clifton. Turn left onto the signed Byway, and follow the road 4 miles to the Conservation Area.

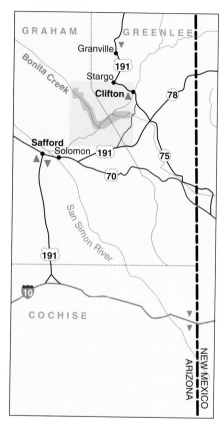

Visitor Activities
Rafting, canoeing, kayaking, picnicking, plant viewing, birdwatching, scenic drives, fishing, wildlife viewing, hiking, sightseeing, historic interpretation, camping, horseback riding, swimming, and hunting.

Permits, Fees, Limitation
Camping is limited to 14 consecutive days in any one location. No permits or fees.

Accessibility
The Bonita Creek Wildlife Viewing Area is wheelchair-accessible.

Camping and Lodging
Camping is permitted at no charge at the Old Bridge Picnic Area, Spring Canyon Picnic Area, and at the mouth of Bonita Creek; the only facilities are tables. Camping is also permitted on adjacent public lands; no facilities are available. Lodging is available in Clifton, 10 miles north on State Highway 191.

Food and Supplies
Food and supplies are available in Clifton, Morenci (south on Highway 191), and in Safford.

First Aid
No first aid is available on-site. The nearest hospitals are in Morenci and Safford.

Additional Information
Major access points are generally reachable by passenger car, but other roads may be rough at times because of infrequent maintenance. Four-wheel drive vehicles are required on many roads. Check with BLM for up-to-date road conditions. Elevations range from 3,100 to 4,400 feet. The Conservation Area is open year-round. Summer temperatures can be extremely hot, and some winter days quite cold. Flooding may occur during winter and summer rainy seasons, as well as during spring run-off.

Sponsoring Partner

Activity Codes

 - canoeing, kayaking, swimming, horseback riding, sightseeing, picnicking

Little Black Mountain Petroglyph Site

Location
10 miles southeast of St. George, Utah

Phone Number   Fax Number
(435) 688-3246   (435) 688-3258

Description
The site contains some outstanding rock art, representing 6,000 years of human habitation and use. The site has over 500 individual rock-art designs and elements on the cliffs and boulders surrounding the base of a 500-foot mesa. The different designs are associated with the cultures of the Great Basin, Western Anasazi and Lower Colorado River, only a few of the many cultures that have passed this way. Some of the representations of turtles, lizards and bear paws may be symbols with social or religious meanings that are now lost to us.

Directions
From St. George, Utah, travel south on River Road 5 miles to the Arizona State Line. Three-tenths of a mile south of the State Line, turn left (east) and drive 4.5 miles to the site.

Visitor Activities
Viewing petroglyph panels.

Permits, Fees, Limitations
None

Accessibility
None

Mailing Address
BLM - Arizona Strip Field Office
345 East Riverside Drive
St. George, UT 84790

Camping and Lodging
No camping or lodging facilities are available on-site. Lodging is available in St. George.

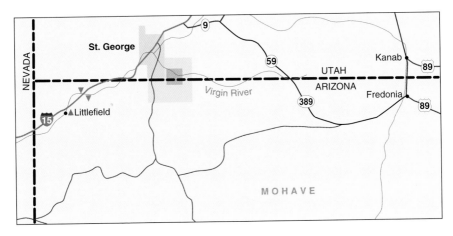

Food and Supplies
No food or supplies are available on-site. Food and supplies are available in St. George.

First Aid
No first aid is available on-site. The nearest hospital is in St. George.

Additional Information
The area is very hot in the summer. A high-clearance vehicle is recommended.

Sponsoring Partner

Activity Codes

  - petroglyphs

Mt. Trumbull

Location
55 miles southwest of Fredonia, Arizona

Description
Mt. Trumbull is centered in the Uinkaret Mountains, just north of the Grand Canyon. The area contains basalt flows and cinder cones draped with ponderosa pine, piñon pine, and juniper. Tassel-eared Kaibab squirrels and wild turkeys are abundant.

Mailing Address
BLM - Arizona Strip Field Office
345 East Riverside Drive
St. George, UT 84790

Phone Number   Fax Number
(435) 688-3246   (435) 688-3258

Directions
From Fredonia, Arizona: Travel 8 miles west on State Highway 389 to its intersection with Toroweap Road (County Road

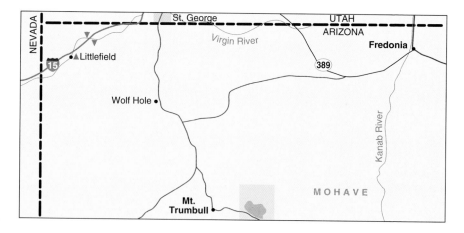

109). Follow Toroweap Road southwest about 38 miles to its intersection with County Road 5. Continue south 6 miles on County Road 5 to its intersection with County Road 115. Bear right, and continue 7 miles east on County Road 5 to Nixon Flat, a large, open meadow at the foot of Mt. Trumbull. From St. George, Utah: Follow the directions to the Mt. Trumbull Schoolhouse site, and continue east from the Schoolhouse on County Road 5 about 10 miles to Nixon Flat.

Visitor Activities
Wildlife viewing, geologic sightseeing, sightseeing, hiking, and scenic drives.

Permits, Fees, Limitations
Vehicles are restricted to existing roads and trails; vehicles and mountain bikes are not permitted in the wilderness areas.

Accessibility
None

Camping and Lodging
No camping facilities or developed campsites are provided on-site. Camping in semi-primitive settings is permitted throughout the area, within 100 yards of existing roads.

Food and Supplies
No food and supplies are available in the area. The nearest sources are in Fredonia and in St. George, Utah, 70 miles northwest on Quail Hill Road.

First Aid
No first aid is available on-site. The nearest hospital is in St. George.

Additional Information
Roads are hazardous when wet. No services are available on-site and the area is about 55 miles from the nearest town. Winter conditions include below-freezing temperatures and muddy or snow-covered

The Mt. Trumbull area is the focus of a major cooperative effort to restore the health of the local ponderosa pine ecosystem. *(Courtesy BLM)*

roads. Spring through fall is the best time to visit. No conveniences are provided.

Sponsoring Partner

Activity Codes

 - geologic sightseeing, sightseeing

Mt. Trumbull Schoolhouse

Location
60 miles southeast of St. George, Utah

Description
This is a historic schoolhouse that has been restored and is open to the public. The old schoolhouse holds fond memories for those who received some or all of their education there. It functioned as a school, church, dance hall, and a town meeting place. People came from miles around to attend dances and listen to music played by local musicians, which were their main sources of entertainment. The first schooling in the area took place in the home of one of the local residents. In order to accommodate a growing student body, a modest schoolhouse was built. Soon it became too small and was moved to make room for the existing building, which was completed in 1922 and continued to be used until 1966.

Mailing Address
BLM - Arizona Strip Field Office
345 East Riverside Drive
St. George, UT 84790

Phone Number   Fax Number
(435) 688-3246   (435) 688-3258

Directions
From Exit 8 on Interstate 15 in St. George, Utah, travel 8 miles south on River Road to the Arizona State Line. Continue south about 18 miles along BLM Road 1069 into Wolfhole Valley. Continue about 34 miles southeast on County Road 5 to the schoolhouse.

Visitor Activities
Scenic drives and historic site.

Permits, Fees, Limitations
None

Accessibility
None

Camping and Lodging
No camping or lodging is available on-site. Call BLM for information on nearby lodging.

Food and Supplies
No food or supplies are available on-site. Call BLM for information on supply sources.

First Aid
No first aid is available on-site. The nearest hospitals are in St. George and Kanab, Utah.

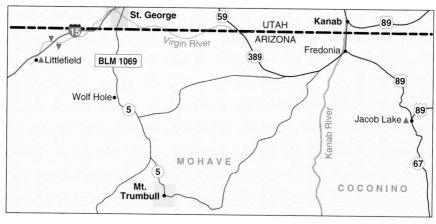

Additional Information
The site is open all year. A visit to this site requires a 120-mile round-trip on unpaved roads that can be impassable when wet. Visitor maps can be obtained from BLM. Be sure to bring enough food, water and supplies for your round-trip. Check weather conditions before leaving.

Sponsor

Activity Codes

 - historic schoolhouse

Muleshoe Ranch
Cooperative Management Area

Location
20 miles west of Willcox, Arizona

Description
This area boasts rugged mountains, canyon streams, saguaro cactus, and mesquite bosques that are home to desert dwellers such as coati mundi, javelina, and a wide variety of neo-tropical migratory birds and native fish. The mosaic of public and private land, which includes the BLM's Redfield Canyon Wilderness, the U.S. Forest Service's Galiuro Wilderness, and The Nature Conservancy's Muleshoe Preserve, offers a diversity of remote recreational opportunities.

Mailing Address
BLM - Safford Field Office
711 14th Avenue
Safford, AZ 85546

Phone Numbers   Fax Number
(520) 348-4400   (520) 348-4450

Directions
From Willcox, take Interstate 10 to exit 340 south. Turn right on Bisbee Avenue, then turn right on Airport Road. After

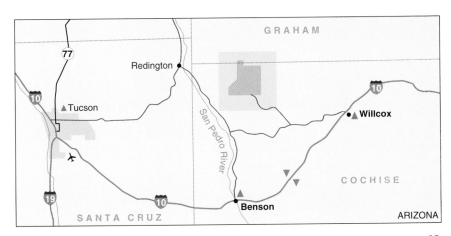

A lone saguaro perches on an escarpment at Muleshoe Ranch, a rugged desert area that is home to such unique wildlife as coati mundis and javelinas. *(Photo by Diane Drobka, Safford Field Office)*

15 miles, bear right at a fork in the road. Drive 14 more miles to The Nature Conservancy's Muleshoe Headquarters.

Visitor Activities
Wildlife viewing, birdwatching, hiking, and scenic drives.

Permits, Fees, Limitations
No fees. Visitors must sign the guest register at Muleshoe Headquarters. All wilderness areas prohibit the use of motorized vehicles; additional specific rules apply in some areas. Hunting is not allowed on The Nature Conservancy's land.

Accessibility
None

Camping and Lodging
The Nature Conservancy's Muleshoe Preserve has casitas for guests. Minimum-impact backpack camping is also allowed on the Preserve. Lodging is available in Willcox and Benson.

Food and Supplies
Supplies are available in Willcox and Benson.

First Aid
First aid is available in Willcox and Benson.

Additional Information
Plan ahead. Bring a good map, water, and food. Spring, fall, and winter are the best times to visit. Learn ahead of time about heat, poisonous wildlife, prickly plants, and thunderstorms, all of which pose potential hazards. All roads are dirt.

Sponsoring Partner

Activity Codes

Murray Springs Clovis Site

Location
6 miles east of Sierra Vista, Arizona

Description
Murray Springs is a significant archaeological site that contains an undisturbed stratigraphic record of the past 40,000 years. Excavations were conducted by the University of Arizona from 1966 to 1971. People first arrived in this area 11,000 years ago. They belonged to what we now call the Clovis Culture and were the earliest known people to have inhabited North America. Named after the distinctive and beautifully crafted Clovis spear points they made, they were expert hunters of the large mammals of the last Ice Age. An interpretive trail leads visitors through the site. (The Murray Springs Clovis Site is within the San Pedro Riparian National Conservation Area, described elsewhere in this guidebook.)

Mailing Address
BLM - San Pedro Project Office
1763 Paseo San Luis
Sierra Vista, AZ 85635

Phone Number
(520) 458-3559

Fax Number
(520) 458-3559

Directions
From Sierra Vista, take State Highway 90 east 6 miles to Moson Road. Turn left, and go about 1.2 miles to the signed turnoff to Murray Springs. The access road is located on the right.

Visitor Activities
Birdwatching, hiking, biking, horseback riding, and archaeological interpretation.

Permits, Fees, Limitations
No firearm discharge is permitted. The site is for day use only.

Accessibility
None

Camping and Lodging
Only back country camping is available. Back country permits can be obtained from the San Pedro House on Highway 90. The nearest lodging is available in Sierra Vista.

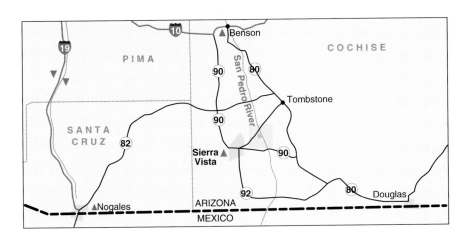

First Aid
There is no first aid available on-site. The nearest hospital is in Sierra Vista.

Additional Information
None

Sponsoring Partner

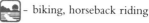
SAA
SOCIETY FOR AMERICAN ARCHAEOLOGY

Activity Codes

- biking, horseback riding

Paria Canyon

Location
30 miles northeast of Page, Arizona

Description
Paria Canyon is part of the larger Paria Canyon-Vermilion Cliffs Wilderness. A scenic river carves a 37-mile canyon through 7 major geologic formations of the Colorado Plateau.

Mailing Address
BLM - Arizona Strip Field Office
345 East Riverside Drive
St. George, UT 84790

Phone Number   Fax Number
(435) 688-3246   (435) 688-3258

Directions
From Page, take U.S. Highway 89 west for 30 miles to the Paria Information Station. Or, from Kanab, Utah, drive 40 miles east on U.S. Highway 89 and turn south at the information station. The trailhead is 2 miles south of the station.

Visitor Activities
Hiking, backpacking, wildlife viewing, geologic sightseeing, and photography.

Permits, Fees, Limitations
Group size is limited to 10 persons for carry-on entry, and requires visitor registration. No campfires or motorized vehi-

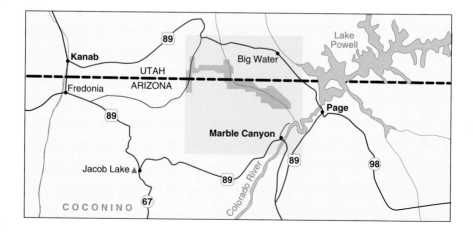

cles are allowed in the canyons. Contact BLM for information on fees.

Accessibility
None

Camping and Lodging
There are 5 walk-in campsites at White House Trailhead. Lodging is available in Page, Marble Canyon (10 miles east), and Kanab.

Food and Supplies
No food or supplies are available on-site. Supplies can be purchased in Kanab, and Page.

First Aid
There is no reliable first aid available on-site. The nearest hospital is in Page.

Additional Information
Paria Canyon is subject to life-threatening flash floods at any time of the year. Temperatures range from lows of 20°F during the winter to highs of over 100°F in the summer. Hiking usually requires frequent wading in shallow water.

Sponsoring Partner

Activity Codes

 - geologic sightseeing, backpacking, photography

Parker Strip Recreation Area

Location
In Parker, Arizona

Description
With an annual visitation of approximately 3 million people, the Parker Strip is one of the BLM's most visited recreation areas. Composed of BLM-operated campgrounds, off-highway vehicle areas, and concessionaire facilities, the Parker Strip provides a wide array of activities for the outdoor enthusiast.

Mailing Address
BLM - Lake Havasu Field Office
2610 Sweetwater Avenue
Lake Havasu City, AZ 86406

Phone Number
(520) 505-1200

Fax Number
(520) 505-1208

Directions
From Interstate 40, go south on State Highway 95 approximately 38 miles, through Lake Havasu City into Parker. Access to camping sites can be made from Highway 95 at Parker Dam, and from the California side of the Colorado River/Parker Dam Road Back Country Byway. Access is also available by traveling on Highway 95 along the Arizona side of the Colorado River and into the town of Parker.

Visitor Activities
Hiking, scenic drives, fishing, boating, swimming, wildlife viewing, birdwatching, wild horse and burro viewing, off-highway touring, and plant viewing.

Permits, Fees, Limitations

Concessionaire-owned facilities are open year-round and restrict visitors to a maximum stay of 150 days per year. At BLM-operated campgrounds, the maximum stay is 14 days and fees are charged. The BLM campgrounds are also open year-round. Contact BLM for a list of concessionaires and their telephone numbers; contact concessionaire-operated facilities directly for rate schedules.

Accessibility

BLM and concessionaire-operated facilities are wheelchair-accessible.

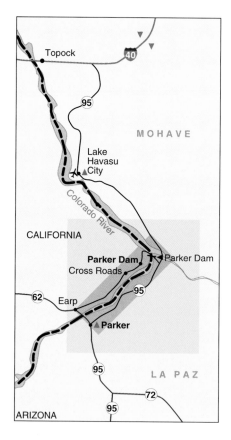

Camping and Lodging

Accommodations are available along both sides of the Colorado River in the Parker Strip Recreation Area. Facilities range from motels to primitive campsites.

Food and Supplies

Several concessionaire-operated facilities along area highways have general stores with food, gasoline, and camping supplies.

First Aid

Emergency services are provided by the San Bernardino County Sheriff and Fire Department. The nearest hospital is located in Parker.

Additional Information

Havasu Resource Area concessions are composed of approximately 2,500 recreation vehicle (RV) sites, 1,300 mobile home sites (limited to 150 days of occupancy per year), general stores, boat launch ramps, RV fueling facilities, RV and boat storage units, restaurants, and overnight accommodations. Concessionaire-operated facilities are used by both winter and summer visitors. Scattered along 11.5 miles of the Colorado River between Parker Dam and the Colorado River Indian Tribal boundary, BLM-operated facilities include boat launch ramps, campsites, several day-use areas, off-highway vehicle areas, and a newly constructed visitor center. Two public fishing docks are available and provide anglers with the best shoreline fishing on the south end of Lake Havasu. Take Off Point and Havasu Springs Dock provide anglers with year-round challenges. The Lake Havasu Fisheries Improvement Program is the largest and most comprehensive warm-water fisheries project ever undertaken in the United States; BLM is the lead agency for the multi-agency partnership. The project goals include increasing sport fishing opportunities in Lake Havasu, improving access and facilities for shoreline anglers, and augmenting the dwindling populations of two endangered fish species in the lake. Low rainfall, mild winters, and hot summers are the norm.

Sponsor

Activity Codes

  - swimming

Presidio Santa Cruz de Terrenate

Location
65 miles east of Tucson, Arizona

Description
The Spanish Presidio Santa Cruz de Terrenate is the most intact remaining example of a once-extensive network of similar presidios. These fortresses marked the northern extension of New Spain into the New World. Only a stone foundation and a few remaining adobe wall remnants mark the location of an isolated and dangerous military station.

Mailing Address
BLM - San Pedro Project Office
1763 Paseo San Luis
Sierra Vista, AZ 85635

Phone Number   Fax Number
(520) 458-3559   (520) 458-3559

Directions
Take Interstate 10 east from Tucson to State Route 90. Go south about 20 miles to State Route 82. Turn east and continue 9 miles to Kellar Road (0.2 mile before

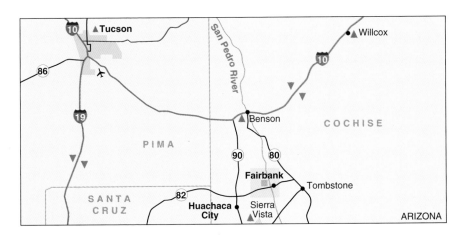

the San Pedro River). Go north about 2 miles to the marked BLM parking lot.

Visitor Activities
Birdwatching, hiking, biking, horseback riding, and archaeological site.

Permits, Fees, Limitations
There are fees for back-country camping.

Accessibility
None

Camping and Lodging
The closest developed camping and lodging is in Tombstone, 10 miles east on State Highway 80. Daily back-country permits can be obtained at Fairbank (see "Additional Information," below). Overnight camping in vehicles or in parking lots is not permitted.

Food and Supplies
Food and supplies can be purchased in Huachaca City, approximately 12 miles southwest on State Highway 90, and in Sierra Vista.

First Aid
The nearest hospital is located in Sierra Vista.

Additional Information
Fairbank is a historic ghost town that provides access to the San Pedro River, trails, picnicking and birdwatching. It is also where the tourist train from Benson, Arizona, stops. It is about 3 miles from the Presidio trailhead, along State Highway 82. There is a full-time volunteer site host, a small information room, and a self-service back-country permit station.

Sponsoring Partner

SOCIETY for
HISTORICAL
ARCHAEOLOGY

Activity Codes

- biking, horseback riding

Route 66 Historic Back Country Byway

Location
6 miles west of Kingman, Arizona

Description
This 42-mile stretch of two-lane blacktop is one of the last and best-preserved segments of the original Route 66, one of America's first transcontinental highways. This portion of the highway once included one of the most fearsome obstacles for "flatland" travelers in the 1930's: the hairpin curves and steep grades of Sitgreaves Pass, which characterize Old Route 66 as it makes its way over the Black Mountains of western Arizona.

Mailing Address
BLM - Kingman Field Office
2475 Beverly Avenue
Kingman, AZ 86401

Phone Number   Fax Number
(520) 692-4400   (520) 692-4414

Directions
From Kingman, travel west on Interstate 40 to Exit 44 (McConnico/Oatman). Follow the Oatman Road west for about 0.5 mile to a left turn on Historic Route 66. The Byway begins here, and ends 42 miles further at the community of Golden Shores.

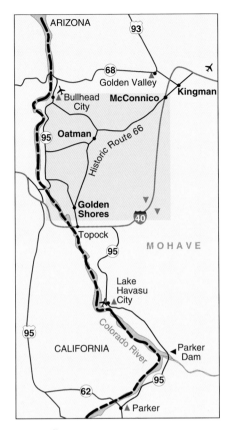

Visitor Activities

Scenic drives, historic site, wild burro viewing, wildlife viewing, plant viewing, and souvenir shopping.

Permits, Fees, Limitations

None

Accessibility

The Byway is driveable in any type of vehicle of less than 40 feet in length. Information kiosks at both ends of the Byway are wheelchair-accessible. No other BLM facilities are present along the route.

Camping and Lodging

Primitive camping without fees is available on public lands year-round. Motel lodging is abundant in Kingman and is limited in Oatman, which is situated in the center of the Byway.

Food and Supplies

Food and supplies are available in nearby Kingman, and along Route 66 in Oatman and Golden Shores.

First Aid

The nearest hospitals are in Kingman and Bullhead City, approximately 28 miles north on State Highway 95. First aid is available from the Oatman Volunteer Fire Department and the Golden Shores Fire Department along Route 66.

Additional Information

Snow is not a constraining factor in traveling this road, but heat can be. The extreme heat of the summer months can limit activity levels outside vehicles. Make sure your car is in good operating condition. Bring plenty of extra water (for drinking and for your radiator) to have in the event of a car breakdown. Many plants and animals in the desert can be hazardous; if the desert is new to you, extreme caution is advised. The Byway can be traveled any time of year. Most of the road is in the open desert, with no facilities other than in Oatman. Plan your trip accordingly. The federally-designated Warm Springs and Mount Nutt Wilderness Area is adjacent to the Byway. Visitors may hand-feed wild burros in Oatman, a historic mining town.

Sponsor

Activity Codes

San Pedro Riparian National Conservation Area

Location
10 miles west of Sierra Vista, Arizona

Description
The San Pedro Riparian National Conservation Area, containing about 40 miles of the upper San Pedro River, was designated by Congress as a National Conservation Area (NCA) in 1988. The primary purpose for the designation was to protect and enhance the desert riparian (streamside) ecosystem, a rare remnant of what was once an extensive network of similar riparian systems throughout the American Southwest. One of the most important riparian areas in the United States, the San Pedro Area runs through the Chihuahuan Desert and the Sonoran Desert in southeastern Arizona along the San Pedro River. The Conservation Area, a 35-mile

The verdant San Pedro Riparian National Conservation Area follows the twisting San Pedro River 35 miles through the Sonoran Desert. *(Photo by David Smith ©, Arizona State Office)*

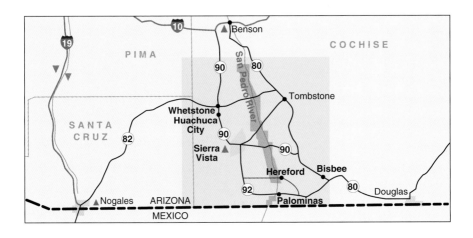

segment of this stretch, is home to 82 species of mammals, 12 species of fish, 47 species of reptiles and amphibians, and 100 species of breeding birds. It also provides invaluable habitat for 250 species of migrant and wintering birds, and contains archaeological sites representing the remains of human occupation from 11,200 years ago to the present. (The Murray Springs Clovis Site, described elsewhere in this guidebook, is located within the Conservation Area.)

Mailing Address
BLM - San Pedro Project Office
1763 Paseo San Luis
Sierra Vista, AZ 85635

Phone Number   Fax Number
(520) 458-3559   (520) 458-3559

Directions
Take Interstate 10 east from Tucson 40 miles to State Highway 90, then follow this highway south through Huachuca City to Fry Boulevard in Sierra Vista. Follow this street for 6 miles east until you reach the San Pedro House.

Visitor Activities
Birdwatching, hiking, fishing, rafting, biking, horseback riding, guided hikes, and weekend children's programs.

Permits, Fees, Limitations
There is an entrance fee, and back-country camping permits are required. Campfires are permitted only in designated areas. Firearm use is permitted only for regulated hunting, and only in certain areas. Contact BLM for specific information on hunting.

Accessibility
Wheelchair-accessible restrooms and trails are under construction.

Camping and Lodging
Only back-country camping is available, and a permit is required. Contact BLM for information on fees and permits.

Food and Supplies
Food and supplies are available in the surrounding communities of Sierra Vista, Whetstone, and Bisbee (approximately 10 miles east), Hereford (within the San Pedro Riparian NCA), and Palominas

(within the San Pedro Riparian NCA).

First Aid
The nearest hospital is in Sierra Vista.

Additional Information
The San Pedro River is subject to seasonal flooding, and summer monsoons are common. Birdwatching is best in the spring and fall. Picnic facilities are available at Fairbank (within the San Pedro Riparian NCA) and at the San Pedro House (also located within the San Pedro Riparian NCA, and run by volunteers). Call ahead for the schedule of guided walks, hikes and children's programs. The San Pedro gift shop/bookstore is open from 9:30 a.m. to 4:30 p.m. daily.

Sponsoring Partners

Activity Codes

 - horseback riding, biking, guided hikes, children's programs, gift shop/bookstore

San Simon Valley

Location
7 miles east of Safford, Arizona

Description
Approximately 500,000 acres of public land in the San Simon Valley provide unlimited recreational opportunities. In addition, the Hot Well Dunes Recreation Area is located in the heart of the San Simon Valley. This Special Recreation Management Area provides unique opportunities for off-highway vehicle riding and hot-water bathing. Wildlife species in the area include quail, dove, deer, and javelina.

Mailing Address
BLM - Safford Field Office
711 14th Avenue
Safford, AZ 85546

Phone Number
(520) 348-4400

Fax Number
(520) 348-4450

Directions
The San Simon Valley can be accessed by three primary routes: (1) Haekel Road: From Safford, travel 7 miles east on State Highway 70. Turn right on BLM's Haekel Road. This road takes you through approximately 33 miles of the San Simon Valley. (2) Fan Road: From Bowie, turn right on Central Avenue and go north to Fan Road, which meets Haekel Road 8 miles further. (3) Tanque Road: From State Highway 191, turn onto Tanque Road near milepost marker 105. Tanque Road runs for 12 miles before meeting Haekel Road.

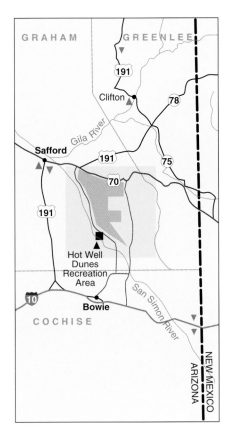

Visitors to Hot Well Dunes Recreation Area are treated to a landscape dotted with rumex and other desert plants, with Javelina Peak looming in the distance.
(Photo by Diane Drobka, Safford Field Office)

Visitor Activities
Hiking, scenic drives, wildlife viewing, horseback riding, sightseeing, photography, hunting, hot-water bathing, and off-highway vehicle driving.

Permits, Fees, Limitations
Fees are charged for the Hot Well Dunes Recreation Area. Camping is limited to 14 days. State hunting and fishing licenses are required.

Accessibility
Most of the San Simon Valley is accessible by standard passenger vehicle, making activities such as sightseeing, off-highway vehicle driving and wildlife viewing available

to individuals with disabilities. The restrooms and hot tubs at Hot Well Dunes Recreation Area are wheelchair-accessible.

Camping and Lodging
Hot Well Dunes Recreation Area, in the center of the San Simon Valley, contains 10 developed campsites with tables, grills, restrooms, and trash cans. No hook-ups are available. The campground is open year-round. Camping is permitted on all public lands in the San Simon Valley, but there are no facilities in these areas. Lodging is available in Safford.

Food and Supplies
Food and supplies are available in Safford and Bowie.

First Aid
The nearest hospital is located in Safford.

Additional Information
The public lands in the San Simon Valley are open all year long, but it is best to visit in the spring, fall and winter. Summer can be quite hot! The roads through the San Simon Valley are not regularly maintained. At certain times of the year, the roads can be very rough and may be impassable after heavy rains.

Sponsoring Partner

Activity Codes

 - hot-water bathing, horseback riding, sightseeing, photography

Sunshine Loop Trail

Location
Northern Arizona, 10 miles southeast of St. George, Utah

Description
This is an 8.5-mile loop trail through fascinating desert scenery. Interesting dry washes, colorful buttes and abruptly-rising escarpments impress mountain bikers all along the trail. The trail is rated "more difficult" to "moderate" because of difficult trail surfaces over some stretches; some portaging may be necessary.

Mailing Address
BLM - Arizona Strip District Office
345 East Riverside Drive
St. George, UT 84790

Phone Number   Fax Number
(435) 688-3246   (435) 688-3258

Directions
In St. George, head south on Main Street. Turn left on Route 700 south. Turn right at the stoplight onto River Road. Turn left onto Route 1460 south, which is the first left immediately after the bridge. Keep heading east (left) at the fork in the road. Follow the signs to Ft. Pearce/Warner Valley. Follow the road past the Warner Valley turn-off for 6.5 miles, always following the road to the left when it forks. At the 6.5 mile mark, drive through a gate in the fence to the right, over a cattle guard, through a wash, to the BLM marked trailhead.

Visitor Activities
Mountain biking and hiking.

Permits, Fees, Limitations
None

Accessibility
None

Camping and Lodging
Primitive camping is allowed at the trailhead. Camping and lodging are available in St. George.

Food and Supplies
No food or supplies are available on-site. The nearest supplies are located in Washington and St. George.

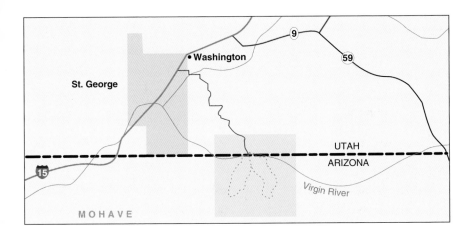

First Aid
No first aid is available on-site. The nearest hospital is in St. George.

Additional Information
Recommended use seasons are fall, winter and spring. Watch for flash floods following precipitation in the region. The trail surface ranges from a two-lane road to a single-lane road, to a 3-foot-wide trail of mostly hard dirt with some stretches of soft sand or rocks. A map is available from BLM.

Sponsoring Partner

Activity Codes

  - mountain biking

Table Top Wilderness

Location
75 miles southeast of Phoenix, Arizona

Description
Dominated by its namesake, the 4,356-foot Table Top Mountain, this 34,000-acre wilderness typifies the landscapes, flora and fauna of the Sonoran Desert of North America. This remote area provides outstanding opportunities for solitude and unconfined recreation. A strenuous, 3.5-mile summit trail (Table Top Trail), along with a more moderate 7.25-mile foothill trail

(Lava Flow Trail) are available for hikers and equestrians. The view from the summit of Table Top Mountain provides a 100-mile panorama of the surrounding mountain ranges and desert.

Mailing Address
BLM - Phoenix Field Office
2015 West Deer Valley Road
Phoenix, AZ 85027

Phone Number   Fax Number
(602) 580-5500   (602) 580-5580

Directions

From Phoenix, take Interstate 10 south to Interstate 8. Take exit 144, Vekol Valley Road. Travel south on Vekol Valley Road 2.1 miles to the Vekol Ranch turnoff and continue south on the dirt-surfaced road to the right. The wilderness boundary may be accessed via this road at the Lava Flow West and South Trailheads and the Table Top Trailhead. Respectively, the Lava Flow West, Table Top, and South Trailheads are 10 miles, 15 miles and 14 miles south of Interstate 8. For other access routes, contact BLM.

Visitor Activities

Hiking, sightseeing, scenic drives, and horseback riding.

Permits, Fees, Limitations

No fees or permits. No motorized vehicles, campfires or wood-collecting are permitted within the wilderness. No pets are allowed on Table Top Trail. Campfires are allowed at trailheads within the fire rings provided.

Accessibility

Trailheads, trails, and the restroom at the Table Top Trailhead are wheelchair-accessible; however, trails are primitive, with portions that would be extremely challenging for wheelchair-bound persons.

Camping and Lodging

Table Top Trailhead Campground is a non-fee site. A small, 3-site campground with picnic tables, fire rings, a vault toilet and day-use parking for about 10 vehicles is available at the Table Top Trailhead. There is a 5-day camping limit at the Table Top Trailhead. Pets must be leashed in the Table Top Trailhead camping area. There is no camping permitted within 200 feet of designated trails. No facilities are available elsewhere in or near the wilderness. The closest lodging is located in Gila Bend and Casa Grande.

Food and Supplies

No food or water is available on-site. Restaurants and markets can be found in Gila Bend and Casa Grande. Two small cafes are also located just north of the wilderness along Interstate 8; both are less than a 1-hour drive from the wilderness by vehicle.

First Aid

No first aid is available on-site. The closest full-service hospital is located in Casa Grande. "Flight for Life" helicopter services may be available from some of the Phoenix and Tucson hospitals.

Additional Information
Because of extreme summer temperatures, activities are best pursued from late October through mid-April. Drinking water is NOT provided, so bring plenty. The main access routes and washes are prone to heavy seasonal rains and flash floods. Check with BLM for up-to-date local conditions. This is a wilderness; recreational opportunities are primitive and access roads are not maintained. No water or trash collection is provided. Plan accordingly.

Sponsoring Partner

AMERICA OUTDOORS

Activity Codes

 - horseback riding, sightseeing

Vermilion Cliffs

Location
10 miles northeast of Page, Arizona

Description
Part of the Paria Canyon-Vermilion Cliffs Wilderness, this 3,000-foot escarpment of colorful sandstone dominates the Marble Canyon area. Seven major geologic formations are exposed in layer-cake fashion.

Mailing Address
BLM - Arizona Strip Field Office
345 East Riverside Drive
St. George, UT 84790

Phone Number
(435) 688-3200

Fax Number
(435) 688-3258

Directions
From Page, take State Highway Alternate 89 for approximately 30 miles to the site. From Kanab, Utah, take State Highway 89 south and then east to Jacob Lake. Turn left on Highway Alternate 89, and proceed to cliffs.

Visitor Activities
Scenic drives, geologic sightseeing, hiking, backpacking, historic site, birdwatching, wildlife viewing, and plant viewing.

Permits, Fees, Limitations
None

Accessibility
None

Camping and Lodging
Three lodges are located just outside the wilderness, west of Marble Canyon Bridge, approximately 3 miles away. Other lodging is available in Page.

Across from the dramatic sandstone cliffs, a roadside marker describes historical expeditions through the Marble Canyon area.
(Photo by David Smith ©, Arizona State Office)

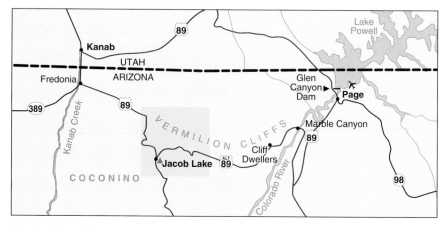

Food and Supplies

Food and supplies are available at the three lodges. The nearest source of food and supplies is Page.

First Aid

No first aid is available within the wilderness. The nearest reliable first aid is at Lees Ferry (National Park Service), approximately 30 miles west of Page. The nearest hospital is in Flagstaff, 125 miles away.

Additional Information

Hiking in foothills may be hazardous because of loose rock, steep slopes, and extreme temperatures in summer. Fall through spring is the best time to visit. No restrooms are provided in the wilderness; the nearest facilities are at the lodges in Page.

Sponsoring Partner

Activity Codes

 - geologic sightseeing, backpacking

Virgin River Canyon
Recreation Area

Location
20 miles southwest of St. George, Utah

Description
The Recreation Area is a scenic canyon with a campground, picnic area, restrooms, group sites and trails.

Mailing Address
BLM - Arizona Strip Field Office
345 East Riverside Drive
St. George, UT 84790

Phone Number   Fax Number
(435) 688-3246   (435) 688-3258

Directions
From St. George, take Interstate 15 south approximately 10 miles.

Visitor Activities
Picnicking, wildlife viewing, birdwatching, plant viewing, hiking, and wading.

Permits, Fees, Limitations
Nightly camping fees are charged. Group site fees depend on the size of the party.

Accessibility
Restrooms and some campsites are wheelchair-accessible.

Camping and Lodging
Seventy-seven campsites are available within the Recreation Area. Lodging is also available in St. George.

Food and Supplies
No food or supplies are available on-site. Food and supplies can be obtained in St. George.

First Aid
There is no first aid available on-site. There is a hospital in St. George.

Additional Information
The area is open all year. Water and flush toilets are available at campsites, but there are no electrical or water hookups.

Sponsoring Partner

Activity Codes

 - picnicking, wading

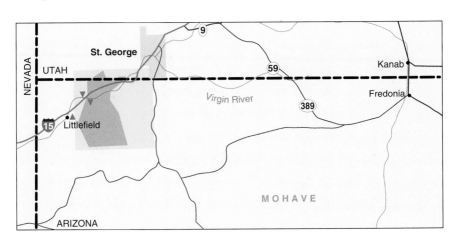

The Lost Coast National Recreation Trail winds through the King Range National Conservation Area, one of the last pristine stretches of California coastline. *(Photo by Bob Wick, Arcata Resource Area)*

California

From the subtle to the sublime, vivid and exciting recreation opportunities abound in California. The 14 million acres of public lands offer remoteness and majesty ranging from the desolation of the Great Basin to the grandeur of the Pacific Ocean. Most of California's public lands are located in the southern California Desert with smaller, but significant concentrations throughout the state. The terrain of these public lands is extremely diverse, ranging from sagebrush plains to old-growth forests, from rolling sand dunes to the rugged Pacific coastline and from lush streamside areas to arid high desert.

No matter what your experience level, you will find myriad adventures to challenge and enlighten. Thrill your senses by passing through tunnels of time along Bizz Johnson National Recreation Trail or careening down one of California's exceptional whitewater runs. Additional not-to-be-missed sites include the King Range National Conservation Area along the north coast and the Imperial Sand Dunes in southern California. The public lands provide recreation opportunities for thousands of visitors through hiking trails, rivers, off-highway vehicle areas, campgrounds, and over 3.5 million acres of wilderness.

The best time to visit California is year-round! California's diverse climate offers everything from desert heat to alpine snow. In the desert, scorching summers turn to sunny and mild autumns for off-highway vehicle play—or solitude. Primeval old-growth forests provide shaded trails away from the desert in the hot months. For winter fun, a blanket of snow and cross-country skiing await on your favorite trail.

Most of California's public lands are accessible from major roadways, but by getting off the highway and exploring a back road or two, you can also escape to some of the more remote regions of the state.

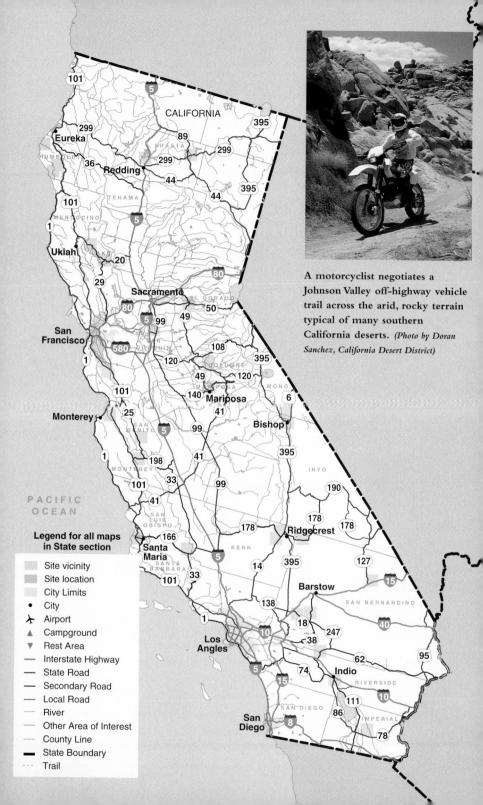

CALIFORNIA

101
5
395
299
Eureka
89
299
36
Redding
299
44
299
44
395
101
MENDOCINO
1
Ukiah
20
80
29
Sacramento
80
50
5 99
49
San
Francisco
108
580
SAN JOAQUIN
120
395
1
101
49
120
140
Mariposa
MONO
41
6
Monterey
25
SAN BENITO
Bishop
1
5
99
395
MONTEREY
198
41
33
99
INYO
101
41
190
PACIFIC
OCEAN
SAN LUIS OBISPO
178
178
178
Ridgecrest
Legend for all maps
in State section
166
395
127
KERN
Santa
Maria
SANTA BARBARA
14
5
Barstow
SAN BERNARDINO
33
138
15
Site vicinity
101
18
40
Site location
1
247
City Limits
10
38
• City
62
95
✈ Airport
Los
Angeles
74
Indio
▲ Campground
5
RIVERSIDE
▼ Rest Area
15
111
10
— Interstate Highway
San
Diego
86
IMPERIAL
— State Road
SAN DIEGO
8
— Secondary Road
78
— Local Road
— River
— Other Area of Interest
— County Line
— State Boundary
··· Trail

A motorcyclist negotiates a
Johnson Valley off-highway vehicle
trail across the arid, rocky terrain
typical of many southern
California deserts. *(Photo by Doran
Sanchez, California Desert District)*

American River Recreation Areas

Locations

North Fork: 6 miles east of Colfax, California

South Fork: 2.5 miles north of Coloma, California

Descriptions

North Fork: The famous Giant Gap 14-mile run of the even more famous North Fork American River is one of California's top whitewater challenges, for experts only. Cliffs tower 2,000 feet above the river. Heaps of mine tailings and old cabin ruins border this roller-coaster ride through the historic Mother Lode. Stop to catch your breath at the Lover's Leap picnic area, which features California's most venerable black oak, estimated to be 350-450 years old.

South Fork: Nicknamed the Gold Rush River, the South Fork of the American River is treasured as the most popular whitewater run in California. Even before James Marshall's fortuitous 1848 gold find, the "Rio de los Americanos" flaunted its reputation as a wild and capricious mountain stream. Today, tempered by upstream dams, the South Fork still lurches and bucks through cataracts of boulders, drops and chutes. The 21-mile run can be negotiated in 1 full day, but most rafters prefer to camp overnight on the river between 2 exciting half-day runs. On the Dave Moore Nature Trail, visitors can still see evidence of the intense mining activity that took place during the great Gold Rush.

Mailing Address

BLM - Folsom Resource Area
63 Natoma Street
Folsom, CA 95630

Phone Number	Fax Number
(916) 985-4474	(916) 985-3259

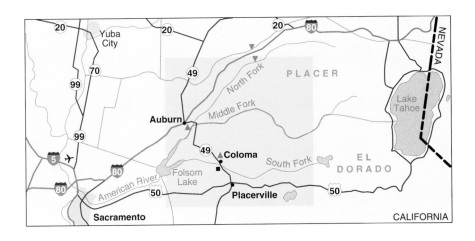

Directions

North Fork: To get to the rafting put-in at Euchre Bar, take the Alta exit off Interstate 80, 30 miles northeast of Auburn, then turn south on Casa Loma Road to the trailhead. The put-in is a 2-mile walk from the trailhead. To get to the rafting take-out from Auburn, travel 15 miles north on Interstate 80 to Colfax. Take the Highway 174 exit, follow the signs to the Iowa Hill Road, and take that road to the Iowa Hill Bridge.

South Fork: From Placerville on U.S. Highway 50, take State Highway 49 north 8 miles to Coloma and the Marshall Gold Discovery State Historic Park. Travel another 2.5 miles to BLM's Dave Moore Nature Area.

Visitor Activities

North Fork: Whitewater rafting, hiking, birdwatching, wildlife viewing, boating, swimming, and picnicking.

South Fork: Historical studies, whitewater rafting, hiking, birdwatching, wildlife viewing, boating, swimming, and picnicking.

Permits, Fees, Limitations

A free county tag is required for private rafting trips and is available through El Dorado County offices in Placerville.

Accessibility

North Fork: The terrain is very rugged and not wheelchair-accessible.

South Fork: The Dave Moore Nature Area has a wheelchair-accessible trail.

Camping and Lodging

North Fork: There is a State Park campground at the Iowa Hill bridge. The nearest lodging is available in Auburn and Colfax. Sacramento, California's capital city, is only 50 miles to the west.

South Fork: Camping is abundant in the area in private, county, and state campgrounds. The American River Recreation Area covers a large geographic area and is located near a major metropolitan center (Sacramento). Visitors are encouraged to contact BLM for recommendations of campgrounds for specific areas. The nearest lodging is available in Auburn and Placerville. Sacramento, California's capital city, is only 50 miles to the west.

Food and Supplies

North Fork: Food and supplies are not available on-site. Supplies can be obtained in Auburn, Colfax, and Sacramento.

South Fork: Food and supplies are available locally through commercial rafting outfitters and others. Supplies are also plentiful in Auburn, Placerville, and Sacramento.

First Aid

North Fork: First aid is available from commercial outfitters and State Park rangers. The nearest hospital is located in Auburn.

South Fork: First aid is available from commercial outfitters and State Park rangers. The nearest hospitals are located in Auburn and Placerville.

Additional Information

North Fork: There are many tourist-oriented services available on-site. The best times to float the river are spring and summer. The river offers Class IV-V rapids on the North Fork, and Class III rapids on the South Fork. If you are planning to go river rafting, go with a professional guide who will prepare you with proper gear and safety information. Contact BLM for a list of permitted outfitters.

South Fork: There are many tourist-oriented services available in the local area, but nothing on-site. Most of the public land parcels are accessible only from the river. The best times to float the river are spring and summer. The river offers Class III rapids on the South Fork. If you are planning to go river rafting, go with a professional guide who will prepare you with proper gear and safety information. Contact BLM for a list of permitted outfitters.

Sponsoring Partner

Activity Codes

 - swimming, picnicking

Big Morongo Canyon

Location
15 miles north of Palm Springs, California

Description
The preserve is an oasis and transition zone between the Mojave and Sonoran deserts. For centuries, it was used by nomadic Native Americans, who found water and game plentiful here. More than 235 bird species have been observed in the preserve, including several rare species. Many additional transient species are present during the spring and fall migration seasons. Water also attracts desert bighorn sheep, raccoons, bobcats, coyotes, and other mammals. The preserve is listed as a Watchable Wildlife site.

Mailing Address
BLM - Big Morongo Canyon Preserve
Attn: Preserve Manager
P.O. Box 780
Morongo Valley, CA 92256

Phone Number   Fax Number
(760) 363-7190   (760) 363-1180

Visitors travel the Big Morongo Canyon's boardwalk, exploring the abundant plant and animal life at this unique desert oasis.
(Photo by Doran Sanchez, California Desert District)

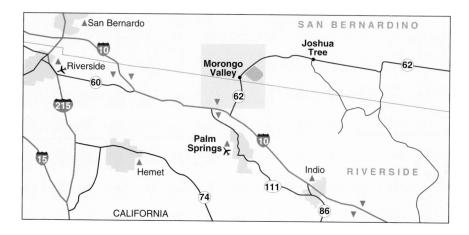

Directions

From Palm Springs, travel west on Interstate 10 to State Highway 62. Travel north on Highway 62 for 11.5 miles to Morongo Valley. Turn right on East Drive and go a short distance to the Preserve entrance on the left.

Visitor Activities

Birdwatching, plant viewing, wildlife viewing, hiking, horseback riding, and guided tours.

Permits, Fees, Limitations

No fees. No unauthorized vehicles or bicycles are permitted beyond the parking lot. No dogs or other pets are allowed in the Preserve. Firearms and hunting are restricted. Smoking is not allowed. Hiking and horseback riding are permitted on designated trails only.

Accessibility

Some portions of the trails are wheelchair-accessible. Please contact the Preserve Manager for details.

Camping and Lodging

Primitive camping is available at Morongo Valley Park, 5 miles north of Big Morongo on U.S. Highway 62. Camping is free. Developed camping is available at the Black Rock Campground in the Joshua Tree National Park, 20 miles north of Morongo on Highway 62. Picnic facilities, toilets, and detailed trail maps are available at the Preserve.

Food and Supplies

Food and supplies are available in Morongo Valley.

First Aid

No first aid is available on-site. The Avalon Urgent Care Center in Yucca Valley is located 10 miles north on U.S. Highway 62. The nearest hospital is located in Joshua Tree.

Additional Information

The Preserve is open daily from 7:30 a.m. to sunset. Winter, fall, and spring are the best times of the year to visit this area. The Preserve has a desert climate with hot, dry summers and moderate winters. Rainfall is scarce, and winter and spring nighttime temperatures can be cool.

National Audubon Society

FOUNDATION FOR NORTH AMERICAN

WILD SHEEP

The Garden Club of America

The Nature Conservancy.

AMERICAN
BIRD
CONSERVANCY

Activity Codes

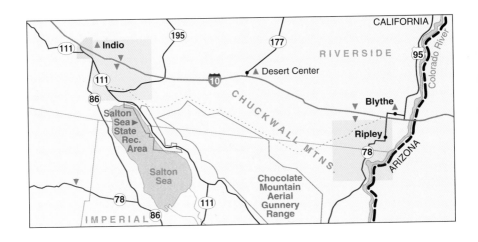 – guided tours, horseback riding

Bradshaw Trail

Location
38 miles southeast of Indio, California

Description
The first road through Riverside County was blazed by William Bradshaw in 1862, as an overland stage route beginning at San Bernardino and ending at La Paz, Arizona (now Ehrenberg, Arizona). The Trail was used extensively between 1862 and 1877 to haul miners and other passengers to the gold fields at La Paz. The Trail is a 65-mile graded road that traverses mostly public land between the Chuckwalla Mountains and the Chocolate Mountain Aerial Gunnery Range. The Trail offers spectacular views of the Chuckwalla Bench, Orocopia Mountains, Chuckwalla Mountains and the Palo Verde Valley.

Mailing Address
BLM – Palm Springs/South Coast
    Resource Area
690 West Garnet Avenue
P.O. Box 2000
North Palm Springs, CA 92258

Phone Number   Fax Number
(760) 251-4800   (760) 251-4899

Directions

From Indio, take Interstate 10 east for about 8 miles to the State Highway 111 exit. Then proceed about 18 miles on State Highway 111 to the Salton Sea State Recreation Area. Across from Park Head-quarters is Parkview Drive. Go left on Parkview Drive for about 1.7 miles, then left on Desert Aire for about 0.5 mile to the Canal Road. Follow Canal Road for about 10 miles to Drop 24 and the begin-ning of the Bradshaw Road (SR 301). Or, from Blythe take Interstate 10 west for about 9 miles to the State Highway 78 exit. Go south on 78 for about 9 miles past the community of Ripley. Look for the Bradshaw Trail sign.

Visitor Activities

Four-wheel-drive vehicle touring, wildlife viewing, plant viewing, birdwatching, scenic drives, and hiking.

Permits, Fees, Limitations

All commercial events require a land-use or special recreation permit from BLM. Primitive vehicular camping is allowed within 300 feet of the trail except in des-ignated wilderness areas. Wilderness boundaries are posted and closed to all motorized vehicles. Fourteen-day camping restrictions apply.

Accessibility

The Wiley's Well Campground is located next to the Trail at the intersection of the Bradshaw Trail and Wiley's Well Road. The campground provides 15 campsites with picnic tables, shade ramadas and grills. Wheelchair-accessible restrooms are available at the campground.

Camping and Lodging

The cities of Indio and Blythe offer com-plete accommodations. Campgrounds are available at Lake Cahuilla (City of La Quinta), Joshua Tree National Park, and Corn Springs (near Desert Center).

Food and Supplies

Food, supplies, and gasoline are available at Indio, Chiriaco Summit, Desert Center, and Blythe.

First Aid

There is no first aid available along the Bradshaw Trail. Hospitals are located in Indio and Blythe.

Additional Information

The Trail is a dirt road graded two or three times per year by the Riverside County Transportation Department. Four-wheel-drive vehicles are recommended be-cause of stretches of soft sand and dry wash conditions. The Chocolate Mountain Naval Gunnery Range is located immedi-ately south of the trail. This is a live bombing range that is closed to all public entry. **DO NOT ENTER THE BOMBING RANGE.** Summers can be extremely hot. Carry plenty of water. Al-ways tell someone your plans, and stick to your itinerary. The Trail can be very sandy in places.

Sponsoring Partner

Activity Codes

Cache Creek

Location
8 miles west of Clearlake Oaks, California

Description
The 50,000-acre Cache Creek management area is cooperatively managed by BLM and the California Department of Fish and Game to enhance wildlife habitat, protect cultural resources, and provide primitive recreational opportunities. It offers visitors spectacular views of the endangered bald eagle, wildflowers, pockets of the rare adobe lily, free-roaming tule elk herds, wild turkey, black bear, blacktail deer, and other upland species.

Mailing Address
BLM - Clear Lake Resource Area
2550 North State Street
Ukiah, CA 95482.

Phone Number
(707) 468-4000

Fax Number
(707) 469-4027

Directions
To Redbud Trail: From Clearlake Oaks, travel east on State Highway 20 for 8 miles to the Redbud Trailhead.

To Blue Ridge Trail: From Clearlake Oaks, travel east approximately 25 miles on State Highway 20 to its junction with State Highway 16. Turn right and travel south on Highway 16 for 10 miles. Turn right on County Road 40, proceed 0.25 mile, and cross Cache Creek on a low-water bridge. Turn onto the access road that parallels the creek, and proceed downstream to the parking area. If the road is closed by winter weather, park at the Cache Creek Regional Park, at the junction of Highway 16 and County Road 40, and walk in. The trailhead is about 150 yards downstream from the low-water bridge on a trail paralleling the creek.

Or, from Woodland, take State Highway 16 north 40 miles to the junction with

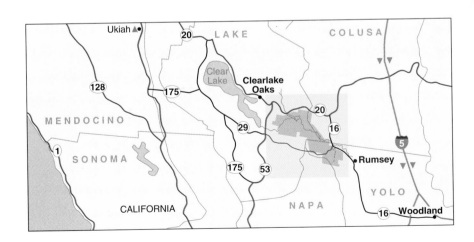

County Road 40 (at Cache Creek Regional Park). The junction is about 5 miles north of the community of Rumsey.

Visitor Activities

Hiking, hunting, wildflower viewing, birdwatching, wildlife viewing, guided tours, and guided wildflower-viewing walks.

Permits, Fees, Limitations

No fees. The Wilson Valley portion of Cache Creek (approximately 6 miles up the trail from the Red Bud Trailhead) is closed for tule elk calving from April 15 to June 30. Campfires may be prohibited during periods of extreme fire danger.

Accessibility

None

Camping and Lodging

Primitive camping is permitted; there are no developed camping areas. Lodging is available in Clearlake Oaks.

First Aid

No first aid is available on-site. The nearest first aid is available at Redbud Hospital in the community of Clear Lake, 15 miles off the Redbud Trailhead via State Highway 20 and State Highway 53.

Additional Information

The best times to visit are fall, winter and spring. Summer provides optimal conditions for rafting, though Cache Creek can be impassable at times of high water.

Restroom facilities are available at the Redbud and Blue Ridge trailheads. No potable water is available on-site. Guided bald eagle tours are popular mid-January to mid-February. Guided wildflower-viewing hikes are popular during Saturdays in April. Call BLM for schedule information on guided bald eagle and wildflower tours.

Sponsoring Partners

Activity Codes

- guided tours, guided wildflower-viewing walks

Caliente Mountains

Location
50 miles east of San Luis Obispo, California.

Description
The Caliente Range forms the western border of the Carrizo Plain Natural Area, and Caliente Mountain is the highest point in San Luis Obispo County. This is an isolated area, with the Cuyama Valley and the Los Padres National Forest situated on the other side of the Range.

Mailing Address
BLM - Bakersfield Field Office
3801 Pegasus Drive
Bakersfield, CA 93308

Phone Number
(805) 391-6000

Fax Number
(805) 391-6040

Directions
From San Luis Obispo take U.S. Highway 101 north to Santa Margarita, then turn east on State Highway 58 and travel 35 miles to Soda Lake Road. Turn south on Soda Lake Road and travel 15 miles to just south of the Painted Rock turnoff. Turn west on Selby Road and follow it about 5 miles to Caliente Ridge in the Carrizo Plain Natural Area. There is a parking area at Caliente Ridge, and a foot trail that continues along the ridge line 10 miles to the top of Caliente Mountain.

Or, from San Luis Obispo, take U.S. Highway 101 south 20 miles to State Highway 166. Turn east on Highway 166 and travel 27 miles to a trail on the left side of the road to Caliente Mountain. Park there and hike 7 miles to Caliente Ridge. The town of New Cuyama is 13 miles further east on State Highway 166.

Visitor Activities
Hunting, hiking, birdwatching, plant viewing, wildlife viewing, and photography.

Permits, Fees, Limitations
No fees. A State of California hunting license is required. Vehicle access is limited; visitors must be prepared to hike into many areas.

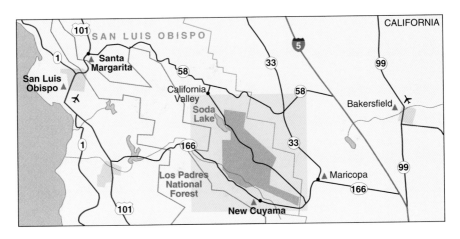

Accessibility
None

Camping and Lodging
There is primitive camping available in the Carrizo Plain Natural Area. Developed campgrounds are located in the Los Padres National Forest, 25-30 miles west on State Highway 166 or 58. The nearest lodging is available in California Valley on Soda Lake Road, about 10 miles north of the Selby Road turnoff, and in New Cuyama.

Food and Supplies
This is a very isolated area with limited services. The nearest food and supplies are located in California Valley on Soda Lake Road, about 10 miles north of the Selby Road turnoff, and in New Cuyama.

First Aid
There is a BLM Fire Station on the Carrizo Plain [Tel.: (805) 391-6108], and a Santa Barbara County Fire Station at New Cuyama [Tel.: (805) 965-5252]. The nearest hospital is located in Santa Maria, 50 miles west on State Highway 166.

Additional Information
This is an undeveloped area with no restroom facilities or potable water. It is hot and dry during the summer, with high wildland fire danger during summer and fall. Winter can be very cold. Most visiting is done during the fall hunting seasons, generally from November to January, when daytime temperatures are very warm and evenings are chilly. The best time to visit for sightseeing is during the spring wildflower season in April.

Sponsoring Partner

Activity Codes

 - photography

Chappie/Shasta Off-Highway Vehicle Recreation Area

Location
10 miles north of Redding, California

Description
Visitors to the rolling, brushy hills near Shasta Lake in northern California will find off-highway vehicle (OHV) riding challenges for all abilities. More than 250 miles of roads and trails are open to motorcyclists, all-terrain vehicle drivers and four-wheelers. The area is near massive Shasta Dam and Shasta Lake, and there are overlooks of the Sacramento River below the dam. Wildlife species in the area include osprey, bald eagle, mule deer, and bear. The area, named for former U. S. Congressman Eugene Chappie, is open year-round.

Mailing Address
BLM - Redding Resource Area
355 Hemsted Drive
Redding, CA 96002

Phone Number   Fax Number
(916) 224-2100   (916) 224-2172

Directions
From Redding, take Interstate 5 north
about 10 miles to the Shasta Dam Exit.
Follow Shasta Dam Boulevard to the dam.
There are directional markings on the
pavement. Continue on the road across the
dam. Turn left past the dam and continue
to a 3-way stop sign, and turn right.
(Streets are not named.) The road leads to

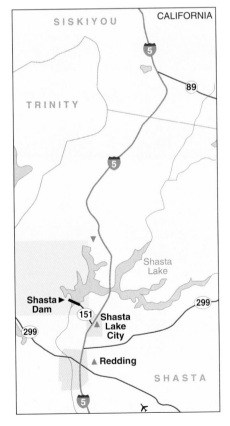

the OHV parking area, about
2.5 miles down.

Visitor Activities
Off-highway vehicle touring, four-wheel-
driving, competitive events, mountain biking, hiking, wildlife viewing, birdwatching, plant viewing, and fishing.

Permits, Fees, Limitations
No fees. California off-highway vehicle
registration is required for all motorized vehicles. Helmets are required for riders of
motorized off-highway vehicles. All engines
must be equipped with spark arresters, and
must meet California noise emission requirements. Engines must not produce
noise exceeding 101 decibels. Sound levels
are measured according to California stan-
dards that vary with engine size.

Accessibility
The campground and 2 river overlooks are
wheelchair-accessible. The overlook is on
Shasta Dam Boulevard, about 6 miles west
of Interstate 5.

Camping and Lodging
Camping is available on-site in a U.S. Forest Service campground offering pit toilets,
potable water and sites for recreational vehicles, but no hookups. There is a daily
campground fee. Motels with a variety of
rates are available in Redding.

Food and Supplies
The nearest supplies are available in Shasta
Lake, 10 miles east on Shasta Dam Boule-
vard (State Highway 151).

Fist Aid
There is no first aid available on-site. The
nearest hospital is located in Redding, 10
miles south on Interstate 5. Camp hosts
with phones are on-site and can assist in
emergencies.

Additional Information

The best times to visit are fall, winter, and spring. Summertime temperatures of over 100°F can make activities very uncomfortable to undertake. Poison oak grows at lower elevations. There is no potable water in the area, except at the campground. There are opportunities for both non-competitive recreational riding and participation in organized competitions, such as the Shasta National Hare Scramble. Information about organized events is published in local newspapers and regional magazines. The OHV area consists of intermingled public lands and private lands. Some private lands, including an active mine, are closed to the public. Visitors should respect private property rights, and heed signs.

Sponsoring Partner

Activity Codes

 - mountain biking
four-wheel driving,
competitive OHV events

Cosumnes River Preserve

Location
20 miles south of Sacramento, California

Description
The Preserve is home to California's largest remaining valley oak riparian forest, and is one of the few protected wetland habitat areas in the state. The Cosumnes River is the only free-flowing river left in California's Central Valley. Only minutes from California's capital, this is a critical stop on the Pacific Flyway for migrating and wintering waterfowl. Over 200 species of birds have been sighted on or near the Preserve, including the state-listed threatened Swainson's hawk, greater and lesser sandhill cranes, Canada geese, and numerous ducks. The Preserve includes 11,500 acres of current and potential wetlands and valley oak forests.

Mailing Address
BLM - Folsom Resource Area
63 Natoma Street
Folsom, CA 95630

Phone Number   Fax Number
(916) 985-4474   (916) 985-3259

Directions
From Sacramento, take Interstate 5 south 20 miles, and exit at Twin Cities Road. Head east 1 mile on Twin Cities Road to Franklin Boulevard, and then head south on Franklin for 2 miles to the Preserve.

Visitor Activities
Hiking, birdwatching, plant viewing, and wildlife viewing.

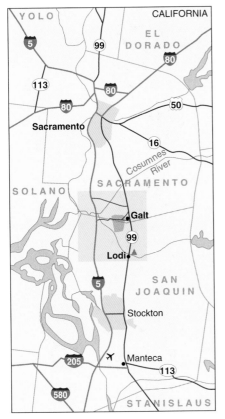

Sacramento, Galt (5 miles south on State Highway 99), and Lodi (20 miles south on Highway 99).

Food and Supplies
Food and supplies are not available on-site. The nearest sources are in Sacramento, Galt, and Lodi.

First Aid
No first aid is available on-site. The nearest hospitals are located in Galt and Lodi.

Additional Information
The best time to observe waterfowl is during the winter months.

Sponsoring Partners

Permits, Fees, Limitations
Visitors are asked to stay on the trails.

Accessibility
The visitor center is wheelchair-accessible.

Camping and Lodging
No camping is available on-site or nearby. Commercial facilities offer lodging in

Activity Codes

Cow Mountain Recreation Area

Location
8 miles east of Ukiah, California

Description
This 60,000-acre area offers a variety of recreational opportunities. The northern area is set aside for non-motorized recreation, and the southern area is for off-highway vehicles. A creek and mountain ridge separate the areas, and the trail systems do not interconnect. The terrain is rugged, and elevations range from 800 to 4,000 feet. The area offers beautiful views of Ukiah and Lake County; pockets of old-growth fir; several species of oak; willows; over 31 miles of stream; 13 reservoirs; and habitat for blacktail deer, bear, wild turkey, and other upland species.

Mailing Address
BLM - Clear Lake Resource Area
2550 North State Street
Ukiah, CA 95482

Phone Number
(707) 468-4000

Fax Number
(707) 468-4027

Directions
From Ukiah, take State Highway 101 south to the Talmage exit. Go east on Talmage Road about 1.5 miles. Turn right at East Side Road. Travel less than 0.5 mile to Mill Creek Road, which is on the left. Continue on Mill Creek Road 3 miles to the turnoff for the North Cow Mountain area, or 5 miles to the entrance to South Cow Mountain.

Or, from the community of Lakeport (State Highway 29, west shore of Clear Lake), take 11th Street to Scotts Valley Road. To reach North Cow Mountain, continue on Scotts Valley Road 6 miles to Glenn Eden Trailhead on the right. Park in signed areas. To access south Cow Mountain from Lakeport, take 11th Street (becomes Riggs Road), turn right on Scotts Creek Road and proceed 2 miles to the end.

Visitor Activities
Hiking, wildlife viewing, birdwatching, plant viewing, sanctioned motorcycle

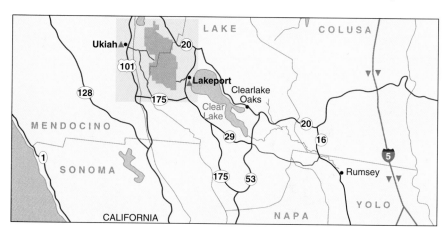

A motorcyclist pauses to take in the grand vista of Lake and Mendocino Counties from a Cow Mountain trail. *(Photo by Jim Pickering, California State Office)*

events, black-powder shoots, and motorcycle and off-highway vehicle driving opportunities.

Permits, Fees, Limitations

There may be seasonal site closures to prevent damage to the roads and trails. Off-highway vehicle use is permitted only in the South Cow Mountain area. Trailers are not recommended on any of the roads leading to the site.

Accessibility

None

Camping and Lodging

There are two developed campgrounds:

Mayacmas Campground: From Ukiah, exit U.S. Highway 101 south at Talmage Road, then go 1.5 miles east to Eastside Road. Turn right and proceed 0.3 mile to Mill Creek Road. Turn left, and proceed 3 miles to Mendo Rock Road, and follow it to the site, about 10 miles. There are 9 campsites, with tables, barbecue grates, and pit toilets.

Red Mountain Campground: From Ukiah, exit U.S. Highway 101 south at Talmage Road, then go 1.5 miles east to Eastside Road. Turn right and proceed 0.3 mile to Mill Creek Road. Follow Mill Creek Road 8 miles to the staging area, veer right where the road forks (there is a directional sign), and continue less than 1 mile to Red Mountain Campground. There are 10 sites, with toilets, barbecue grates, and picnic tables.

Food and Supplies

The nearest location for supplies is in Ukiah.

First Aid

No first aid is available on-site. The nearest hospital is located in Ukiah. For emergencies, dial 911.

Additional Information

The best times to visit are fall, winter, and spring. On South Cow Mountain, there are about 125 miles of off-highway-vehicle trails and roads. The access from Scotts

Creek Road is a rugged, unimproved dirt road, which is impassable during the winter because of high water at a creek crossing. Before exploring the Cow Mountain Recreation area, obtain a free map from BLM. All roads are steep and winding and not recommended for recreational vehicles. There is no potable water at site campgrounds.

Sponsoring Partner

Activity Codes

 - sanctioned motorcycle events, blackpowder shoots

Fish Slough Area of Critical Environmental Concern

Location
5 miles north of Bishop, California

Description
The 36,000-acre Fish Slough Area of Critical Environmental Concern (ACEC) is a place where geographic isolation, geology, climate, and hydrology have created a rare and irreplaceable ecosystem. Located in the transition between the Mojave Desert and Great Basin biomes, Fish Slough encompasses an array of plant communities, including wetlands, alkali meadows, and uplands. With 126 taxa described, Fish Slough represents one of the richest wetland floras in the Great Basin. The ACEC also provides habitat for rare endemic plants, such as the Fish Slough milk-vetch and the alkali Mariposa lily.

Mailing Address
BLM - Bishop Resource Area
785 North Main Street, Suite E
Bishop, CA 93513

Phone Number   Fax Number
(760) 872-4881   (760) 872-2894

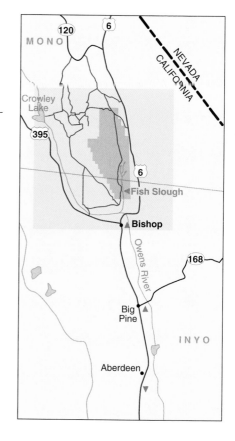

Directions

From Bishop, take U.S. Highway 6 north for 1.4 miles. Turn left on Five Bridges Road and proceed 2.4 miles to Fish Slough Road. Turn right. The ACEC entrance is 0.5 mile beyond.

Visitor Activities

Horseback riding, hiking, rock art, scenic drives, wildlife viewing, plant viewing, birdwatching, and nature interpretation.

Permits, Fees, Limitations

No fees. Visitors, including hikers, are asked to stay on developed roads. Contact the Bishop Resource Area office for other specific information.

Accessibility

This site is accessible to persons with disabilities.

Camping and Lodging

The nearest BLM campground is Horton Creek, approximately 8.5 miles northwest of Bishop on U.S. Highway 395. Call BLM for more information on the campground season. Private and county campgrounds are also available in the area. Call the Bishop Visitor's Center [Tel.: (760) 873-8405] for more information on these. Bishop also has a variety of motels and restaurants.

Food and Supplies

No supplies or facilities are located on-site. The nearest sources are located in Bishop.

First Aid

No first aid is available on-site. The nearest hospital is located in Bishop.

Additional Information

Fish Slough is very hot in the summer and snow is possible in the winter. However, at any time of the year, visitors can find inclement weather in the area. The best times to visit Fish Slough are fall, winter, and spring, but no matter what time of year you visit, remember to bring along drinking water.

BLM and the Audubon Society offer a variety of interpretive activities in the

The Sierra Mountain Range provides a stunning backdrop for the rich wetlands of Fish Slough. *(Photo by Jim Pickering, California State Office)*

Slough throughout the year. Contact BLM for further information.

Much of the Slough area is visible from roads, but be sure that the vehicle you take to the area is suitable for dirt roads. The main dirt roads are very well-maintained, but secondary roads require high-clearance vehicles and possibly four-wheel-drive vehicles. Secondary roads may be impassable in winter or following episodes of heavy precipitation.

Sponsoring Partner

Activity Codes

 - horseback riding, rock art, nature interpretation

Fort Ord

Location
5 miles north of Monterey, California

Description
This 7,200-acre portion of the former Army base at Fort Ord is now public land managed by BLM. The elaborate system of trails left behind by the military is well-suited to hiking, biking and equestrian use. An additional 8,000 acres is expected to be transferred by the year 2002. Fort Ord contains one of the largest maritime chaparral areas in all of California, as well as oak woodlands, rolling grassy hills, wetlands and ponds. Forty-six different rare plants and animals thrive in the rugged hills, including the coast wallflower, marine chaparral, tiger salamander, fairy shrimp, and mountain lion.

Once a training ground for the U.S. Army, Fort Ord's grassy hills now delight nature lovers. *(Photo by Steve Addington, Hollister Resource Area)*

Mailing Address
BLM - Hollister Resource Area
20 Hamilton Court
Hollister, CA 95023

Phone Number   **Fax Number**
(408) 637-8183   (408) 637-5218

Directions

From Monterey, travel 5 miles north on State Highway 1 to the Fort Ord/California State University Monterey Bay main entrance. Make a right onto North-South Road, travel 1 mile, and then make a right onto Parker Flats Cut-Off. Travel 4 miles and then make a left onto Park Flats Road. Travel 5 miles to Eucalyptus Road

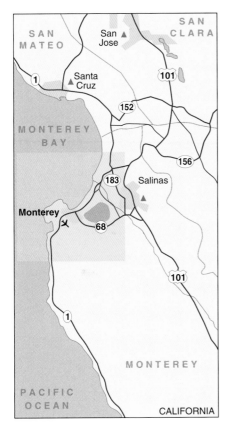

and the BLM office. Most back country roads are closed to vehicle traffic. Parking areas are available for access to hiking, bicycle and equestrian trails.

Visitor Activities

Horseback riding, hiking, biking, interpretive exhibits and trails, environmental education programs, scientific research, scenic drives, plant viewing, wildlife viewing, and birdwatching.

Permits, Fees, Limitations

No fees. Prohibited activities include shooting, off-highway vehicle use and off-trail travel.

Accessibility

Special trail map descriptions are being prepared for people with physical limitations. Contact BLM for more information regarding these maps.

Camping and Lodging

No camping is permitted on-site. Camping is available in Monterey County Parks [Tel.: (908) 646-3866]. Lodging is available on-site at the Sun Bay Resort [Tel.: (805) 394-0136]. Off-site lodging can be found throughout the Monterey Peninsula and in Salinas, 12 miles southeast on State Highway 68.

Food and Supplies

A restaurant and food store are located on-site. Food and supplies are also available in Marina and Seaside, which are immediately adjacent to Fort Ord on State Highway 1.

First Aid

First aid is available on-site through the Fort Ord Fire Department. The nearest hospitals are located in Monterey and Salinas.

Additional Information
Weather can be cold at any time of the year. Spring is probably the best time of the year to visit.

Sponsoring Partners

Activity Codes

- horseback riding, biking, interpretive exhibits, environmental education, scientific research

Jawbone/Butterbredt Area of Critical Environmental Concern

Location
15 miles southwest of Ridgecrest, California

Description
With less than 5 inches of precipitation annually, including some snowfall, the dryness of the climate causes rapid evaporation at this site. Some water seeps underground to feed area springs that provide water, which is essential to wildlife. Butterbredt Spring supports desert wildlife while also providing water and habitat for waterfowl migrating in the spring and fall. The land at the spring is privately owned, and vehicle travel and hunting in the area is restricted. The Audubon Society, in cooperation with the private landowner, has established the spring as a wildlife sanctuary.

Mailing Address
BLM - Ridgecrest Resource Area
300 South Richmond Road
Ridgecrest, CA 93555

Phone Number
(760) 384-5400

Fax Number
(760) 384-5499

Directions
From State Highway 178 east of Bakersfield or west of Inyokern, take the Kelso Valley Road 38 miles south to the site.

Or, from State Highway 14 south of Red Rock, take Jawbone Canyon Road 14 miles west to the site.

Or, take State Highway 14 west to designated routes such as Cow Heaven Canyon Route (#SC-51), Sage Canyon Route (#SC-56), and Horse Canyon Route (#SC-65). The SC routes are for four-wheel-drive vehicles only.

From Ridgecrest, travel west on State Highway 178 to State Highway 14, then travel south for 27 miles to Jawbone Canyon Road.

Visitor Activities
Hunting, wildflower viewing, birdwatching, wildlife viewing, hiking, off-road touring, and scenic drives.

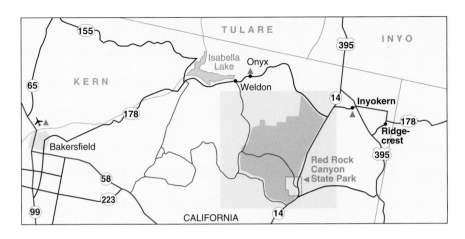

Permits, Fees, Limitations
Visitors are urged to stay on designated routes of travel and avoid damage to grasses and other plants that provide feed for livestock and wildlife.

Accessibility
None

Camping and Lodging
No facilities are available on-site. Primitive camping is permitted. Lodging is available in Inyokern and Ridgecrest.

First Aid
No first aid is available on-site. The nearest hospital or place for other assistance is located in Ridgecrest.

Additional Information
The best times to visit are fall, winter and spring. Dirt roads can become impassable after a rain.

Sponsoring Partners

National
Audubon
Society

AMERICAN
BIRD
CONSERVANCY

Activity Codes

 - wildflower viewing

Johnson Valley Off-Highway Vehicle Recreation Area

Location
35 miles east of Victorville

Description
The 189,000-acre Johnson Valley Off-Highway Vehicle (OHV) Recreation Area offers outstanding trails for competitive off-highway motorcycle racing, enduro and trial events, and day play-riding. Sloping bajadas, narrow canyons, flat dry lakes, sand dunes, and twisting trails through low rocky mountains provide a variety of experiences for all levels of riders. The Johnson Valley Yucca Rings Area of Critical Environmental Concern (ACEC), Soggy Lake Creosote Rings ACEC, Cougar Buttes' huge rock slabs, ruins of historic mines, range cattle, and a wide variety of desert animal and plant life offer unique nature and touring experiences.

Address
BLM - Barstow Resource Area
150 Coolwater Lane
Barstow, CA 92311

Phone Number
(619) 255-8760 (BLM California Desert Information Center)

Fax Number
(619) 255-8766 (BLM California Desert Information Center)

Directions
From Victorville travel 25 miles east on State Highway 18 to Lucerne Valley. Continue north on State Highway 247 to Camp Rock Road (5 miles from Lucerne Valley), Bessemer Mine Road (13 miles) or Boone Road (24 miles). There are a number of access routes into the OHV area off these roads; just follow the signs.

Visitor Activities
"Hare and hound" competitions, European scrambles, car/truck races, enduros, trial events, OHV races, recreational OHV riding, scenic drives, land sailing, model-rocket flying, wildlife viewing, photogra-

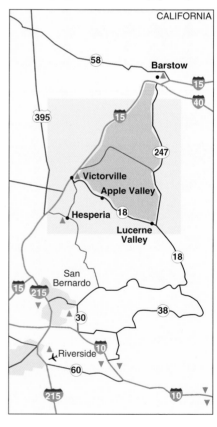

phy, hiking, rockhounding, hunting, and rock climbing.

Permits, Fees, Limitations

California Department of Motor Vehicle "Green Sticker" OHV registration is mandatory for ALL vehicles that are not "street legal." Spark arresters are necessary and must satisfy U.S. Forest Service requirements. Vehicles must have legal headlights and taillights if they are used at night. All competitive events, such as dual sport rides, enduro and "hare and hound" races, require a BLM permit. Contact the California Desert Information Center for more information.

Accessibility

None

Camping and Lodging

Camping is permitted anywhere in the open area, but is limited to a maximum of 14 days. There are no designated campgrounds or designated sites. Lodging is available in Victorville, Apple Valley, Hesperia, Lucerne Valley (10 miles southwest of the OHV area) and Barstow (35 miles northwest on State Highway 247).

Food and Supplies

Food and supplies are available in Victorville, Lucerne Valley, Barstow, Apple Valley, Hesperia, and Flamingo Heights (10 miles south of the OHV area on State Highway 247).

First Aid

There is no first aid available on-site. The nearest medical assistance is the California Department of Forestry station on State Highway 247 in Lucerne Valley. The nearest hospitals are located in Victorville and Apple Valley.

Additional Information

This site is open year-round. Rockhounds may keep what they find, within limits; please contact the California Desert Information Center for more information.

Sponsoring Partners

Activity Codes

 - land sailing, rock climbing, rockhounding, model-rocket flying, competitive off-highway events, photography

Juniper Flats

Location
7 miles south of Apple Valley, California

Description
Juniper Flats is an area of public and private lands in the northern foothills of the San Bernardino Mountains. The public route network in this area connects San Bernardino National Forest with Victor Valley to the northwest. Juniper Flats is a diverse landscape of mountains, canyons and washes. Wildlife viewing is best in the early morning and evening hours. In the washes, birds tend to gather in thick vegetation.

Mailing Address
BLM - Barstow Resource Area
150 Coolwater Lane
Barstow, CA 92311

Phone Number
(619) 255-8760 (BLM California Desert Information Center)

Fax Number
(619) 255-8766 (BLM California Desert Information Center)

Directions
Just south of Victorville, turn east from Interstate 15 onto Bear Valley Road and drive 10 miles to Central Avenue. Turn south on Central Avenue and drive about 3 miles to Roundup Way. Turn east on Roundup Way and go for 2.3 miles to Bown Ranch Road. Turn south on Bown Ranch Road and follow it into the Juniper Flats area.

Visitor Activities
Off-highway-vehicle touring, wildlife viewing, plant viewing, birdwatching, hiking, horse packing, horseback riding, and hunting.

Permits, Fees, Limitations
This is a "shotgun only" hunting area, and is closed to night shooting and recreational target shooting. Washes are marked as follows: brown markers — open to motorized vehicles; red markers or no markers — closed to motorized vehicles.

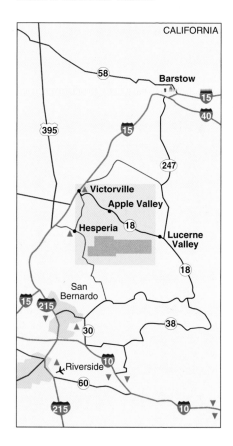

Accessibility
None

Camping and Lodging
Camping is allowed on public lands within 300 feet of a BLM "Open Route." Fourteen-day camping limits apply. Campfire permits are required and can be obtained from BLM. Lodging is available in Hesperia and Apple Valley.

Food and Supplies
Food and supplies are available in Apple Valley, Hesperia, Victorville, and Lucerne Valley.

First Aid
There is no first aid available on-site. The nearest hospital is located in Apple Valley.

Additional Information
Thunderstorms can cause flash flooding in canyons and washes. Please respect the rights of private land owners. Bring your cameras and binoculars.

Sponsoring Partner

Activity Codes

- horseback riding

King Crest Trail

Location
28 miles west of Redway, California

Description
This is a rugged, 10.5-mile hiking trail to the top of King Peak, elevation 4,087 feet, the highest point in the King Range National Conservation Area. The hike is challenging, but hikers find rewarding ocean views high above the fog. The trail is narrow and winding with many switchbacks, and is not recommended for horses.

Mailing Address
BLM - Arcata Resource Area
1695 Heindon Road
Arcata, CA 95521

Phone Number	Fax Number
(707) 825-2300	(707) 825-2301

Directions
From Willits, travel 90 miles north on U. S. Highway 101 to the Redway exit. Go west for 22 miles on Briceland Road, which later becomes Shelter Cove Road. Then turn north on Kings Peak Road, and continue 6 miles to Saddle Mountain Road. Continue 2 miles to the trailhead.

Visitor Activities
Hiking, wildlife viewing, plant viewing, photography, and birdwatching.

Fees, Permits, Limitations
Fees and permits are required for organized commercial groups. Campfire permits are required year-round, including for use of portable stoves. All permits are available from BLM.

Camping and Lodging

The nearest developed campground is the Horse Mountain Campground on Kings Peak Road, near the junction with the Saddle Mountain Road turnoff. The closest lodging is located in Shelter Cove, 12 miles from the trailhead via Saddle Mountain, King Peak and Shelter Cove Roads.

Food and Supplies

The nearest supplies are located in Shelter Cove.

First Aid

The closest first aid is available in Shelter Cove. The nearest hospital is located in Garberville, 35 miles west on Shelter Cove Road.

Additional Information

Hikers should carry plenty of water; there are no water sources along the trail. The trail is high-elevation and very hot in summer months. It is very windy along the summit. Hikers should also be watchful for poison oak, and be aware that they are hiking in mountain lion and bear habitat. Hikers should also watch for ticks and rattlesnakes. The trail is very steep and winding, gaining 2,300 feet in elevation between the south trailhead and the summit. Hikers should be in good physical shape. Hikers must negotiate heavy brush in some areas.

Sponsoring Partner

 American Hiking Society

Activity Codes

 - photography

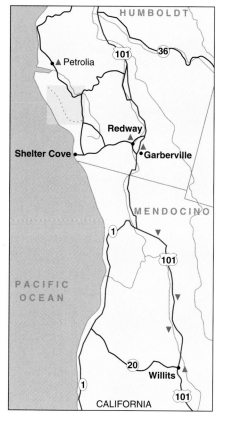

King Range
National Conservation Area

Hikers marvel at the majesty of land meeting sea in the King Range National Conservation Area. *(Photo by Bob Wick, Arcata Resource Area)*

Location
5 miles southwest of Petrolia, California

Description
You don't just stumble across the King Range National Conservation Area (KRNCA)—you have to hunt for it. But this dramatic meeting of land and sea will reward you for your effort. The King Range, located along the northern California coast, rises from sea level to over 4,000 feet in less than a mile. Rugged topography and record rainfalls create over 60,000 acres of desolate grandeur. Its mountains, streams, forests, and beaches are ideal for fishing, hunting, and sightseeing. The highlight of the King Range is the Lost Coast National Recreation Trail, which winds hikers down 26 miles of secluded coastline.

Mailing Address
BLM - Arcata Resource Area
1695 Heinden Road
Arcata, CA 95521-4573

Phone Number
(707) 825-2300

Fax Number
(707) 825-2301

Directions
From Eureka, travel 10 miles south on U.S. Highway 101 to the Ferndale exit. Proceed 5 miles on County Road 211 onto Main Street in Ferndale. Follow Main Street approximately 1 mile to its end. Turn right on Ocean Street, then immediately left on Wildcat Road. Continue 45 miles to Petrolia. Turn right on Lighthouse Road and travel 5 miles to Mattole Campground.

Or, from U.S. Highway 101 at Garberville, take Shelter Cove Road 23 miles west to the community of Shelter Cove, also an access point for the King Range.

Visitors Activities
Hiking, hunting, fishing, wildflower viewing, sightseeing, scenic drives, birdwatching, wildlife viewing, and picnicking.

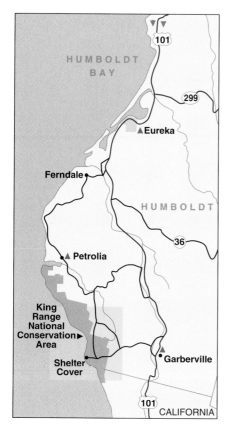

Nadelos Campground, or 2.5 miles to Wailaki Campground. Both have pit toilets, fire rings, and potable water.

To Horse Mountain and Tolkan Campgrounds: From Shelter Cove, drive 4 miles on Shelter Cove Road to King Peak Road. Turn left on King Peak Road and continue 5 miles to Tolkan Campground, or 7 miles to Horse Mountain Campground. Both have pit toilets, fire rings, and potable water.

Lodging is available in Shelter Cove and in Garberville.

First Aid

First aid is available in Shelter Cove and Garberville. Neighboring fire departments provide full medical aid for various areas of KRNCA. The nearest hospital is located in Garberville. For emergencies, dial 911.

Additional Information

Tide tables should be consulted when planning any hike along the beach. Hikers can expect frequent and dense morning fog. The best times to visit are April, May, September, and October. Water sources are scarce along the upland trails; hikers should carry drinking water. This is one of the wettest spots along the Pacific Coast Trail. Several parcels of private property are located along the coastline; visitors should respect landowners' private property rights.

Sponsoring Partner

Activity Codes

– sightseeing, picnicking, wildflower viewing

Permits, Fees, Limitations

None

Accessibility

Near the community of Shelter Cove are 2 campgrounds, Wailaki and Nadelos, that are accessible to persons with disabilities.

Camping and Lodging

There are 4 developed campgrounds: Wailaki, Nadelos, Tolkan and Horse Mountain, all within 10 miles of the community of Petrolia on Lighthouse Road.

To Wailaki and Nadelos Campgrounds: From Shelter Cove, drive 5 miles east on Shelter Cover Road to Chemise Mountain Road. Turn right and continue 2 miles to

Kingston Range Wilderness

Location
50 miles northeast of Baker, California

Description
The Kingston Range covers over 200,000 acres, including 17 miles of continuous ridgeline above 6,000 feet, capped by the 7,300-foot Kingston Peak. A small stand of white fir survives on Kingston Peak, and over 500 plant species make this a botanically diverse wilderness area. It is one of 4 areas where banded gila monsters have been sighted. Year-round water and wetland habitat provide food and shelter for diverse birds, fish, mammals, and insects.

Mailing Address
BLM - Needles Resource Area
101 West Spikes Road
Needles, CA 92363

Phone Number   **Fax Number**
(760) 326-3896   (760) 326-4079

Directions
Access the wilderness from State Highway 127 in the vicinity of Silurian Lake, or from the Old Spanish Highway in the vicinity of Tecopa, or from the Excelsior Mine Road via Cima Road off Interstate 15 in the vicinity of the Shadow Mountains. (The very fact of its being a wilder-

Desert flora thrive in the botanically diverse Kingston Range Wilderness. *(Courtesy BLM)*

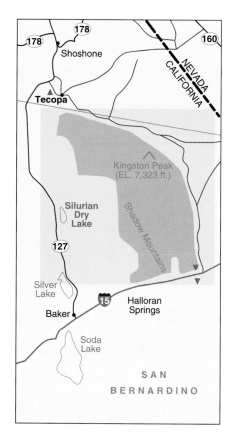

Camping and Lodging
Primitive camping is available. There are no developed campsites. Lodging is available in Baker and in Stateline, Nevada.

Food and Supplies
Food and supplies are available in Baker and Stateline.

First Aid
Ambulance service is available in Baker and Stateline. The nearest hospital is located in Las Vegas, 160 miles east on Interstate 15.

Additional Information
The best times to visit are spring and fall; however, the area is open year-round. Be aware of the hazards of desert travel, both in winter and summer. Plan your trip carefully, tell someone where you are going and stick to your itinerary. Always carry appropriate maps and know how to use them. Dress properly, and don't forget a hat, sunglasses, and sunscreen. Carry plenty of drinking water (at least 1 gallon per person per day). Stay out of abandoned mine shafts. Keep your vehicle well-maintained, and remember to also carry extra water for your vehicle.

Sponsoring Partner

Activity Codes

 - photography

ness area means that the Kingston Range has no defined entrance, campgrounds, or other facilities.)

Visitor Activities
Hiking, hunting, wildlife viewing, bird-watching, and photography.

Permits, Fees, Limitations
No fees. No commercial uses are allowed. No use of motorized vehicles of any kind (off-road vehicles, motorcycles, bicycles, hang-gliders, motorized equipment, or motorboats) is allowed. No facilities are available.

Accessibility
None

Merced River Recreation Area

Location
15 miles north of Mariposa, California

Description
Beginning in the high country of Yosemite National Park, the Merced River makes a headlong rush through glacially-carved canyons, rugged mountains and foothills to the San Joaquin Valley. Ample access points allow you to float rapids at your own pace. Come ashore long enough to watch an eagle dive for its dinner. Hook a trout and plunk it in a pan over an open fire at Railroad Flat or McCabe Flat campgrounds.

Mailing Address
BLM - Folsom Resource Area
63 Natoma Street
Folsom, CA 95630

Phone Number
(916) 985-4474

Fax Number
(916) 985-3259

Directions
From Merced, located on State Highway 99, travel 40 miles east on State Highway 140 to Mariposa. Then travel another 15 miles on Highway 140 to the Briceburg Visitor Center.

Visitor Activities
Whitewater rafting (Class III-V), boating, fishing, wildlife viewing, birdwatching, plant viewing, hiking, camping, picnicking, hobby gold prospecting, horseback riding, and swimming.

Permits, Fees, Limitations
A daily camping fee is charged.

Accessibility
Campgrounds are accessible to persons with disabilities.

Camping and Lodging
There are three BLM campgrounds along the Merced River between Briceburg and

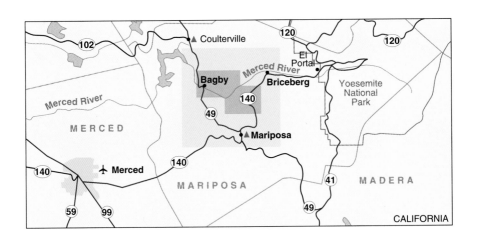

Bagby. They are the McCabe Flat Campground, Railroad Flat Campground, and Willow Placer Campground. The campgrounds are only accessible by crossing the bridge at Briceburg and heading downriver on the Merced River Trail (vehicles allowed). The campgrounds are about 2.5 miles apart. Commercial lodging is available in Mariposa.

Food and Supplies:
Food and supplies are available in Mariposa.

First Aid
BLM crews with emergency medical technicians are on duty on weekends during the rafting season, which is generally from April through July, depending on weather and the amount of snowpack in the mountains. The County Sheriff and Fire Department also provide first aid. The Mariposa County Sheriff can be reached at (209) 966-3614, and the Mariposa County Fire Department can be reached at (209) 966-3621.

Additional Information
The best times to visit are spring and summer. The Merced River Recreation Area is near the entrance to Yosemite National Park, and provides overflow or alternative camping for Park visitors, as well as a beautiful setting for river enthusiasts. Many commercial raft outfitters, licensed and supervised by BLM, offer trips on the Merced River. Contact BLM for a list of approved commercial raft operators and their schedules.

Sponsoring Partner

Activity Codes

 - horseback riding, swimming, hobby gold prospecting, picnicking

Merced River Trail

Location
15 miles north of Mariposa, California

Description
This ungroomed and, for the most part, unshaded 18-mile trek for hikers, mountain bikers and horseback riders follows the old Yosemite Railroad grade from the Briceburg Visitor Center to the Highway 49 bridge at Bagby. Along the way, you'll pass vestiges of a water diversion from the turn of the century, or perhaps encounter a crew of contemporary '49-ers combing the shoals with a gold dredge. Be careful where you step — the tiny creature peeking out from under that nearby rock just might be a rare limestone salamander!

Mailing Address
BLM - Folsom Resource Area
63 Natoma Street
Folsom, CA 95630

Phone Number
(916) 985-4474

Fax Number
(916) 985-3259

Directions
From Merced, located on State Highway 99, travel 40 miles east on State Highway

140 to Mariposa. Then travel another 15 miles on Highway 140 to the Briceburg Visitor Center.

Visitor Activities
Mountain biking, wildlife viewing, bird-watching, plant viewing, hiking, and horseback riding.

Permits, Fees, Limitations
A daily camping fee is charged.

Accessibility
Campgrounds are accessible to persons with disabilities.

Camping and Lodging
There are three BLM campgrounds along the Merced River between Briceburg and Bagby. They are the McCabe Flat Campground, Railroad Flat Campground, and Willow Placer Campground. The campgrounds are only accessible by crossing the bridge at Briceburg and heading down river on the Merced River Trail (vehicles allowed). The campgrounds are about 2.5 miles apart. Commercial lodging is available in Mariposa.

Food and Supplies
Food and supplies are available in Mariposa.

First Aid
BLM crews with emergency medical technicians are on duty on weekends during the rafting season, generally April through July. The County Sheriff and Fire Department also provide first aid. The Mariposa County Sheriff can be reached at (209) 966-3614, and the Mariposa County Fire Department can be reached at (209) 966-3621.

Additional Information
Commercial raft trips are available. Many commercial raft outfitters, licensed and supervised by BLM, offer trips on the Merced River. Contact BLM for a list of approved commercial raft operators and their schedules. Campgrounds are open to Yosemite National Park visitors.

Sponsoring Partner

Activity Codes

   - mountain biking, horseback riding

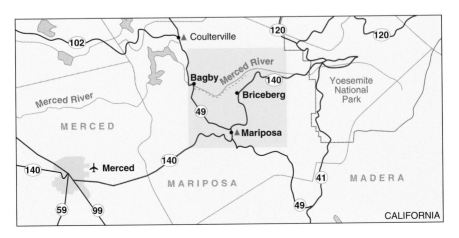

Molina Ghost Run Trail

Location
40 miles south of Hollister, California

Description
This 10-mile trail for the hardy four-wheel-drive enthusiast traverses the BLM Clear Creek Management Area. Named for the abandoned Molina Mercury Mine, which began operation in the 1850's along with the New Idria Mine, this trail is technically difficult and ruggedly spectacular. The Molina Trail offers scenic vistas, and an unusual and bizarre landscape resulting from a large serpentine rock formation un-

derlying most of the Clear Creek area. The Trail begins at the Oak Flat Campground, climbs about 2,000 feet, winds around Goat Mountain past the base of Picacho Peak, and continues to the perennial Clear Creek, ending at the town of New Idria.

Mailing Address
BLM - Hollister Resource Area
20 Hamilton Court
Hollister, CA 95023

Phone Number   Fax Number
(408) 637-8183   (408) 637-5218

Directions
From Hollister, travel south on State Highway 25. Twenty miles past the turn-off for Pinnacles National Monument, turn left on the Coalinga-Los Gatos Road. Twelve miles down, at the BLM sign, turn left on Clear Creek Road, and follow the road 2 miles to Oak Flat Campground, where the Trail begins.

Visitor Activities
Wildlife viewing, hunting, birdwatching, geologic sightseeing, off-road touring, plant viewing, scenic drives, and historic site.

Permits, Fees, Limitations
No fees. Travel only on designated routes throughout the Clear Creek area. The San Benito evening primrose grows in the area and is an endangered species. Fences have been placed around populations of the plant for their protection. Please observe all route restrictions.

Accessibility
None

Camping and Lodging
Camping is available at the Oak Flat campground. Lodging is available in Hollister.

Food and Supplies
Food and supplies are not available on-site. Some country stores are located 25 miles north on State Highway 25.

First Aid
First aid is available on-site from the resident BLM Ranger. The nearest hospital is in Hollister.

Additional Information
The area is open year-round. Travel is recommended during the wetter months of November through March. This is a rugged and remote area with limited visitor services. The area's serpentine-rich rock contains natural asbestos, which easily becomes airborne in dry weather. Posted signs warn of the potential hazard of breathing airborne asbestos fibers. Please call BLM about road and asbestos conditions before your trip.

Sponsoring Partner

Activity Codes

 - geologic sightseeing

North Algodones Dunes Wilderness

Location
26 miles east of Brawley, California

Description
The Algodones Sand Dune system covers 1,000 square miles, making it one of the largest dune complexes in North America. The dunes are interrupted in places by basins of flats, which support mesquite, smoke tree, ironwood, palo verde, and desert willow trees. The flat-tailed horned lizard, desert tortoise, and Colorado desert fringe-toed lizard have all been spotted in the region. The 32,000-acre North Algodones Wilderness Area provides ample opportunities for solitude and primitive recreation.

Mailing Address
BLM - El Centro Resource Area
1661 South 4th Street
El Centro, CA 92243

Phone Number
(760) 337-4400

Fax Number
(760) 337-4490

Directions
From Brawley, take State Highway 78 east approximately 26 miles. The wilderness lies along the north side of the highway.

Visitor Activities
Hunting, scenic drives, birdwatching, wildlife viewing, plant viewing, and hiking.

The sweeping North Algodones Dunes offer visitors unparalleled opportunities for solitude. *(Photo by Doran Sanchez, California Desert District)*

Permits, Fees, Limitations

No fees. No commercial uses are allowed. No use of motorized or mechanized vehicles of any kind (off-road vehicles, motorcycles, bicycles, hang-gliders, motorized equipment, or motorboats) is allowed. No facilities are available.

Accessibility

None

Camping and Lodging

Primitive camping is available. There are no developed sites. Developed campgrounds are available along Gecko Road, immediately south of the wilderness area and Highway 78, in the designated off-highway vehicle area. These campgrounds offer restrooms and flat pads, but do not have water. Lodging is available in Brawley.

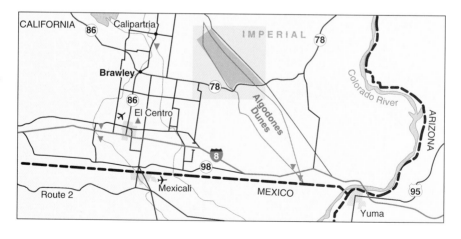

Food and Supplies
Food, gas and supplies are available at the Glamis store located immediately south of Highway 78, on the eastern edge of the Dunes.

First Aid
Cahuilla Ranger Station, located immediately south of Highway 78, is open on weekends from October through April. The nearest hospital is located in Brawley.

Additional Information
The area is open year-round. The best time to visit is from fall through spring. Summer is extremely hot, with temperatures of over 120°F during the day, and 100°F at night, so be sure to bring water. Visitors should be aware that the sand limits mobility. This area is a designated Watchable Wildlife site.

Sponsor

Activity Codes

Owens Peak Wilderness Area (Short Canyon)

Location
15 miles northwest of Ridgecrest, California

Description
The majority of this wilderness is composed of the rugged eastern faces of the Sierra Nevada Mountains. Owens Peak, the high point of the southern Sierra Nevadas, rises to more than 8,400 feet. The mountainous terrain has deep, winding, open and expansive canyons, many of which contain springs with extensive riparian vegetation. Vegetation varies considerably within the site, with a creosote desert scrub community on the bajadas, scattered yuccas, cacti, annuals, cottonwood, and oak trees in the canyons and valleys, and a juniper-piñon woodland with sagebrush and digger/grey pine on the upper elevations. Wildlife includes mule deer, golden eagle, and prairie falcon.

Mailing Address
BLM - Ridgecrest Resource Area
300 South Richmond Road
Ridgecrest, CA 93555

Phone Number
(760) 384-5400

Fax Number
(760) 384-5499

Directions
From Bakersfield, take State Highway 178 east 57 miles to State Highway 14 and then take Highway 14 north for 9 miles to the signed Short Canyon turnoff to the west.

Or, from Ridgecrest, travel west on State Highway 178 to State Highway 14, and then go north on Highway 14 for 3 miles to the Short Canyon turnoff to the west.

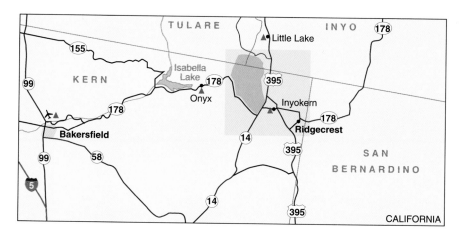

Visitor Activities
Hiking, wildlife viewing, plant viewing, birdwatching, and photography.

Permits, Fees, Limitations
No fees. No commercial uses are allowed. No use of motorized vehicles of any kind (off-road vehicles, motorcycles, bicycles, hang gliders, motorized equipment, or motorboats) is allowed. No facilities are available.

Accessibility
None

Camping and Lodging
Primitive camping is available; there are no developed sites. Lodging is available in Ridgecrest.

First Aid
There is no first aid available on-site. The nearest hospital is located in Ridgecrest.

Additional Information
The site is open year-round. Spring is the best time to view wildflowers in Short Canyon, which is an easy hike from a nearby parking area. Good hiking shoes or walking shoes are recommended. Indian Wells and Short and Sand Canyons offer vehicle access to the wilderness boundary. There is also access to the Pacific Crest Trail. A popular section of the Trail can be accessed from Walker Pass on State Highway 178, which is 8 miles west of State Highway 14.

Sponsoring Partner

Activity Codes

 – photography

Pacific Crest National Scenic Trail - Owens Peak Segment

Location
60 miles east of Bakersfield, California

Description
The Pacific Crest National Scenic Trail is a continuous hiking trail from the Mexican border to the Canadian border. The Owens Peak Segment begins at Walker Pass in Kern County, and extends 41 miles north to the Sequoia National Forest at Rockhouse Basin, where the Domelands Wilderness begins. Elevations range from 5,245 feet at Walker Pass to 7,600 feet on Bear Mountain. The Trail offers spectacular views of the surrounding mountains and valleys.

Mailing Address
BLM - Bakersfield Field Office
3801 Pegasus Drive
Bakersfield, CA 93308

Phone Number	Fax Number
(805) 391-6000	(805) 391-6040

Directions
From Bakersfield, take State Highway 178 east about 60 miles to Walker Pass. Or, from Ridgecrest, travel 20 miles west on State Highway 178 to Walker Pass.

Visitor Activities
Hiking, hunting, horse packing, plant viewing, birdwatching, and wildlife viewing.

Permits, Fees, Limitations
No fees. A California campfire permit is required if you intend to have a campfire. Permits are available from BLM, the U.S. Forest Service, and California Department of Forestry offices. The Trail is for hiking and equestrian use only; no bicycles or motorized vehicles are permitted.

Accessibility
None

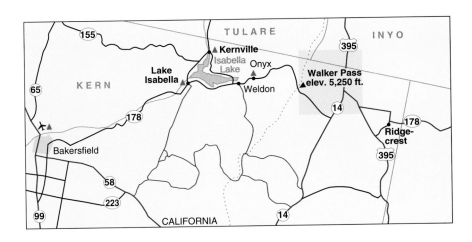

Camping and Lodging

Camping is available at the Walker Pass Trailhead campground, which has water (from April to October), toilets, parking, fire grates, and corrals. Chimney Creek campground is a primitive campground with water that may not be potable because of the area's naturally-occurring uranium. The campground is located on Canebrake Road off State Highway 178, but hikers can access it from the trail (0.25 mile off the trail and marked by a sign). Lodging is available in Lake Isabella, Kernville, and Ridgecrest. Lake Isabella is 25 miles west of Walker Pass on State Highway 178. Kernville is 15 miles west on 178, then 10 miles north on State Highway 155. Ridgecrest is 20 miles east on State Highway 178.

Food and Supplies

Food and supplies are available in Onyx, 15 miles west of Walker Pass on State Highway 178, or Inyokern, 15 miles east on State Highway 178.

First Aid

First aid is available at the BLM South Fork Fire Station [Tel.: (619) 378-3317], located on Highway 178, 10 miles west of Walker Pass, or at the BLM Chimney Peak Fire Station [Tel.: (619) 371-5326], located on Canebrake Road and accessible from the trail. The nearest hospital is located in Ridgecrest.

Additional Information

Be prepared for all weather conditions. Summer temperatures range from 32°F to over 100°F. The trail is usually free of snow by mid-May, but sudden and severe snowstorms can still occur at that time. Springtime means strong winds, and summer thunderstorms bring lightning and the possibility of fire and flashfloods. Extreme care is advised. There are small springs and streams in the Spanish Needles area (the trail passes through this back country area), but it is best to pack your own water.

Sponsoring Partners

Activity Codes

Panoche/Tumey Hills

Location

30 miles south of the State Highway 152/Interstate 5 junction, in the Central Valley of California

Description

The Panoche/Tumey Hills, rising out of the west side of the San Joaquin Valley, are rich in upland game, provide significant habitat for endangered species of plants and animals, and contain significant paleontological resources. There are 2 Areas of Critical Environmental Concern (ACEC's) and 2 Wilderness Study Areas (WSA's) within the Panoche/Tumey Hills. One ACEC was established for the protection of rare plants and animals, and the other is for the protection of the paleontological resources. The 2 WSA's are located in the Panoche Hills and must be managed so as not to diminish existing wilderness values. Although located near a heavily traveled highway, the Panoche/Tumey Hills area has been isolated over the years, with much of the area only recently opened to public access.

Mailing Address
BLM - Hollister Resource Area
20 Hamilton Court
Hollister, CA 95023

Phone Number   Fax Number
(408) 637-8183   (408) 637-5128

Directions
From State Highway 152, travel 30 miles south on Interstate 5 to the Little Panoche Road/Mercy Hot Springs exit. Follow the signs to Panoche/Tumey Hills.

Visitor Activities
Hunting, wildlife viewing, plant viewing, birdwatching, horse packing, horseback riding, paleontological site, and star-gazing.

Permits, Fees, Limitations
Because of extreme fire danger, the area is closed to vehicles from April 15 until the opening of the upland game bird season in mid-October, or even longer if the fire hazard remains extreme. The area is off-limits to motorcycles and all-terrain vehicles. Four-wheel-drive vehicles are restricted to existing roads. Since there are no equestrian pass-throughs available, horses are also effectively barred from the area during the vehicle closure. The area is open to foot and bicycle traffic year-round. The Panoche/Tumey Hills are popular with upland game hunters, and a hunting packet is available for purchase from BLM. A State of California hunting license is required for hunting, and a campfire permit, available from BLM, the U.S. Forest Service, or California Department of Forestry offices, is required for campfires. Check with BLM for seasonal restrictions on campfires or other activities due to fire danger. Written permission is required from BLM in order to study or remove any paleontological resource.

Accessibility
None

Camping and Lodging
There are no developed campgrounds in the area. Primitive camping is allowed as

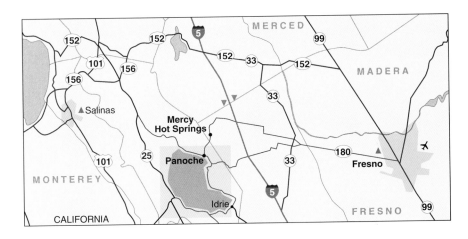

long as vehicles stay within 15 feet of an existing road. Lodging is available at several locations along Interstate 5, where clusters of services are at most major exits.

Food and Supplies
There are several gas stations, stores and motels along Interstate 5. The best selection for shopping is along Interstate 5, at the Panoche Road exit.

First Aid
There is no first aid available on-site. The closest hospitals are in Fresno, west on State Highway 198.

Additional Information
Pack in your own water. The area is hot and dry with no visitor facilities. Vehicle traffic is restricted during spring and summer. Early spring after the winter rainfall is the best time to visit. There is a brief but spectacular spring wildflower season.

Sponsoring Partner

Activity Codes

 - horseback riding, star-gazing

Point Sal

Location
5 miles west of Guadalupe, California

Description
Point Sal is a 77-acre promontory on the coast of northern Santa Barbara County near the north end of Vandenberg Air Force Base. It is a fragile area, with sandy soil and a unique blend of wildlife. Sea lions, mussels, and deer can be found just yards from one another. Threatened or endangered species such as the peregrine falcon, California brown pelican, California least tern, southern sea otter, and California gray whale are regulars at Point Sal. The area is also a unique meeting point and transition zone for tidepool life and plant life common to the northern and southern coasts of California. There is abundant evidence of Native American occupation as recently as 250 years ago and as far back as 4,800 years ago. Rock rings where homes once stood, grinding stones, and other Native American artifacts are easily visible. Point Sal is managed by BLM as an Area of Critical Environmental Concern.

Mailing Address
BLM - Caliente Resource Area
3801 Pegasus Drive
Bakersfield, CA 93308

Phone Number	Fax Number
(805) 391-6000	(805) 391-6040

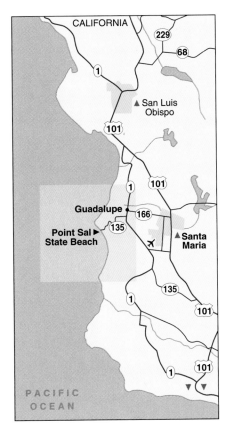

Permits, Fees, Limitations
No fees. Pedestrians are required to stay on designated trails.

Accessibility
None

Camping and Lodging
Camping and lodging are available in Guadalupe or Santa Maria, 15 miles east on State Route 135. No camping is available in the area.

Food and Supplies
Food, supplies and water are not available on-site. There are stores in Guadalupe.

First Aid
First aid is not available on-site. The closest hospital is in Santa Maria, 15 miles east on State Route 135. This is also the location of the nearest first aid.

Additional Information
Weather can be cold at any time of year. The best times to visit are spring and fall. There are no bathrooms or other facilities on-site. Visitors must be well-prepared, since it is a 2- to 3-hour hike back to the parking area from the far end of the trail, and then a 15-20 minute drive to any services.

Sponsoring Partner

Activity Codes

Directions
From Guadalupe, travel 5 miles west on State Route 135 to the Point Sal State Beach. Park in the parking lot and hike to Point Sal. It is a difficult 2-mile, 2- to 3-hour hike each way, on a narrow, cliff-side trail.

Visitor Activities
Hiking, wildlife viewing, birdwatching, plant viewing, and historic and archaeological sites.

Punta Gorda Lighthouse

Location
6 miles southwest of Petrolia, California

Description
Located along the Lost Coast in the King Range National Conservation Area, the Punta Gorda fog station began operating on June 22, 1888, and the lighthouse on January 15, 1912. Isolated and lonely, the lighthouse was reported to be the "Alcatraz" of lighthouses, a place where employees were stationed as a punishment for misconduct. Throughout its operation, the lighthouse remained a frontier settlement in the midst of a modernizing world. During good weather, a keeper would ride horseback into the village of Petrolia to carry back what fresh supplies he could. For much of the winter, flooded streams and fierce winds kept the area cut off from civilization. The lighthouse was in service for 39 years until it was taken over by the U.S. Coast Guard during World War II and finally closed in 1951. The property was transferred to BLM in 1963, and was placed on the National Register of Historic Places on October 5, 1976.

Mailing Address
BLM - Arcata Resource Area
1695 Heinden Road
Arcata, CA 95521-4573

Phone Number
(707) 825-2300

Fax Number
(707) 825-2301

Directions
From Eureka, travel 10 miles south on U.S. Highway 101 to the Ferndale exit. Proceed 5 miles on County Road 211 to Main Street in Ferndale. Follow Main Street approximately 1 mile to its end. Turn right on Ocean Street, then immediately left on Wildcat Road. Continue 45 miles to Petrolia. Turn right on Lighthouse Road and travel 5 miles to Mattole Campground. The Lost Coast Trail begins at the Mattole information kiosk, and leads south 3 miles to the lighthouse.

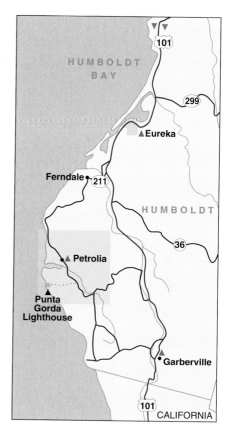

Visitor Activities

Hiking, wildlife viewing, birdwatching, wildflower viewing, picnicking, and historic and archaeological sites.

Permits, Fees, Limitations

None

Accessibility

None

Camping and Lodging

Mattole Campground has no hookups or potable water, but offers pit toilets. Lodging is available in Petrolia and in Garberville, 60 miles south of Eureka on U.S. Highway 101.

Food and Supplies

Food and supplies are available in Petrolia.

First Aid

The Petrolia Fire Department provides full medical aid for this site. The emergency number is 911. The nearest hospital is in Garberville. From the campground, Garberville is accessible by returning to U.S.

Highway 101 via Petrolia and Ferndale.

Additional Information

Frequent and dense morning fog should be expected. The best months to visit are April, May, September, and October. It is one of the wettest spots along the Lost Coast Trail. From the Mattole Campground to the lighthouse, allow at least 5 hours for the 6-mile round-trip hike, as the soft sand makes for slow going. Bring at least 2 quarts of water per person and plan to hike during low tide, as this short stretch of the Lost Coast Trail may be impassable at high tide. Tide tables are posted at Mattole kiosk.

Sponsoring Partner

 SOCIETY *for* HISTORICAL ARCHAEOLOGY

Activity Codes

 - picnicking, wildflower viewing

Red Elephant Mine Trail

Location

15 miles south of Lower Lake, California

Description

This challenging off-highway vehicle trail is about 8 miles long. Beginning near the top of Round Mountain, the first section of the trail winds around 2 wildlife watering ponds. A steep downhill section leads to a narrow ridge top, overlooking grasslands and streams leading to Hunting Creek. The trail continues to a challenging stream crossing, then back up a nar-

row cross-hill section to a series of clifftop switchbacks. From the switchbacks, a rider can see the site of the old Red Elephant Mine and view eagles and other raptors as they fish the creeks. The trail continues through large cypress and manzanita forests and across grass-covered meadows to Knoxville Road. The scenery and weather in the area vary dramatically with the seasons. In winter and spring, grasses and flowers are vibrant; in summer, the region is extremely hot and dry.

An off-road motorcyclist is airborne amid the cypress trees and red rocks of the Red Elephant Mine Trail. *(Photo by Jim Pickering, California State Office)*

Mailing Address
BLM - Clear Lake Resource Area
2550 North State St.
Ukiah, CA 95482

Phone Number   Fax Number
(707) 468-4000   (707) 468-4027

Directions
From State Highway 53 in Lower Lake, turn south on Morgan Valley Road. Travel for about 12 miles to the north entrance of BLM's Knoxville Recreation Area. Take an immediate left turn over the low-water crossing. Proceed 0.6 mile and take the first right turn. Continue 0.5 mile to the Knoxville North staging area. The trailhead is marked with a BLM sign and is directly opposite the staging area.

Visitor Activities
Motorcycle and off-highway-vehicle riding, target shooting, hunting, swimming and rockhounding.

Permits, Fees, Limitations
Motorized vehicles are permitted on existing roads and trails; cross-country travel is prohibited. There are no site-specific permits or fees required.

Accessibility
None

Camping and Lodging
A day-use staging area is located at the northern end of the trail. A 4-site primitive campground is located at Hunting Creek, about 7 miles from the southern end of the trail. The nearest lodging is located in Clearlake, 20 miles north of Knoxville on State Highway 53.

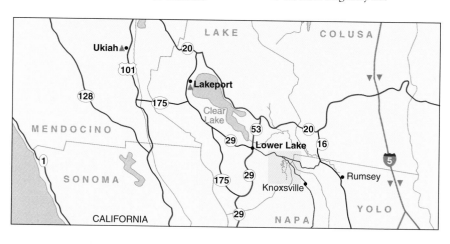

Food and Supplies
The nearest food and supplies are located in Lower Lake.

First Aid
No first aid or emergency services are available in the Knoxville Recreation Area. The nearest hospital is located in Clearlake.

Additional Information
The Red Elephant Mine Trail and the Knoxville Recreation Area are most pleasant in the winter and spring months, though hunters favor the fall. The summers are hot and dry; swimming in the local creeks is popular. Two organized target shooting areas are available to the public.

Sponsoring Partner

Activity Codes

 - target shooting, swimming, rockhounding

Red Hills Area of Critical Environmental Concern

Location
0.5 mile south of Chinese Camp, California

Description
The Red Hills is a region of 7,100 acres of public land located just south of the historic town of Chinese Camp in Tuolumne County. The Red Hills are noticeably different from the surrounding countryside. The serpentine-based soils in the area support a unique assemblage of plant species. Included among the thorny buckbrush and scraggly foothill pine is a rich variety of annual wildflowers, which put on a showy display every spring. The endangered bald eagle is a winter resident of the area.

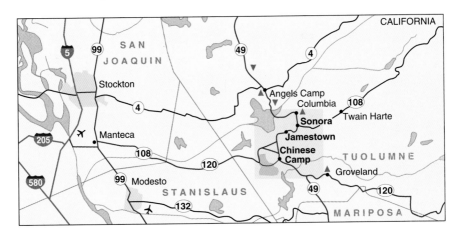

Mailing Address
BLM - Folsom Resource Area
63 Natoma Street
Folsom, CA 95630

Phone Number   Fax Number
(916) 985-4474   (916) 985-3259

Directions
From Sonora, take State Highway 49
south 15 miles to Chinese Camp, then
drive south on Red Hills Road for 0.5
mile.

Visitor Activities
Horseback riding, wildflower viewing,
wildlife viewing, plant viewing, birdwatching, hiking, picnicking, hunting, and
mountain biking.

Permits, Fees, Limitations
No fees. No overnight stays are permitted.
Target shooting is prohibited.

Accessibility
None

Camping and Lodging
No camping is available on-site. Lodging is
available in Jamestown, approximately 5
miles north on State Highway 49, and in

Sonora, about 10 miles in the same direction.

Food and Supplies
Food and supplies are available in Chinese
Camp.

First Aid
No first aid is available on-site. The nearest hospital is located in Sonora. First aid is
available through the Volunteer Fire Department in Chinese Camp. Contact them
by going to the Chinese Camp store.

Additional Information
The best time to view wildflowers is late
March through early May.

Sponsoring Partner

Activity Codes

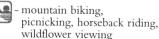 - mountain biking,
picnicking, horseback riding,
wildflower viewing

Timbered Crater
Wilderness Study Area

Location
10 miles north of Fall River Mills, California

Description
The Timbered Crater Wilderness Study Area is an outstanding showcase for the geology of extinct volcanic craters. The alternating depressions and buttes are dominated by a 500-foot butte at the rim of the crater. The crater provides the only northeastern California habitat for the Baker cypress tree. Because Timbered Crater lies at the junction of the Great Basin and Cascade Mountains ecosystems, there is a unique blend of desert and mountain plant communities. Vegetation ranges from pine, western juniper and Oregon white oak to desert plants such as big sagebrush, needle grass, and blue grass.

Mailing Address
BLM - Alturas Resource Area
608 West 12th Street
Alturas, CA 96101

Phone Number   Fax Number
(916) 233-4666   (916) 233-5696

Directions
From Fall River Mills, travel 4 miles east on State Highway 299 to Shasta County Road A-19, also called McArthur Road, and turn left. Follow the road 4.8 miles to a fork/junction with Spring Creek Road, and turn right. Continue 5.7 miles to Forest Service Road 39N03 and follow the signs.

Visitor Activities
Hiking, photography, plant viewing, geologic sightseeing, birdwatching, and wildlife viewing.

Permits, Fees, Limitations
No fees. No motorized vehicles are permitted inside the area. Temporary restrictions may be imposed on the use of fire during periods of high fire danger. Fire conditions are posted.

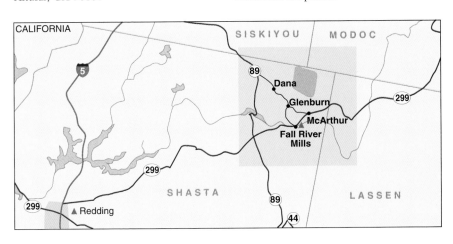

Accessibility
None

Camping and Lodging
Primitive camping is allowed throughout the area. The closest lodging is in the community of Dana, 6 miles north of Timbered Crater on Glen Burn Road.

Food and Supplies
The nearest location for supplies is Fall River Mills.

First Aid
No first aid is available on-site. The nearest hospital is in Fall River Mills.

Additional Information
Travel is over very rough lava rock; high-clearance and four-wheel-drive vehicles are strongly recommended. Access is difficult during wet weather, and winters can be harsh. There is no potable water available at the site.

Sponsoring Partner

Activity Codes

 - photography, geologic sightseeing

Trona Pinnacles

Location
20 miles east of Ridgecrest, California

Description
The Trona Pinnacles are some of the most unique geological features in the California Desert Conservation Area. The unusual landscape consists of more than 500 tufa spires, some as high as 140 feet, rising from the bed of the Searles Dry Lake basin. The pinnacles vary in size and shape from short and squat to tall and thin, and are composed primarily of calcium carbonate (tufa). The Trona Pinnacles have been featured in many commercials, films, and still-photo shoots.

Mailing Address
BLM - Ridgecrest Resource Area
300 South Richmond Road
Ridgecrest, CA 93555

Phone Number
(760) 384-5400

Fax Number
(760) 384-5499

Directions
From Ridgecrest, travel 20 miles east on State Highway 178 to its intersection with Trona-Red Mountain Road. Continue east on Highway 178 for 7.7 miles, and access the site by a dirt road leading off Highway 178 to the south.

Visitor Activities
Hiking, picnicking, photography, and geologic sightseeing.

Permits, Fees, Limitations
Visitors are urged to remain on designated routes or trails.

Accessibility
None

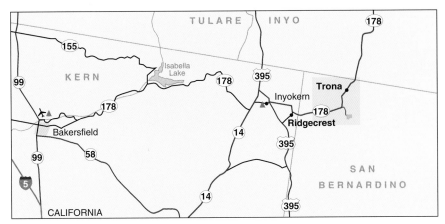

Camping and Lodging
Primitive camping is permitted; there are no developed sites. Lodging is available in Ridgecrest.

Food and Supplies
Food and supplies are available in Ridgecrest.

First Aid
The nearest hospital or place for other assistance is Ridgecrest.

Additional Information
The site is open year-round; the best times to visit are fall, winter and early spring.

Good hiking and walking shoes are recommended. The dirt access road is usually accessible by two-wheel-drive vehicles. Following a rain, however, the road may be impassable to all vehicles, including four-wheel-drive vehicles.

Sponsor

Activity Codes
  – photography, geologic sightseeing, picnicking

Ancient tufa spires create an eerie desert "moonscape" enjoyed by recreationists and filmmakers alike. *(Photo by Doran Sanchez, California Desert District)*

Volcanic Tablelands

Location
6 miles north of Bishop, California

Description
The Volcanic Tablelands is a vast volcanic landscape that was formed over 700,000 years ago by materials spewing from the Long Valley caldera, located to the northwest.

Mailing Address
BLM - Bishop Resource Area
785 North Main Street, Suite E
Bishop, CA 93514

Phone Number
(760) 872-4881

Fax Number
(760) 872-2894

Directions
From Bishop, take State Highway 6 north to Five Bridges Road, then turn left. Proceed on Five Bridges Road 5 miles until it turns into a dirt road. At the entrance to the area, there is a BLM kiosk that provides map and route information for the Tablelands.

Visitor Activities
Four-wheel driving, off-highway touring, scenic drives, hunting, plant viewing, geologic sightseeing, wildlife viewing, birdwatching, horseback riding, horse packing, mountain biking, and hiking.

Permits, Fees, Limitations
No fees. Four-wheel-drive and motorcycle touring are permitted on established routes only.

Accessibility
None

Camping and Lodging
Camping is available at BLM's Horton Creek Campground, located 8.5 miles north on U.S. Highway 395. Take a left on Millpond Road, then follow signs. Various types of lodging are available in Bishop.

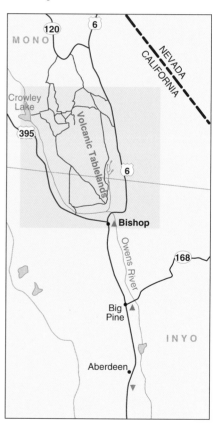

Food and Supplies
Food and supplies are available in Bishop.

First Aid
No first aid is available on-site. The closest hospital is located in Bishop.

Additional Information
The area is a primitive recreation area with no visitor facilities. Spring, fall, and winter are the best seasons to visit.

Sponsoring Partner

Activity Codes

 - geologic sightseeing, horseback riding, mountain biking

Brilliantly colored spring wildflowers line the Alpine Loop as it winds through Colorado's snow-capped San Juan Mountains. *(Courtesy BLM)*

Colorado

About 8 percent of the state of Colorado, or 8.3 million acres, is public land. Concentrated primarily in the western portion of the state, these lands showcase spectacular terrain, from alpine tundra to arid and colorful canyons and mesas. The range of elevation from 4,000 to 14,000 feet provides for a variety of climate and vegetation.

Recreational opportunities are plentiful throughout the state all year. Winter sports include cross- country skiing, snowshoeing, and snowmobiling. Warmer seasons entice visitors to whitewater adventures, fishing, hunting, camping, hiking, mountain biking, off-road vehicle activities, world-renowned rock climbing, wildlife viewing, and spectacular sightseeing.

Public lands throughout the state also provide important habitat for deer, elk, and antelope, as well as threatened and endangered species. Premier cultural sites abound. Ruins of the prehistoric Anasazi culture are being preserved on the public lands in the Four Corners region where Colorado meets Arizona, New Mexico, and Utah. The Anasazi Heritage Center houses an impressive collection of ancient artifacts. The Center helps visitors learn about the prehistoric Anasazi culture, which flourished on the high plateau of the southwestern United States for thousands of years before settlement by Europeans.

Most public lands are accessible from major freeways, highways, and county roads. In fact, many beautiful Colorado vistas can be experienced from the comfort of an automobile. How about a ride on the historic Gold Belt Scenic Byway, for example? Escapes to remote areas are also possible, except during wintry months which frequently extend beyond the traditional seasons. It is always wise to check with local BLM offices for access before starting out to experience the public lands in Colorado.

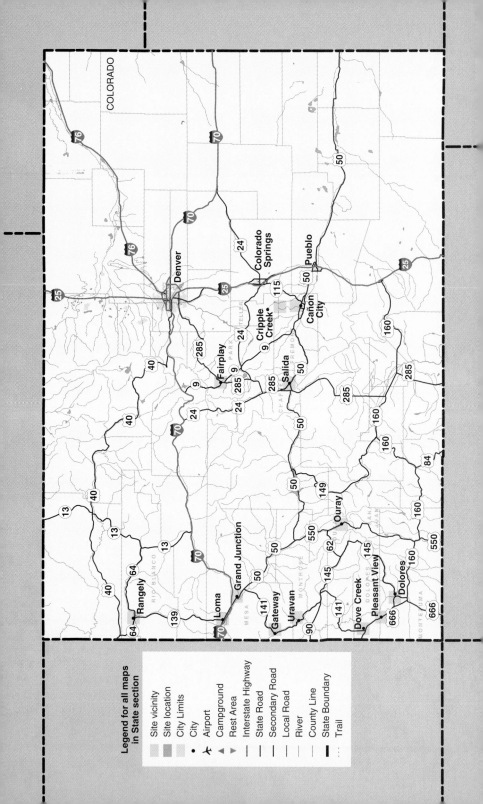

Legend for all maps
in State section

Site vicinity
Site location
City Limits
City
Airport
Campground
Rest Area
Interstate Highway
State Road
Secondary Road
Local Road
River
County Line
State Boundary
Trail

COLORADO

76

70

70

76

Denver

24

Colorado
Springs

Pueblo

25

25

25

50

115

Cripple
Creek

50

Cañon
City

285

Fairplay

9

24

9

285

9

285

Salida

50

FREMONT

285

24

24

50

160

285

70

50

285

160

149

160

40

550

Ouray

62

84

13

40

50

160

13

13

550

Grand Junction

50

145

550

70

50

145

Dolores

160

40

Rangely

64

RIO BLANCO

Loma

141

Gateway

Uravan

90

145

Dove Creek

145

Pleasant View

160

64

139

70

MESA

MONTROSE

DOLORES

141

666

666

666

MONTEZUMA

SAN JUAN

Alpine Loop

Location
The Loop is a network of jeep roads that weave through the San Juan Mountains between the towns of Lake City, Silverton and Ouray in southwestern Colorado.

Description
This National Back Country Byway will take you on a day-long, 50-mile loop through spectacular alpine scenery surrounded by 14,000 foot peaks. The area is dotted with ghost towns and historic mining sites.

Mailing Addresses
BLM - San Juan Resource Area
701 Camino del Rio
Durango, CO 81301

BLM - Gunnison Resource Area
216 North Colorado Street
Gunnison, CO 81230

Phone Numbers
(970) 247-4874 (San Juan Resource Area)
(970) 641-0471 (Gunnison Resource Area)

Fax Numbers
(970) 385-1375 (San Juan Resource Area)
(970) 641-1928 (Gunnison Resource Area)

Directions
The Silverton and Ouray entrances to the Loop can be accessed via U.S. Highway 550 south of Montrose or north of Durango. The Lake City entrances are accessed via State Highway 149 south of Gunnison or north of Creede.

Visitor Activities
Four-wheel driving, scenic drives, fishing, hiking, photography, mountain biking, and visiting ghost towns.

Spectacular scenery, historic ghost towns, and four-wheel-drive roads make a tour of the Alpine Loop a high-country treat. *(Photo by Rick Athearn (retired), Colorado State Office)*

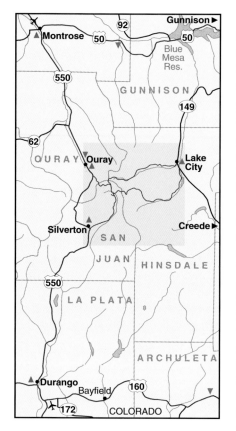

First Aid

Some medical services are available in nearby towns. The nearest hospitals are 35-50 miles away, in Montrose, Gunnison, and Durango.

Additional Information

The visitor centers in Silverton, Ouray, and Lake City provide information and maps. There are 10 restrooms along the Loop. This area is in the high Colorado Rockies, and is subject to changing weather. The route is usually open from early June to mid-October, and is closed during the winter. Short thundershowers are common on summer afternoons. While much of the Loop is accessible by ordinary passenger vehicle, you will need a four-wheel-drive vehicle to complete the Loop over Cinnamon and Engineer Passes. To protect this fragile environment, vehicle use is limited to designated roads. An informative, 20-page area visitor's guide, called "The Alpine Explorer," is available for purchase from BLM. It includes a detailed map, points of interest, history, safety tips, and much more.

Permits, Fees, Limitations

Fees are charged only for overnight camping in developed campgrounds.

Accessibility

Most facilities along the way are wheelchair-accessible.

Camping and Lodging

Camping and lodging are available in Silverton, Ouray and Lake City. There are three developed campgrounds on the Lake City side of the route. Primitive camping is allowed on public lands.

Food and Supplies

Food and supplies are available in Lake City, Silverton, and Ouray.

Sponsoring Partner

SCENIC AMERICA

Activity Codes

- four-wheel driving, photography, ghost town, mountain biking

Anasazi Heritage Center

Location
3 miles west of Dolores, Colorado.

Description
This unique archaeological museum features the history and culture of the Four Corners region. The Center's films, hands-on discovery area, interactive computer programs and exhibits explore archaeology, local history, and the lifeways of the Pueblo, Ute and Navajo peoples. Visitors to the Center are invited to "touch the past": grind corn, weave on a loom, use microscopes, and examine actual artifacts. Special exhibits are complemented by lectures, demonstrations and visitor activities. Two stabilized and interpreted archaeological sites are accessible from a 0.5-mile paved trail. The Center grounds also offer spectacular views of McPhee Lake, Four Corners mountain ranges, and the Great Sage Plain.

Mailing Address
BLM - Anasazi Heritage Center
27501 Highway 184
Dolores, CO 81323

Phone Number
(970) 822-4811

Fax Number
(970) 822-7035

Directions
From Dolores, travel west on State Highway 145, then turn west (right) on State Highway 184.

Visitor Activities
Archaeological sites, hands-on activities, interactive computer programs, exhibits, theater, and traveling exhibits.

Permits, Fees, Limitations
There is an admission fee. Golden Eagle, Access and Age passes are honored.

Accessibility
This is a fully-accessible site.

Camping and Lodging
No camping is allowed at the Anasazi Heritage Center. Lodging is available in Dolores and in Cortez (1 mile east on State Highway 184 and 9 miles south on State Highway 145). McPhee Campground (U.S. Forest Service) is located 3 miles west of the Center on State Highway 184. Commercial camping is available in Dolores and Cortez.

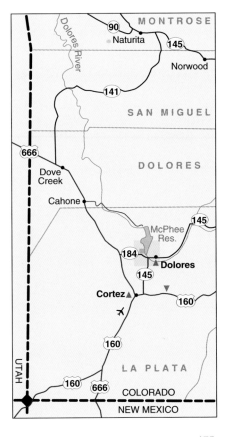

Food and Supplies
Food and supplies are available in Dolores and Cortez.

First Aid
There is limited first aid available on-site. The nearest hospital is in Cortez.

Additional Information
The Anasazi Heritage Center is a visitor-friendly museum and interpretive site that is open 7 days a week, year-round, except for Thanksgiving, Christmas and New Year's Day. There are restrooms, as well as a theater and bookstore.

Sponsor

Activity Codes

 - interactive displays, theater

Arkansas Headwaters Recreation Area

Location
From Leadville, Colorado, along the Arkansas River to the Pueblo Reservoir.

Description
This area is one of the most popular river-rafting spots in the United States, and also provides some of the best fishing in Colorado. The spectacular scenery is high-lighted by the steep, narrow, rocky canyons that provide excellent opportunities to view Rocky Mountain bighorn sheep. There are over 25 developed river-access areas. Popular activities include rock-hounding at Ruby Mountain, fishing for brown trout at Hecla Junction, and wildlife-watching at the Five Points Watchable Wildlife Area in Bighorn Sheep Canyon. The area is jointly managed by BLM and the Colorado Division of Parks and Outdoor Recreation.

Mailing address
BLM - Arkansas Headwaters Rec. Area
P. O. Box 126
Salida, CO 81201

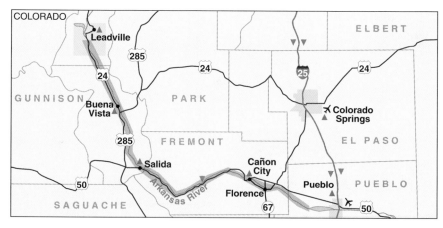

Phone Number   Fax Number
(719) 539-7289   (719) 539-3771

Directions
The Arkansas Headwaters Recreation
Area extends about 148 miles from
Leadville to the Pueblo Reservoir through
the towns of Buena Vista, Salida, Cañon
City, and Florence.

Visitor Activities
Fishing, sightseeing, photography, rafting,
wildlife viewing, and picnicking.

Permits, Fees, Limitations
Commercial rafting outfitters are required
to have a permit. Check with the Colorado Division of Wildlife for fishing license requirements [Tel.: (719) 539-3529].
There are fees for all campsites, and a daily
charge at all day-use sites.

Accessibility
Most facilities are new and include accessible restrooms, picnic areas, parking, and
campsites.

Camping and Lodging
Camping is available at Hecla Junction,
Rincon, Five Points, Ruby Mountain, and
Railroad Bridge. No water or electricity is
provided at campsites. Lodging is available
in Leadville, Buena Vista, Salida, Cañon
City, and Pueblo.

Food and Supplies
Food and supplies are available in
Leadville, Buena Vista, Nathrop, Salida,
Howard, Cotopaxi, Texas Creek, Cañon
City, Florence, and Pueblo.

First Aid
There is no first aid available on-site. The
nearest hospitals are in Leadville, Salida,
Cañon City, and Pueblo.

Additional Information
This is a very well-developed recreation
area complex. Access is very easy from 3

major highways (Highways 50, 24 and
285). The site is open year-round. Visitor
centers are located in Buena Vista, Salida,
Cañon City, and Florence.

Sponsoring Partner

FOUNDATION FOR
NORTH AMERICAN
WILD SHEEP

Activity Codes

 - photography, picnicking, sightseeing

**Intrepid rafters rush headlong down Col-
orado's Arkansas River, one of the most
popular whitewater destinations in the
country.** *(Photo by Rick Athearn (retired), Colorado
State Office)*

Calamity Camp Mining Site

Location

50 miles southwest of Grand Junction, Colorado

Description

This remote, historic site contains one of the last standing vanadiun-radium-uranium camps in Colorado. Calamity Camp is an example of the historic mining camps that were active during the uranium booms from 1916 to 1980. The site has several well-preserved structures, including a cookhouse. **NOTE: There is some residual radiation at this site, because of radioactive minerals in the area. Please call BLM for details.**

Mailing Address

BLM - Grand Junction Resource Area
2015 11 Road
Grand Junction, CO 81506

Phone Number   Fax Number
(970) 244-3000   (970) 244-3083

Directions

From Grand Junction, travel U.S. Highway 50 south 10 miles to State Highway 141. Travel 42 miles west, toward Gateway. Turn off at Niche Road, 4 miles east of Gateway. Follow Niche Road 16 miles to Calamity Mesa. It is recommended that maps be purchased from BLM before visiting the site.

Visitor Activities

Self-guided historic tour and scenic drives.

Permits, Fees, Limitations

None

Accessibility

None

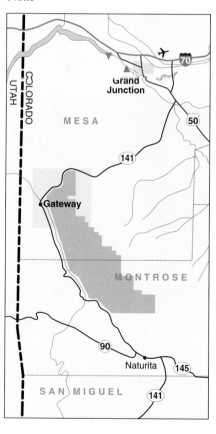

Well-preserved stone structures highlight the remote Calamity Camp, a historic mining camp that was active until 1980.
(Photo by Rick Athearn (retired), Colorado State Office)

Camping and Lodging
Camping is allowed on the public lands. Lodging is available in Gateway and Grand Junction.

Food and Supplies
The nearest source for food and supplies is Gateway.

First Aid
The nearest first aid is available in Gateway.

Additional Information
This is an extremely remote area. Roads are limited to high-clearance or four-wheel-drive vehicles. Sedans and station wagons are not recommended, and there is no help if you break down. The roads can be very slippery when wet. The area is not accessible during winter because of snow. There is no drinking water available. **WARNING: There is a potential radiation hazard because of open uranium mines/pits in the area.**

Sponsoring Partner

 SOCIETY for HISTORICAL ARCHAEOLOGY

Activity Codes

  - self-guided historic tour

Canyon Pintado
National Historic District

Location
Begins 3 miles south of Rangely, Colorado

Description
Canyon Pintado National Historic District encompasses over 16,000 acres of public land along 15 miles of State Highway 139. Canyon Pintado (Spanish for "Painted Canyon") received its name in 1776 when Fathers Dominguez and Escalante noted numerous examples of ancient Native American rock art as they traveled through the Douglas Creek Valley.

The prehistoric Fremont culture and the historic Ute Indians left much of the rock art that is visible in the Canyon today. Seven rock art sites are open to public viewing within the Historic District, right along the highway. A large Kokopelli (fertility) figure is displayed at the ramada interpretive kiosk in the Canyon.

Mailing Address
BLM - White River Resource Area
P.O. Box 928
73544 Highway 64
Meeker, CO 81641

Phone Number
(970) 878-3601

Fax Number
(970) 878-5717

Directions
From Rangely, Colorado (junction of State Highways 64 and 139), travel south on Highway 139. The District begins about 3 miles south and continues for 15 miles.

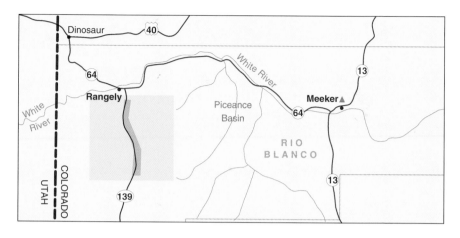

Visitor Activities
Picnicking, hiking, photography, sightseeing, rock art, mountain biking, and scenic drives.

Permits, Fees, Limitations
None

Accessibility
Only the Kokopelli viewing site is currently wheelchair-accessible, with an accessible toilet.

Camping and Lodging
Primitive camping is allowed on public lands. Lodging and a developed campground are available in Rangely.

Starting out from this information kiosk, visitors can view the "Painted Canyon," which is decorated with 1,000-year-old rock art. *(Photo by Rick Athearn (retired), Colorado State Office)*

Food and Supplies
Food and supplies are available in Rangely.

First Aid
There is no first aid available on-site. The nearest hospital is in Rangely.

Additional Information
All trails to sites in the District are primitive and receive little maintenance. The only facilities are a kiosk, picnic ramada, and toilet located in the southern end of the District. There are additional rock art sites open to the public in the Rangely area.

Sponsor

Activity Codes

 - photography, sightseeing, rock art, picnicking, mountain biking

Dolores River

Location
30 miles north of Cortez, Colorado

Description
Across western Colorado, the Dolores River runs from the rugged La Plata Mountains through deep-red canyons toward the Colorado River in Utah. The Dolores features outstanding scenic values, wildlife viewing, rare plants, and cultural resources.

Mailing Address
BLM - San Juan Resource Area
701 Camino del Rio
Durango, CO 81301

Phone Number   **Fax Number**
(970) 247-4874   (970) 385-1375

Directions
From Cortez, travel 30 miles north on U.S. Highway 666. The put-in is at the Bradfield Bridge Recreation Site, 6 miles east of Cahone, Colorado

Visitor Activities
Fishing, whitewater rafting, canoeing, wildlife viewing, sightseeing, birdwatching, plant viewing, and scenic drives.

Permits, Fees, Limitations
A permit is required for commercial rafting, but not for private boaters. Check with the Colorado Division of Wildlife for fishing license requirements [Tel.: (970) 247-0855].

Accessibility
None

Camping and Lodging
There are 18 campsites at the Bradfield Ranch Recreation Site. Dispersed camping is also permitted along the river. Lodging is available in Cortez.

Food and Supplies
Food and supplies are available in Naturita, Dolores, and Norwood.

Western Colorado's Dolores River twists and turns its way through brilliantly colored "layer-cake" canyons. *(Photo by Rick Athearn (retired), Colorado State Office)*

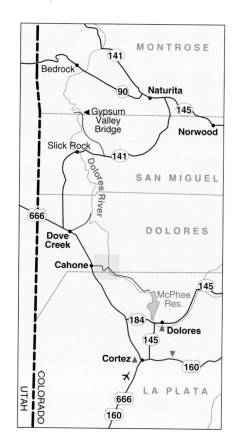

First Aid
First aid is not available on-site. The nearest hospital is in Cortez.

Additional Information
The Dolores River is a primitive recreation area with few visitor facilities. Bring drinking water, food, and appropriate clothing for rapidly changing weather conditions. Restrooms are located at Bradfield Bridge and Mountain Sheep Point Recreation Site, located 8 miles east of Dove Creek.

Sponsoring Partner

Activity Codes

     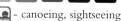

 - canoeing, sightseeing

Garden Park Fossil Area

Location
6 miles north of Cañon City, Colorado

Description
Fossils of well-known species of large dinosaurs have been discovered at this site over the last 120 years. Many of the dinosaur fossils discovered at this site are on exhibit at museums around the country, including the Denver Museum of Natural History, and the Smithsonian Institution's Museum of Natural History in Washington, D.C. Fossils of two-legged, plant-eating dinosaurs, dinosaur eggs, and dinosaur tracks have also been discovered in the Garden Park Fossil Area. In addition to dinosaur bones, Garden Park contains 2 significant, rare plant species, Brandegee wild buckwheat and inch milkweed. Plans are in place to build a world-class paleoenvironmental museum here in the year 2000; activities will include interpretation of present-day native plants as well as those that are part of the fossil record. Garden Park is a BLM Area of Critical Environmental Concern, a Colorado Re-

search Natural Area, and a National Natural Landmark.

Mailing Address
BLM - Royal Gorge Resource Area
3170 East Main Street
Cañon City, CO 81212

Phone Number   Fax Number
(719) 269-8500   (719) 269-8599

Directions
From Cañon City, go about 6 miles north on Shelf Road. This is part of the Gold Belt Back Country Scenic Byway. There are 2 small pull-outs with marked interpretive signs.

Visitor Activities
Scenic drives, photography, hiking, birdwatching, plant viewing, and wildlife viewing.

Permits, Fees, Limitations
None

Accessibility
The Cleveland Quarry pull-off is wheelchair-accessible.

Camping and Lodging
Primitive camping is available on-site. The nearest lodging is in Cañon City.

Food and Supplies
Food and supplies are available in Cañon City.

First Aid
No first aid is available on-site. The nearest hospital is in Cañon City.

Additional Information
General information about the area is posted at the Cleveland Quarry pull-off. Dinosaur tours of the area can be obtained for a fee by contacting the Dinosaur Depot in Cañon City [Tel.: (719) 269-7150]. The Dinosaur Depot also features inter-

pretive exhibits about the Garden Park Fossil Area. The Cleveland Quarry streamside interpretive kiosk has a restroom and picnic area. The Marsh Quarry Interpretive Trail includes a 0.25-mile self-guided interpretive trail.

Sponsoring Partner

Activity Codes

 - dinosaur quarry, photography

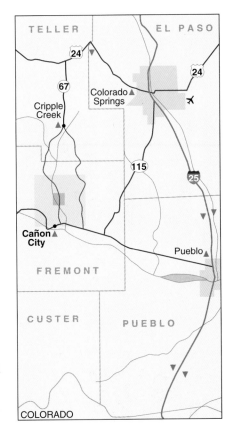

Gold Belt Scenic Byway

Location

The Byway travels through the towns of Cañon City, Florence, Victor, Cripple Creek, and Florissant, Colorado.

Description

Travel on a historic, narrow-gauge railroad bed, an old stage road, and a county road on the Gold Belt Scenic Byway. The Byway retraces the historic travel routes connecting Cripple Creek and Victor Mining District, site of the world's largest Gold Rush. Cripple Creek now caters to gamblers and other visitors. The 3 legs of the route, which form a loop, have a total length of about 131 miles.

Mailing Address
BLM - Royal Gorge Resource Area
3170 East Main Street
Cañon City, CO 81212

Phone Number   Fax Number
(719) 269-8500   (719) 269-8599

Directions
The Byway is located just 1 hour from Colorado Springs or Pueblo, Colorado. From the north, it can be reached from

Colorado's historic Gold Belt invites visitors to travel the route taken by old-time Gold Rush prospectors. *(Photo by Rick Athearn (retired), Colorado State Office)*

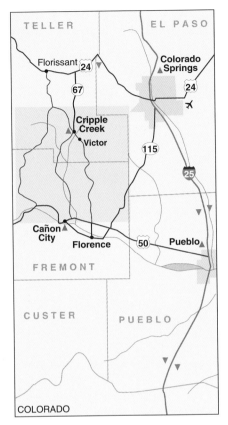

U.S. Highway 24; the southern end can be reached from U.S. Highway 50.

Visitor Activities
Photography, birdwatching, wildlife viewing, plant viewing, interpretive signs, scenic drives, hiking, and biking.

Permits, Fees, Limitations
Two Byway routes (Shelf Road and Phantom Canyon Road) are winding and narrow, and in places are limited to 1 lane. There are restrictions on the use of trailers, campers, and motor homes. No vehicles over 25 feet in length are permitted.

Accessibility
Many of the rest areas and parks located along the Byway include accessible restrooms, picnic areas, and parking.

Camping and Lodging
Primitive camping is allowed on public lands, and there are several private campgrounds along the Byway. Lodging is available in Cañon City, Florence, Cripple Creek, and Victor.

Food and Supplies
Food and supplies are available in Cañon City, Florence, Florissant, Victor, and Cripple Creek.

First Aid
There is no first aid available on-site. The nearest hospital is in Cañon City.

Additional Information
The route is driveable by passenger vehicle, except for Shelf Road, which may require a four-wheel-drive vehicle under certain conditions of heavy rain or snow. The Phantom Canyon Road is very narrow and cannot accommodate oversize vehicles, tractor-trailers, or large towed trailers. Roads can be slippery when wet.

Sponsoring Partner

SCENIC AMERICA

Activity Codes

 - photography, biking, interpretive signs

Kokopelli's Trail

Location
The east end of the trail is located near Loma, Colorado, and the west end is at Moab, Utah.

Description
Discover one of Colorado's and Utah's premiere mountain bike trails. Stretching 140 miles with elevations that rise to 8,400 feet, this trail is made up of improved roads, four-wheel-drive roads, and single-track roads. Kokopelli's Trail begins at the Loma boat launch parking lot and ends in Moab, Utah. The trail is named for Kokopelli, the hunchbacked flute player and fertility symbol in the Native American cultures of the Colorado Plateau.

Mailing Address
BLM - Grand Junction Resource Area
2815 H Road
Grand Junction, CO 81506

Phone Number
(970) 244-3000

Fax Number
(970) 244-3083

Directions
From Grand Junction, travel west on Interstate 70 about 15 miles. Take the Loma exit (exit 15), then travel south. The trailhead is at the Loma boat launch. Look for signs.

Visitor Activities
Mountain biking, hiking, and picnicking.

Permits, Fees, Limitations
None

Accessibility
There is a wheelchair-accessible restroom at the Loma Launch Parking area.

Camping and Lodging
No camping is allowed at the Loma trailhead. Primitive camping is available on nearby public lands. The nearest lodging is 5 miles away in Fruita.

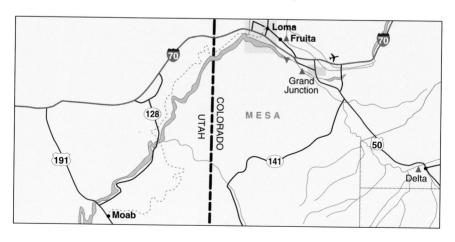

Food and Supplies
Food and supplies are available in Fruita.

First Aid
The nearest hospital is in Fruita.

Additional Information
This is a primitive bike trail in an undeveloped area. It is very hot in the summer and subject to intense thunderstorms. The trail can be very slippery when wet. Drinking water is not available.

Sponsoring Partner

I·M·B·A
INTERNATIONAL MOUNTAIN BICYCLING ASSOCIATION

Activity Codes

 –mountain biking, picnicking

Lowry Ruins
National Historic Landmark

Location
18 miles north of Cortez, Colorado

Description
Visit a 1,000-year-old ancestral Puebloan (Anasazi) ruin, which includes a 40-room village. The Lowry Pueblo site was first excavated in 1931 and became a National Historic Landmark in 1967. It is one of the most significant BLM archaeological sites in the Four Corners region, where Colorado, Utah, New Mexico, and Arizona meet.

Mailing Address
BLM – San Juan Resource Area Office
701 Camino del Rio
Durango, CO 81301

The 1,000-year-old walls of Lowry Ruins enclose a 40-foot village once inhabited by the Anasazi people. *(Photo by Rick Athearn (retired), Colorado State Office)*

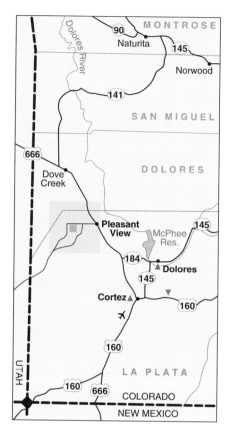

Permits, Fees, Limitations
None

Accessibility
None

Camping and Lodging
Camping is not allowed at Lowry Ruins. Camping and lodging are available in Cortez and Dolores (9 miles south on U.S. Highway 666 and 8 miles east on State Highway 184).

Food and Supplies
Food and supplies are available in Cortez and Dolores.

First Aid
No first aid is available on-site. The nearest hospital is in Cortez. First aid and a phone are available in Pleasant View

Additional Information
Lowry Ruins has a restroom and a graveled parking lot. Drinking water is not available at the site.

Sponsoring Partner

SAA
SOCIETY FOR AMERICAN ARCHAEOLOGY

Phone Number
(970) 247-4082

Fax Number
(970) 385-4818

Directions
From Cortez, travel about 18 miles north on U.S. Highway 666 to the "Pleasant View and Lowry" sign. Turn west and follow the signs.

Visitor Activities
Self-guided historic/archaeological tour and picnicking.

Activity Codes

  – picnicking, self-guided archaeological tour

Mosquito Peaks

Location
10 miles west of Fairplay, Colorado

Description
This beautiful high-alpine tundra and Area of Critical Environmental Concern contains significant biodiversity. There are several small parcels of BLM land here, with unique geological formations and 18 rare plant species. There are also views of historic mining buildings in the town of Leadville, 8 miles away.

Mailing Address
BLM - Royal Gorge Resource Area
3170 East Main Street
Cañon City, CO 81212

Phone Number
(719) 269-8500

Fax Number
(719) 269-8599

Directions
From Fairplay, go west on Mosquito Pass Road for about 10 miles.

Visitor Activities
Four-wheel driving, sightseeing, plant viewing, historic sites, hiking, and wildlife viewing.

Permits, Fees, Limitations
No permits or fees. There is limited access to the area; a high-clearance or four-wheel-drive vehicle is required.

Accessibility
None

Camping and Lodging
Primitive camping is allowed on public lands. Lodging is available in Fairplay and also in Leadville.

Food and Supplies
Food and supplies are available in Leadville and Fairplay.

First Aid
No first aid is available on-site. The near-

The seemingly barren high-alpine tundra of Mosquito Peaks is actually home to 18 rare plant species. *(Photo by Andy Senti, Colorado State Office)*

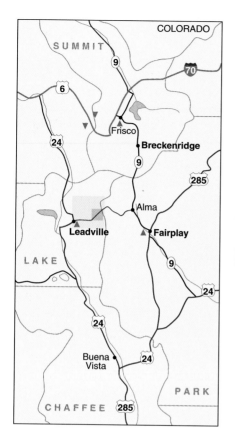

est hospital is about 20 miles away in Breckenridge on State Highway 9.

Additional Information
This is alpine tundra with elevations between 13,000 and 14,000 feet. It is rugged and subject to harsh and suddenly changing weather. Summer storms produce lightning and hail. The area is closed from September to June.

Sponsoring Partner

Activity Codes

 - four-wheel-driving, sightseeing

Rabbit Valley
Trail Through Time

Location
30 miles west of Grand Junction, Colorado

Description
At the Rabbit Valley Trail Through Time site, view the fossils of 140-million-year-old dinosaurs at a working fossil quarry with an interpretive trail. There is also an interpretive kiosk that describes the numerous dinosaurs that have come from

Rabbit Valley. This is a designated Area of Critical Environmental Concern.

Mailing Address
BLM - Grand Junction Resource Area
2815 H Road
Grand Junction, CO 81506

Phone Number   Fax Number
(970) 244-3000   (970) 244-3083

Directions

From Grand Junction, drive 30 miles west on Interstate 70 to the Rabbit Valley exit (exit 2). Turn right into the site parking lot.

Visitor Activities

Interpretive kiosk and hiking trail.

Permits, Fees, Limitations

None

Accessibility

The trail to the quarry, kiosk, and restroom is wheelchair-accessible. The Trail Through Time is about 1 mile long and is not wheelchair-accessible.

Camping and Lodging

Camping is permitted in Rabbit Valley south of Interstate 70. Three developed camping areas are available. Lodging is available in Fruita, 20 miles east on Interstate 70, and in Grand Junction.

Food and Supplies

Food and supplies are available in Fruita.

First Aid

The nearest first aid is available at the hospital in Fruita.

Additional Information

The weather is very hot in summer. Drinking water is not available on-site. During winter, the trail may become impassable because of snow. The trail is slippery when wet.

Sponsor

Activity Codes

 - interpretive kiosk

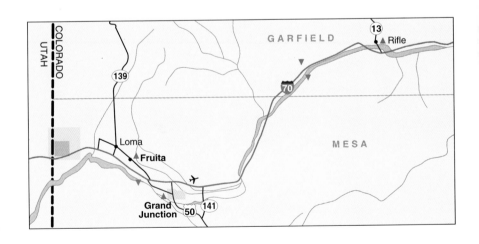

Ruby Canyon/Colorado River

Location
15 miles west of Grand Junction, Colorado

Description
The Colorado River runs though Ruby Canyon into Utah. Rafting is the primary recreational activity. The canyon is very scenic, but is generally accessible only by river.

Mailing Address
BLM - Grand Junction Resource Area
2815 H Road
Grand Junction, CO 81506

Phone Number   Fax Number
(970) 244-3000   (970) 244-3083

Directions
From Grand Junction, travel west on Interstate 70 about 15 miles to the Loma exit, State Highway 139. Use the Loma boat ramp to launch rafts. The site is well-marked.

Visitor Activities
Fishing, wildlife viewing, birdwatching, plant viewing, rafting and sightseeing.

Accessibility
Restrooms are wheelchair-accessible.

Permits, Fees, Limitations
No fees. Floaters are required to sign in at the visitor registration station. Commercial rafters must have a permit. Portable toilets and fire pans are required for all overnight trips. Check with the Colorado Division of Wildlife for fishing license requirements [Tel.: (970) 248-7175].

Camping and Lodging
There is no camping available at the Loma site. Camping is available in Rabbit Valley, 15 miles west on Interstate 70. Lodging is available in Fruita (5 miles away) and Grand Junction.

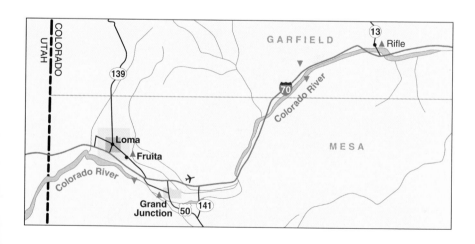

Food and Supplies
Food and supplies are available in Grand Junction and Fruita.

First Aid
The nearest first aid is available at the hospital in Fruita.

Additional Information
The Loma boat ramp has an interpretive sign, parking area and restrooms. Floaters are required to sign in at the visitor registration area. Sudden weather changes can occur along the river. This is a desert area, which is very hot in the summer. Drinking water is not available. Be prepared for difficult conditions, and bring all supplies.

Sponsoring Partner

Activity Codes

 - sightseeing

San Miguel River Special Management Area

Location
16 miles northwest of Telluride, Colorado

Description
The San Miguel River corridor is a fragile ecosystem containing outstanding riparian, recreational, scenic, and wildlife values. A scenic drive along the corridor provides beautiful views and several access points to the river along the way.

Mailing Address
BLM - Uncompaghre Resource Area
2505 South Townsend
Montrose, CO 81401

Phone Number   Fax Number
(970) 240-5300   (970) 240-5367

Directions
From Placerville, take State Highway 145 north along Uniweep-Tabeguache Scenic Byway for about 33 miles to Naturita.

There are several access points for fishing along the way. The northern part of the Special Management Area is accessible via the river, or from the State Highway 90 turn-off, 3 miles east of Naturita.

Visitor Activities
Fishing, rafting, picnicking, sightseeing, and scenic drives

Permits, Fees, Limitations
No fees or permits. Check with the Colorado Division of Wildlife [Tel.: (970) 249-3431] for fishing license requirements.

Accessibility
None

Camping and Lodging
Camping and lodging are available in Telluride and Naturita. Telluride is located on the San Juan Skyway, 16 miles south of

Morning mist rises from the sparkling waters of the San Miguel River, an important riparian area for recreationists and wildlife. *(Photo by Rick Athearn (retired), Colorado State Office)*

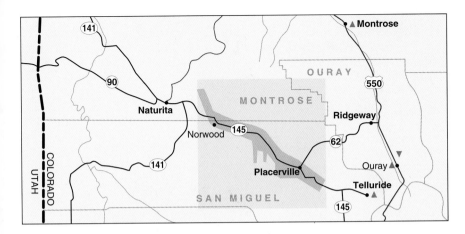

the junction of State Highways 62 and 145 at Placerville. Camping along the river corridor on Highway 145 is limited to designated areas, with a 7-day limit.

Food and Supplies
Food and supplies are available in Telluride, Placerville, and Naturita.

First Aid
There is no first aid available on-site. The nearest hospital is 65 miles north of Telluride via Highway 550, in Montrose. There are medical clinics in Telluride and Ridgeway.

Additional Information
The river has been preserved by BLM and The Nature Conservancy as a BLM Area of Critical Environmental Concern. It is jointly managed along a 28-mile corridor.

Sponsoring Partner

Activity Codes

- sightseeing, picnicking

The clear waters of Minnesota's Lake Vermilion are dotted with wooded islands representing some of the last public land remaining in the eastern United States. *(Photo by Syvlia Jordan, Milwaukee District Office)*

Eastern States

There are about 30,000 acres of scattered public lands in the 31 states bordering upon and east of the Mississippi River. While the surface area of this public land may be comparatively small, their locations make them very important.

Cooperative agreements between the BLM and state and local governments in the East provide key recreation sites such as the Lake Vermilion islands in Minnesota. Lake Vermilion offers excellent boating and fishing areas, and the small public islands are wonderful for picnicking and birdwatching.

The America's Outdoors Center for Conservation, Recreation and Resources in the Federal Building in Milwaukee, Wisconsin, is a good place to find brochures about many local recreation areas. Visitors also can buy a Federal Recreation Passport or find out about community-based conservation projects there. America's Outdoors is a joint effort by the BLM, the U.S. Forest Service, and the National Park Service to provide a single location for obtaining recreation, environmental, and conservation materials.

Visitors to the General Land Office (GLO) Records Automation Project in Springfield, Virginia, can quickly find documentation about when, where, and who obtained land from the federal government during the time of the westward expansion. There, BLM maintains more than 9 million historic GLO records that date back to 1787.

Horse lovers may want to make a trip to the Cross Plains Wild Horse Adoption/Holding facility in Cross Plains, Tennessee. There, visitors can view horses and burros as they await adoption by qualified individuals.

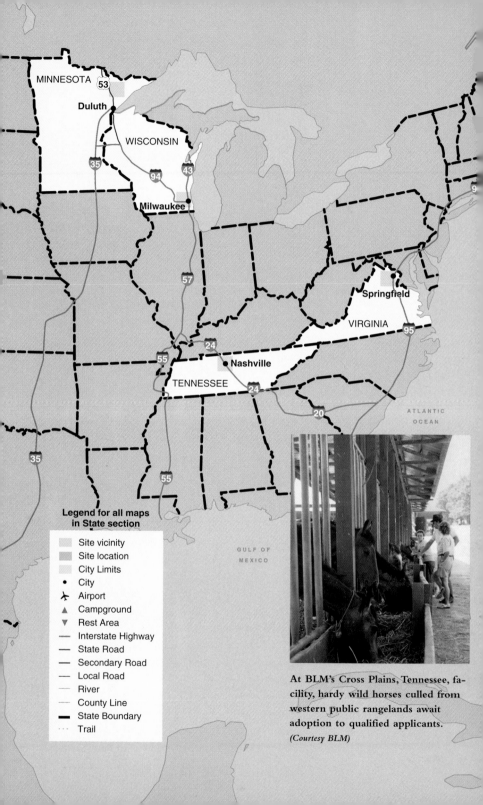

MINNESOTA 53

Duluth

WISCONSIN

35

94 43

Milwaukee

57

9

Springfield

VIRGINIA 95

55 24

Nashville

TENNESSEE 24

20

ATLANTIC OCEAN

35

55

Legend for all maps in State section

	Site vicinity
	Site location
	City Limits
•	City
✈	Airport
▲	Campground
▼	Rest Area
—	Interstate Highway
—	State Road
—	Secondary Road
—	Local Road
—	River
—	County Line
—	State Boundary
⋯	Trail

GULF OF MEXICO

At BLM's Cross Plains, Tennessee, facility, hardy wild horses culled from western public rangelands await adoption to qualified applicants.
(Courtesy BLM)

America's Outdoors, Center for Conservation, Recreation and Resources

Location
Ground floor, Reuss Federal Plaza, Milwaukee, Wisconsin

Description
America's Outdoors is a public information center that provides recreation information on national, state, and local outdoor areas; environmental education materials; and a professional staff to assist with citizen-based conservation projects. The Center also has automated General Land Office Records documenting the transfer of lands from U.S. ownership to private landowners. These services are provided by BLM, the National Park Service and the U.S. Forest Service.

  The Center is a single, convenient location for planning a visit to a National Forest or Park, buying a Golden Eagle Passport, browsing through a wide range of educational materials, or learning about conservation of rivers and other natural areas.

Mailing Address
America's Outdoors, Center for Conservation, Recreation and Resources
310 W. Wisconsin Avenue, Suite 100E
Milwaukee, WI 53203

Phone Number
(414) 297-3693

Fax Number
(414) 297-3660

Directions
The Reuss Federal Plaza building is situated on the corner of Wisconsin Avenue and 4th Street, directly across from the Grand Avenue Mall in downtown Milwaukee. America's Outdoors is located in the southeast corner of the building, on the first floor, just past the elevators.

Visitor Activities
Environmental education and genealogical research.

Permits, Fees, Limitations
None

Accessibility
The Center is wheelchair-accessible.

Camping and Lodging
Lodging is available at several nearby hotels. Local camping information can be obtained from the Center.

Food and Supplies
Restaurants and stores are located within walking distance, along the Grand Avenue Mall.

First Aid
First-aid kits are maintained at this facility. The nearest hospital is Sinai Samaritan in downtown Milwaukee.

Additional Information
America's Outdoors is open Monday through Friday, 9 a.m.- 5 p.m., year-round, except for federal holidays.

Sponsor

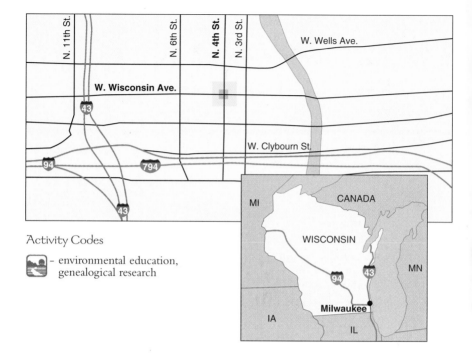

N. 11th St.
N. 6th St.
N. 4th St.
N. 3rd St.
W. Wells Ave.

W. Wisconsin Ave.

43

W. Clybourn St.

94   794

43

Activity Codes

- environmental education,
genealogical research

MI   CANADA

WISCONSIN

MN

94   43

Milwaukee

IA

IL

Eastern United States Wild Horse and Burro Adoption/Holding Facility

Location
35 miles north of Nashville, Tennessee

Description
Wild horses and burros, the descendants of herds brought to the West by explorers and pioneers, have thrived on western rangelands, to the point where they may pose a threat to their own habitat. BLM carefully removes selected wild horses and burros from public rangelands in the West to protect and maintain healthy herds and to preserve their habitat for future genera-

tions. These excess animals are then offered for adoption to qualified people through the BLM Adopt-A-Horse-or-Burro Program, which places these "living legends" in good homes.

The site is a contract-operated facility located in Cross Plains, Tennessee. The facility's owners provide humane animal care, and conduct adoptions of wild horses and burros gathered from western public rangelands. The facility can accommodate up to 170 wild horses and burros at a time.

Eligible adopters get "two for one" when a wild mare and her foal are candidates for adoption at BLM's Tennessee wild horse and burro adoption facility. *(Courtesy BLM)*

Mailing Address
BLM – Eastern States Office
7450 Boston Boulevard
Springfield, VA 22153

Phone Number   Fax Number
(703) 440-1679   (703) 440-1701

Directions
From Nashville, take Interstate 65 north to Exit 112. Take Highway 25 west for 4 miles to Cross Plains. Follow signs to the Adoption/Holding Facility.

Visitor Activities
Wild horse and burro viewing.

Permits, Fees, Limitations
No fees. The facility is open to the public only during special adoption events. Please call BLM or the Adopt-a-Horse-or-Burro hotline (1-800-417-9647) for event dates and times.

Accessibility
Weather conditions can affect accessibility around the Wild Horse and Burro Adoption/Holding Facility. Terrain is slightly- to moderately-sloped bare ground and grassland. The main parking area offers a reasonable view of the animal pens.

Camping and Lodging
Lodging is available in the nearby towns of Springfield and White House. Additional accommodations are available in Nashville.

Food and Supplies
Food is not available at the Adoption/ Holding Facility. The town of Cross Plains offers a rural drug store with an old-fashioned soda fountain and lunch counter.

First Aid
First-aid kits are maintained at the site. The nearest medical facility is located in

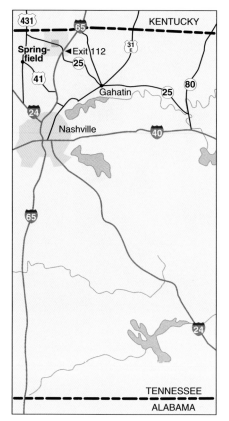

Springfield. Several large hospitals serve the Nashville area.

Additional Information
When the facility is open for a special adoption event, visitors may view the wild horses and burros that are available for adoption. Persons who have met BLM's adoption requirements, and who have applied in advance, may select and take animals home with them on the day of the event. "Satellite" wild horse and burro adoptions are also conducted frequently in various parts of the eastern United States. Please call BLM or the Adopt-a-Horse-or-Burro hotline for adoption requirements, or contact BLM for a brochure.

Sponsor

Activity Codes

General Land Office Records Project

Location
BLM Eastern States Office, Springfield, Virginia

Description
A historian's and genealogist's dream! As the successor agency to the original General Land Office, BLM Eastern States maintains more than 9 million historical land documents — survey plats and field notes, homesteads, patents, military war-

rants, and railroad grants. These historic documents were among the very first land records to develop from the Land Ordinance of 1785, which authorized the disposal of public lands.

For genealogists, these records can be a valuable resource. For example, a surveyor may have recorded the names of settlers, and included a description of land formations, climate, soil and plant and animal life in his field notes. The patent (deed) contained the new landowner's name, the legal land description, and date of issue. Often, the information derived from a patent can be the link needed to piece together a family's history.

Mailing Address
BLM – Eastern States Office
7450 Boston Boulevard
Springfield, VA 22153

Phone Number   Fax Number
(703) 440-1713   (703) 440-1701

Directions
From Springfield, take Interstate 95 south 2 miles to the Backlick Road/Fullerton Road exit. Turn right at the first light onto Fullerton Road. Turn left at the third light onto Boston Boulevard. BLM Eastern States is approximately 0.25 mile on the right. The visitor entrance and parking are located at the rear of the building.

Visitor Activities
Genealogical and historical research.

Permits, Fees, Limitations
Various fees are charged for manual and online research and for copy work. Food and beverages are not permitted in the research area.

Accessibility
The research room, vending room, and restrooms are wheelchair-accessible.

Camping and Lodging
Camping is available at many of the nearby Northern Virginia Regional Parks. For specific information and directions, contact the Northern Virginia Regional Park Headquarters at (703) 352-5900.

Food and Supplies
Restaurants are located within walking distance. Snack foods and soft drinks are available from vending machines in the office.

First Aid
First-aid kits are maintained at this facility. The nearest hospital is located in Fairfax, 10 miles away via Interstate 95 north and Interstate 495 west.

Additional Information
The office is open to the public for research from 8 a.m. to 4:30 p.m., Monday through Friday, excluding federal holidays.

BLM Eastern States safeguards the first land conveyance records for the public domain states of Alabama, Arkansas, Florida, Illinois, Indiana, Iowa, Louisiana, Michigan, Minnesota, Mississippi, Missouri,

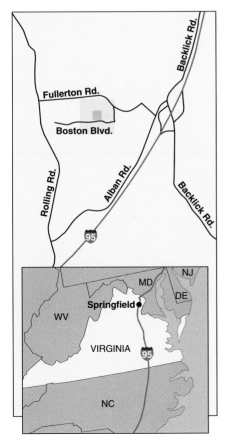

Ohio, and Wisconsin. * Many of these documents are computerized and can be accessed via office terminals. Those documents that are not yet automated may be manually researched with the assistance of BLM personnel. Research can also be conducted via modem or compact disc from the comfort of your own office or home. For information on dial-in access or compact disc purchase, contact BLM.

* Because the 13 original colonies and their territories were not part of the federal lands acquired during national expansion, BLM does not maintain the land records of 18 eastern non-public-lands states, nor the District of Columbia. Those states are Connecticut, Delaware, Georgia, Kentucky, Maine, Maryland, Massachusetts, New Hampshire, New Jersey, New York, North Carolina, Pennsylvania, Rhode Island, South Carolina, Tennessee, Vermont, Virginia, and West Virginia. Inquiries concerning land records for these states should be directed to the individual states' archives or land record offices.

Sponsoring Partner

 SOCIETY *for* HISTORICAL ARCHAEOLOGY

Activity Codes

 - genealogical and historical research

Lake Vermilion Public Islands

Location
Near Tower (St. Louis County), Minnesota

Description
Seventy small, widely-scattered public islands are located in 40-mile-long Lake Vermilion, which is one of the largest lakes in northeastern Minnesota to allow motorized boats. The small islands are delightful stops to make in the midst of pursuing other activities on the lake. Fishing is the most common form of recreation associated with the public islands (their shores provide excellent fish habitat), and some of the larger islands provide good sites for lakeside lunches.

Mailing Address
BLM - Milwaukee District Office
310 West Wisconsin Avenue, Suite 450
Milwaukee, WI 53203

Phone Number   Fax Number
(414) 297-4400   (414) 297-4409

Directions
From Duluth, take Highway 53 north through the town of Virginia. Continue on U.S. Highway 53 to Cook to access the west end of Lake Vermilion, or take State Highway 169 to Tower to access the east end.

Visitor Activities
Boating, fishing, picnicking, houseboat mooring, wildlife viewing, and sightseeing.

Permits, Fees, Limitations
None

Accessibility
The Wakemup Bay public water-access site (west end of Lake Vermilion) provides universal access.

Under clear Minnesota skies, canoeists island-hop in Lake Vermilion's cerulean waters.
(Photo by Sylvia Jordan, Milwaukee District Office)

Camping and Lodging

Three developed campgrounds are located on the southern shore of Lake Vermilion.

Numerous lodges and cabins are also located in the area.

Food and Supplies

Food and supplies are available in Cook and Tower.

First Aid

First aid is available in Cook and Tower. A hospital is located in the town of Virginia.

Additional Information

The Minnesota Department of Natural Resources maintains free, public, water-access sites. Privately-maintained boat-access sites are also available. The lake receives heaviest use from Memorial Day to Labor Day; less use occurs in late spring and early fall.

Sponsor

Activity Codes

 – picnicking

Idaho's public lands, shaped by fire and flood, feature a variety of unique landforms. *(Photo by © Ravi Miro Fry)*

Idaho

It's not just the natural splendor of Idaho's public lands that enchants visitors. It's also the seclusion. With a million residents scattered across 53 million acres, Idaho offers ample opportunity to find peace and solitude on the public lands, which comprise 22 percent of the state.

The opportunities for adventure on Idaho's public lands range from the plush to the primitive. Visitors who want to venture outdoors without leaving the comforts of home will enjoy exploring public land in the resort atmosphere of Lake Coeur d'Alene, while travelers who want a more rugged and remote experience will find it in the Owyhee Canyonlands. Although summer is "high season" on Idaho's public lands, the other seasons offer adventures as well. In the fall, hunters will find abundant birds and big game; in the winter, hearty souls can cross-country ski, snowmobile, and ice fish; and in the spring, everyone will find the wildflowers worth a visit.

Travelers from around the world visit Idaho to see eagles and other birds of prey soaring in the sky at what may be the world's largest raptor nesting site, the Snake River Birds of Prey Conservation Area. Anglers relish the opportunity to cast a line in cool, clear river waters in hopes of landing a trophy cutthroat trout. Amateur and professional historians alike retrace the footsteps of pioneers who trekked West in the 1800's on emigrant trails. You can still see the ruts carved into the earth by settlers' wagon wheels, mute testament to early American courage and an adventurous spirit. And truly wild whitewater awaits the intrepid—and well-prepared—rafter in Idaho's spectacular canyons.

The sites listed in this guide are just a few of the many opportunities for adventure on Idaho's public lands.

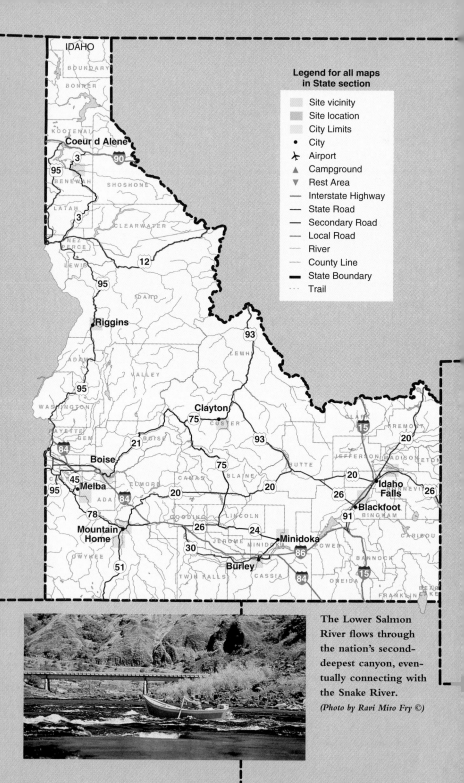

IDAHO

Coeur d Alene

Riggins

Clayton

Boise

Melba

Mountain
Home

Burley

Minidoka

Idaho
Falls

Blackfoot

The Lower Salmon
River flows through
the nation's second-
deepest canyon, even-
tually connecting with
the Snake River.
(Photo by Ravi Miro Fry ©)

Baker Caves

Location
11 miles northeast of Minidoka, Idaho

Description
View an important archaeological site that was occupied by Native Americans 1,000 years ago, and learn about early Native American culture at this ancient volcanic lava flow, estimated to be more than 2,000 years old.

The Baker Caves were formed when lava cooled, leaving pockets (blisters) and tunnels (tubes) in the ground. Evidence found at the site, including bison remains, arrowheads, and knives, indicates that about 1,000 years ago, a small group of Native Americans lived in the main cave.

Mailing Address
BLM - Snake River Resource Area
15 East 200 South
Burley, ID 83318

Phone Number
(208) 678-5514

Fax Number
(208) 677-6699

Directions
From Minidoka, drive 8 miles east on the road that parallels the railroad. Then travel north across the railroad tracks and follow the signs that provide directions to the caves. Drive about 3 miles until you see 4 large signs to the east. The caves take time to locate.

Visitor Activities
Exploring the volcanic rock and lava flow caves.

Permits, Fees, Limitations
None

Accessibility
None

Camping and Lodging
There is no camping on-site. Lodging is available in the towns of Rupert and Burley.

Food and Supplies
Food and supplies are available in Minidoka.

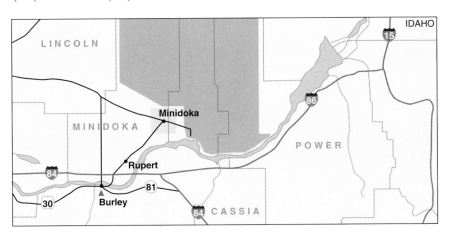

First Aid

First aid is available from the Minidoka Sheriff's Department. The nearest hospital is in Rupert.

Additional Information

The best time to visit the caves is in late spring or fall.

Sponsoring Partner

SAA
SOCIETY FOR AMERICAN ARCHAEOLOGY

Activity Codes

- lava flows, caves

Bonneville Point
Section of the Oregon Trail

Location

7 miles east of Boise, Idaho

Description

At Bonneville Point, visitors can see ruts carved more than 150 years ago by the wagon wheels of westbound emigrants on the Oregon Trail and learn about the pioneers' long westward journey and how the city of Boise got its name. The site also features outstanding panoramic views of the Boise Valley and the Snake River Plain.

Mailing Address

BLM - Bruneau Resource Area
3948 Development Avenue
Boise, ID 83705

Phone Number	Fax Number
(208) 384-3300	(208) 384-3310

Directions

From Boise, travel east 2.5 miles on Interstate 84 to the Blacks Creek exit. Turn left onto Blacks Creek Road; drive about 3.5 miles; turn left at the sign marked "Histor-

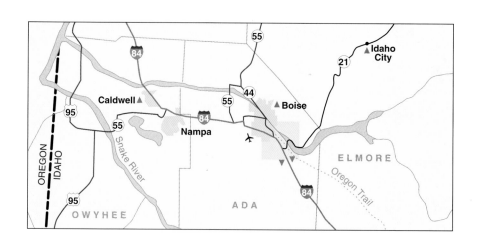

ical Site"; and proceed for 1 mile to the site.

Visitor Activities
Exploring, viewing historical remnants, hiking and mountain biking. A mountain biking trail runs west from Bonneville Point to Discovery Park and eventually connects with the Boise Greenbelt System.

Permits, Fees, Limitations
None

Accessibility
The site can be accessed by wheelchair on a concrete sidewalk.

Camping and Lodging
No camping is available on-site. Lodging and camping are available in Boise.

Food and Supplies
Food and supplies are available in Boise.

First Aid
Two hospitals are located in Boise.

Additional Information
To make your trip more rewarding, read the book *Emigrant Trails of Southern Idaho*, available from BLM. No restrooms or water are available on-site.

Sponsoring Partner

Activity Codes
 - mountain biking, historical remnants

Bruneau - Jarbidge Rivers

Location
8 miles southeast of Bruneau, Idaho

Description
The Bruneau and Jarbidge rivers flow through deep, narrow canyons from the mountains of northern Nevada through the remote high desert of the Owyhee Uplands to the Snake River in southern Idaho. The sheer-walled rhyolite canyons and rock spires provide a first-class wilderness experience for self-sufficient, experienced boaters. There are about 40 miles of Class II-V whitewater, which take between 2 and 6 days to run. This river is only for experienced boaters who are well-versed in self-supported wilderness travel.

Mailing Address
BLM - Bruneau Resource Area
3948 Development Avenue
Boise, ID 83705

Phone Number
(208) 384-3300

Fax Number
(208) 384-3310

Directions
This is a very rugged and remote area. For directions, contact BLM.

Visitor Activities
Whitewater rafting, kayaking, hiking, fishing, and wildlife viewing.

Permits, Fees, Limitations
There are no fees for non-commercial boating, but boater registration is required. Check with the Idaho Department of Fish and Game for fishing license requirements [Tel.: (208) 334-3700].

Accessibility
None

Camping and Lodging
Small, primitive campsites are available all along the river. Campsites cannot be occupied for more than 14 consecutive days.

Equipped with bright protective gear, experienced rafters paddle through challenging whitewater in one of the Bruneau River System's narrow, rocky canyons. *(Photo by © Glade Walker)*

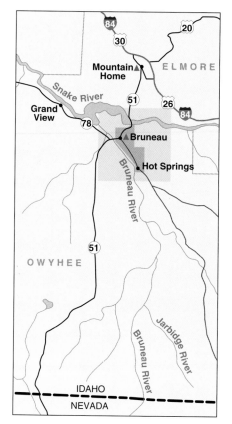

Additional Information

This is a rugged and remote area for experienced wilderness explorers only. There are no trails or developed facilities. Four-wheel-drive vehicles are required for access to the Bruneau River put-in, at Indian Hot Springs. Two-wheel-drive vehicles are sufficient to reach the Jarbidge put-in at Murphy Hot Springs. Rivers are usually boatable by raft or hard-shell kayak from April 1 to June 15. In late June and early July, the rivers can usually be floated with inflatable kayaks. Redband trout and smallmouth bass are plentiful. There are opportunities to view birds, otters, and rare California bighorn sheep. The "Owyhee and Bruneau River Systems Boating Guide" is available from BLM. The area is also serviced by commercial outfitters.

Sponsoring Partners

Lodging is available in the town of Mountain Home.

Food and Supplies

Food and supplies are available in Mountain Home.

First Aid

Ambulances staffed with Emergency Medical Technicians are available in the town of Grandview. The nearest hospital is located in Mountain Home.

Activity Codes

 - kayaking

Coeur d'Alene Lake Special Recreation Management Area

Location
Immediately south of Coeur d'Alene, Idaho

Description
The sparkling waters of Lake Coeur d'Alene, considered one of the most beautiful lakes in the world, offer many different kinds of outdoor recreational activities year-round in a setting of exceptional scenic beauty.

Mailing Address
BLM - Emerald Empire Resource Area
1808 N. Third Street
Coeur d'Alene, ID 83814

Phone Number   Fax Number
(208) 769-5000   (208) 769-5050

Directions
The best way to see Lake Coeur d'Alene is by boat. However, visitors can also take a scenic drive around the lake by traveling east from Coeur d'Alene on Interstate 90, then south on State Highway 97 and State Highway 3 to the town of St. Maries. Proceed west on State Highway 5 to Plummer, and then north back to Coeur d'Alene on Interstate 95. The total distance is about 115 miles.

Visitor Activities
Boating, fishing, swimming, wildlife viewing, hiking, and hunting.

Permits, Fees, Limitations
Camping fees are charged; check with BLM for details. A 14-day stay limit applies. Alcohol and firearms are prohibited at the Mica Bay Boater Park, located 15 miles south of Coeur d'Alene off Interstate 95. Check with the Idaho Department of Fish and Game for hunting and fishing license requirements [Tel.:(208) 334-3700].

Accessibility
The Beauty Bay picnic site and trail, located 20 miles east of Coeur d'Alene off State Highway 97, are fully accessible. Accessibility of other developed sites varies.

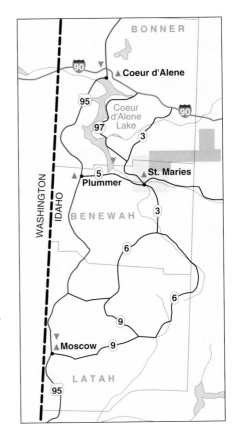

Camping and Lodging
Camping is available at Mica Bay, located about 7 miles south of Coeur d'Alene off U.S. Highway 95, and Windy Bay, located about 18 miles south of Coeur d'Alene off U.S. Highway 95. Windy Bay is accessible only by boat. Lodging is available in Coeur d'Alene.

Food and Supplies
Food and supplies are available in Coeur d'Alene.

First Aid
Kootenai County operates a 911 emergency dispatch. The Kootenai Medical Center is located in Coeur d'Alene.

Additional Information
At an elevation of 2,152 feet, temperatures in the Coeur d'Alene area range from an average of 64°F in the summer to an average of 32°F in the winter. Average annual rainfall is 26 inches. Winter offers a unique opportunity to see migrating bald eagles fish for spawning kokanee salmon.

Sponsor

Activity Codes

- swimming

East Fork, Salmon River Canyon

Location
20 miles southwest of Challis, Idaho

Description
The roads that parallel the East Fork of the Salmon River and its feeder streams offer visitors an opportunity to see a wide variety of wildlife as well as engage in a multitude of outdoor recreational activities. The roads climb from sagebrush plains at 5,400 feet through alpine forests at 10,000 feet. Chukars, red-tailed hawks, and mule deer frequent the lower elevations, while Rocky Mountain bighorn sheep, elk, and golden eagles can be seen at higher elevations.

Mailing Address
BLM - Challis Resource Area
Route 2, Box 610
Salmon, ID 83467

Phone Number
(208) 756-5400

Fax Number
(208) 756-5436

Directions
From Challis, travel south on State Highway 75 for 17 miles and turn left onto East Fork Road.

Visitor Activities:
Wildlife viewing, wild horse viewing, hiking, horseback riding, off-highway vehicle riding, mountain biking, fishing, and hunting.

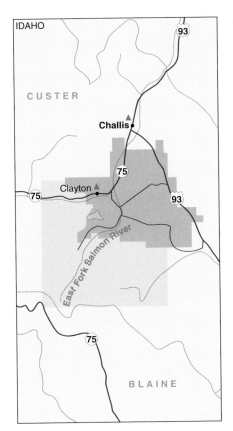

junction of State Highway 75 and East Fork Road, and at the Boulder Creek Campground (no fee), located on East Fork Road about 22 miles south of the junction with State Highway 75. Dispersed camping is also available.

Food and Supplies
Food and supplies are available in Challis.

First Aid
The closest medical clinic is located in Challis.

Additional Information
During most winters, much of East Fork Road is open and plowed. However, the stretch of East Fork Road that begins about 19 miles south of State Highway 75 is closed from November 30 through May 1 to protect wintering big game. All roads leading from the East Fork are gravel or dirt and are subject to intermittent closure due to inclement weather.

Sponsor

Permits, Fees, Limitations
None

Accessibility
None

Camping and Lodging
Camping is available at the East Fork Campground (fee charged), located at the

Activity Codes

 - horseback riding, mountain biking

Hell's Half Acre Lava Flow

Location
15 miles south of Idaho Falls, Idaho

Description
Visitors who take the time to walk through this approximately 4,000-year-old lava flow can learn how it was created and how plants and animals have managed to adapt to this harsh environment. Interpretive signs are located along the trails.

Mailing Address
BLM - Idaho Falls District
1405 Hollipark Drive
Idaho Falls, ID 83401

Phone Number
(208) 524-7500

Fax Number
(208) 524-7505

Directions
From Idaho Falls, take Interstate 15 south for 15 miles to either of 2 rest areas, and look for directional signs to the trails from the parking lots.

Visitor Activities
Hiking, geologic interpretation, bird-watching, plant viewing, and wildlife viewing.

Permits, Fees, Limitations
None

Accessibility
The Interstate 15 southbound trail features a wheelchair-accessible loop. The Interstate 15 northbound trails are not wheelchair-accessible.

Camping and Lodging
Camping is not available on-site. Camping and lodging are available in Idaho Falls.

Food and Supplies
Food and supplies are available in Idaho Falls.

First Aid
The Eastern Idaho Regional Medical Center is located in Idaho Falls.

Additional Information
The Interstate 15 southbound trail is a 1-mile walking trail with moderate slopes and a 0.5-mile wheelchair-accessible loop.

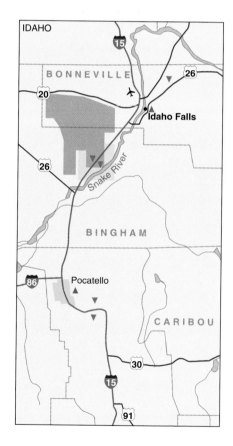

The northbound trail features 0.5-mile and 1.2-mile loops.

Summer temperatures can reach the mid-90's. Since lava retains heat, walkers should take precautions to prevent heat exhaustion or sun stroke. Information about additional recreational opportunities is available from the Eastern Idaho Visitor Information Center, 505 Lindsay Boulevard, Idaho Falls, ID 83402, Tel.: 1-800-634-3246.

Sponsor

Activity Codes

 – geologic interpretation

Lower Salmon River

Location
20 miles east of Riggins, Idaho

Description
This river features 112 miles of Class III-IV whitewater in the second-deepest canyon in the United States. About 53 miles of the river, from White Bird downstream to the confluence of the Snake and Salmon Rivers, are roadless and accessible only by boat.

Mailing Address
BLM - Cottonwood Resource Area
Route 3, Box 181
Cottonwood, ID 83522

Fifty-three miles of the Lower Salmon River corridor, a world–class whitewater destination, are roadless and accessible only by boat. *(Photo by © Ravi Miro Fry)*

Phone Number   Fax Number
(208) 962-3245   (208) 962-3245

Directions
Access is via U.S. Highway 95 through
Riggins and White Bird, Idaho.

Visitor Activities
Whitewater rafting, boating, fishing, and
hunting.

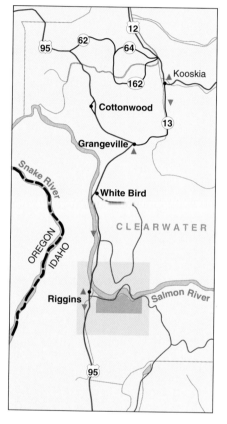

Permits, Fees, Limitations
Boating permits are required. Check with
the Idaho Department of Fish and Game
for hunting and fishing license requirements [Tel.: (208) 334-3700].

Accessibility
The Hammer Creek Recreation site, located 1.5 miles northwest of White Bird,
and the Slate Creek Recreation site, located 8 miles south of White Bird, are
fully accessible.

Camping and Lodging
Camping is available for a fee at the Hammer Creek and Slate Creek Recreation
sites. Lodging is available in Riggins, Cottonwood, and Grangeville.

Food and Supplies
Food and supplies are available in Riggins
and Cottonwood.

First Aid
There is a medical clinic in Riggins and
hospitals are located in Cottonwood and
Grangeville. Emergency medical technicians are located in Riggins and White-
bird.

Additional Information
July through October are best for boating,
with generally hot, dry conditions. The
mild winter months are best for fishing;
steelhead trout are plentiful. High water
from snowmelt in May and June creates
dangerous boating conditions. Commercial
outfitter services are available.

Sponsoring Partner

Activity Codes

Milner Historic/Recreation Area

Location
9 miles west of Burley, Idaho

Description
This 2,055-acre area, located on the banks of the Snake River, provides visitors with opportunities to experience the Oregon Trail, an important part of Idaho's past, and enjoy myriad modern outdoor recreation activities.

Mailing Address
BLM - Snake River Resource Area
15 East 200 South
Burley, ID 83318

Phone Number
(208) 678-5514

Fax Number
(208) 677-6699

Directions
From Burley, drive about 9 miles west on U.S. Highway 30. Signs mark the Milner turnoff.

Visitor Activities
Viewing of Oregon Trail remnants, wildlife viewing, fishing, boating, picnicking, and snowmobiling.

Permits, Fees, Limitations
There are daily per-vehicle entrance and camping fees. Check with the Idaho Department of Fish and Game for hunting license requirements [Tel.: (208) 334-3700].

Accessibility
Vault toilets and a number of picnic tables are fully accessible at 3 sites within the area: Perch Point, the Bicentennial site, and the boat ramp.

Camping and Lodging
Camping is available at Perch Point, Bass Point, Cedar Point, Muskrat Bend, and the boat ramp, as well as several other spots

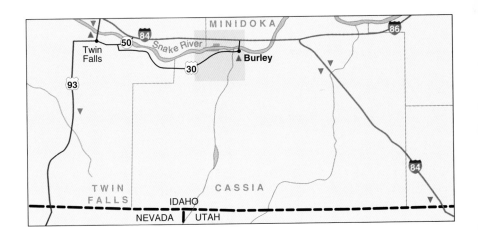

within the recreation area. Lodging is available in Burley.

Food and Supplies
Food and supplies are available in Burley.

First Aid
The Cassia County Sheriff's Department can provide first aid. The nearest hospital is in Burley.

Additional Information
During late winter, the area can get very muddy and some of the roads are closed.

Sponsor

Activity Codes

 - snowmobiling, picnicking

Owyhee Canyonlands and Little Jacks Creek

Location
60 to 100 miles south of Boise, Idaho

Description
These vast, high-desert canyons are home to the largest populations of California bighorn sheep in the United States. Rugged driving, spectacular desert scenery and splendid isolation await the visitor who is prepared to be entirely self-sufficient.

Mailing Address
BLM - Owyhee Resource Area
3948 Development Avenue
Boise, ID 83703

Phone Number
(208) 384-3300

Fax Number
(208) 384-3493

Directions
Call BLM for directions to the area.

Visitor Activities
Wildlife viewing, cross-country hiking, wilderness boating, and off-highway touring.

Permits, Fees, Limitations
None

Accessibility
None

Camping and Lodging
Camping is available at the North Fork Campground, located about 50 miles southwest of Grandview. Lodging is available in the town of Mountain Home and in Boise.

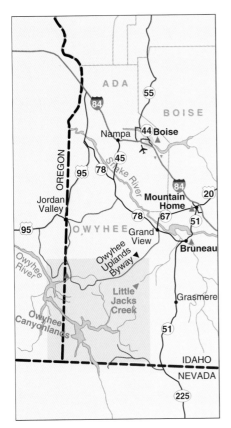

First Aid

Travelers must possess at least basic first-aid skills, since assistance is some distance away. Ambulances are available in Grandview and Bruneau. Hospitals are located in Mountain Home and Boise.

Additional Information

Hiking is best in spring and fall. The floating season is short, typically May through June. A boaters' guide is available from BLM. Visitors should purchase the appropriate 1:100,000-scale BLM surface management maps and U.S. Geological Survey 7.5' topographic quadrangles for areas they intend to explore.

Sponsoring Partner

Food and Supplies

Food and supplies are available in Grandview, Bruneau, and Boise, Idaho, as well as Jordan Valley, Oregon.

Activity Codes

Snake River Birds of Prey National Conservation Area (NCA)

Location
20 miles south of Boise, Idaho

Description
This 485,000-acre area, located along 81 miles of the Snake River, is home to the densest population of nesting birds of prey in North America and perhaps the world. Approximately 800 pairs of hawks, eagles, falcons, and owls nest in the lava cliffs and surrounding desert plateau. The area can best be seen by driving a 56-mile loop. Visitors can also see raptors by taking a raft or canoe trip through the area in the spring. Boating and fishing are popular activities spring through fall, on the Snake River and at C.J. Strike Reservoir. Many miles of trails offer outstanding hiking, horseback riding, and mountain biking. Prehistoric Indian rock art can be seen at nearby Celebration Park.

Mailing Address
BLM - Bruneau Resource Area
3948 Development Avenue
Boise, ID 83705

Phone Number   Fax Number
(208) 384-3300   (208) 384-3326

Directions
From Boise, take Interstate 84 west 10 miles to the Meridian exit, #44. Turn left onto State Highway 69, drive 8 miles south to the town of Kuna and turn south onto Swan Falls Road. Follow signs to the area.

Visitor Activities
Birdwatching, rafting, boating, canoeing, prehistoric rock art, photography, hunting, hiking, horseback riding, mountain biking, and scenic drives.

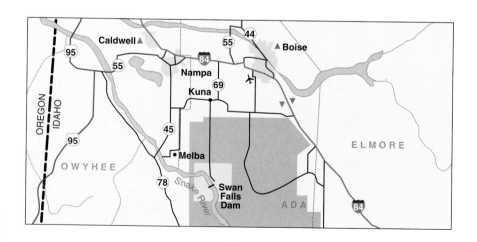

Permits, Fees, Limitations

No permits or fees. Shooting restrictions are in effect in some areas. Check with the Idaho Department of Fish and Game [Tel.: (208) 334-3700] for hunting and fishing license requirements. All vehicles must stay on designated routes.

Accessibility

Wheelchair-accessible restrooms are available at Dedication Point, located 16 miles south of Kuna on Swan Falls Road; Swan Falls Dam, located 21 miles south of Kuna on Swan Falls Road; and Celebration Park, located 21 miles west of Kuna. Call BLM for directions.

Camping and Lodging

Cove Recreation Site on C.J. Strike Reservoir is the only improved public camping facility in the area. West of Cove Recreation Site, Black Sands RV Resort offers campsites with full hookups, resturant/bar, and boat launch. Primitive camping is allowed throughout the National Conservation Area, but campers should avoid areas where birds are nesting. Use of fire pans is recommended. Lodging is available in the towns of Meridian, Nampa, and Caldwell, and in Boise.

Food and Supplies

Food and supplies are available in the towns of Kuna, Melba, Meridian, and in Boise.

First Aid

An Emergency Medical Technician Quick Response Unit is located in the town of Melba. Hospitals are located in Nampa, Meridian, and Boise.

Additional Information

The best viewing of birds of prey is at the Dedication Point Overlook between March 1 and June 15. A visitor contact station in Kuna can provide more information about the area and local conditions. A visitor's guide with map is available for purchase from BLM. Other brochures and handouts are available from BLM free of charge.

Sponsoring Partners

Activity Codes

 - horseback riding, mountain biking, canoeing, prehistoric rock art, photography.

South Fork Snake River Special Recreation Management Area

Location
The first river access site is located about 15 miles north of Idaho Falls, Idaho.

Description
This highly diverse river corridor, which stretches for 62 miles, contains one of the largest cottonwood ecosystems in the world, and is home to 10 nesting pairs of bald eagles.

Mailing Address
BLM - Idaho Falls District Office
1405 Hollipark
Idaho Falls, ID 83442

Phone Number
(208) 524-7543 or (208) 523-1012

Fax Number
(208) 524-7505

Directions
From Idaho Falls, take U.S. Highway 26 east 15 miles.

Visitor Activities
Fishing, boating, hiking, environmental education, scenic drives, mountain biking, off-highway touring, birdwatching, wildlife viewing, and picnicking.

Permits, Fees, Limitations
Permits are required to camp in 15 designated, signed areas along 12 miles of the river between Conant Boat Access and Lufkin Bottom. Fees are charged at some of these campgrounds, which are only accessible by boat. Portable toilets are required in this section. To protect bald eagle nesting sites, a number of areas are closed to riverbank occupancy between February 1 and July 31 each year. Check with the Idaho Department of Fish and Game for fishing license requirements [Tel.: (208) 334-3700].

Accessibility
Accessible restrooms, picnic areas, and a boat ramp are available at the Byington

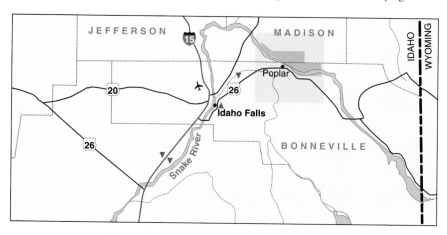

Anglers seeking cutthroat trout drift past waterfalls on the South Fork of the Snake River. *(Photo by Don Smurthwaite, Idaho State Office)*

Boat Access, located off State Highway 26 about 22 miles southeast of Idaho Falls. Accessible facilities are available at the Conant Boat Access, located off State Highway 26 about 40 miles southeast of Idaho Falls. Accessible restrooms are available at Kelly Island Campground, located off State Highway 26, about 25 miles southeast of Idaho Falls. A wheelchair-accessible fishing dock is available at the Palisades Creek Boat Access, located off State Highway 26, about 50 miles southeast of Idaho Falls.

Camping and Lodging

Camping is available from April 1 to November 1 at the following locations: Kelly Island Campground, Wolf Flat Dispersed Campsites, Falls Creek Campground, Falls Creek Group Area, and Tablerock Campground. Lodging is available in Idaho Falls.

Food and Supplies

Food and supplies are available in Idaho Falls.

First Aid

The nearest hospital is located in Idaho Falls.

Additional Information

The South Fork of the Snake River is a flat-water river, but hazards do exist. If you are not an experienced boater, please call BLM for specific information before your visit. Developed and undeveloped launch areas offer river access for fishing and boating. Designated motorized, non-motorized, and environmental education trails offer excellent hiking, mountain biking, and off-road vehicle riding. Excellent wildlife viewing and picnicking opportunities are also available. Additional information about outdoor recreational opportunities in the area is available from the Eastern Idaho Visitor Information Center, 505 Lindsay Blvd., Idaho Falls, ID 83402, Tel.: 1-800-634-3246.

Sponsor

Activity Codes

 - mountain biking, environmental education, picnicking

The Lower Blackfoot River sets a scene typical of Montana's big sky, spectacular mountains and clear water. *(Photo by Greg Albright, Montana State Office)*

Montana North & South Dakota

The journals of the Lewis and Clark Expedition chronicled the natural beauty and diversity of the region. Later, the promise of precious metals and homesteading lands lured miners, farmers, and ranchers to settle the area. Today, the spectacular scenery, uninterrupted vistas, clean air, and an abundance of elbow room are attracting people to Montana as well as North and South Dakota.

The public lands in Montana, North Dakota, and South Dakota represent tremendous diversity in topography, climate, and natural resources. Encompassing 8 million acres in Montana and 339,000 acres in the Dakotas, public lands range from the vast high plains of the western Dakotas and eastern Montana to the majestic peaks of the Rocky Mountains in western Montana. Included are semi-arid regions as well as high elevation areas where snow can fall in any given month. Temperatures range as widely as the geography and can accommodate activities in all seasons.

Visitors will enjoy exploring historical sites and viewing wildlife as well as a host of recreational activities including cross-country skiing, camping, fishing the famous blue-ribbon trout streams, or driving scenic highways and byways. Whether you seek an area with primitive solitude or a more developed and populated area, public lands in Montana and North and South Dakota will fit the bill.

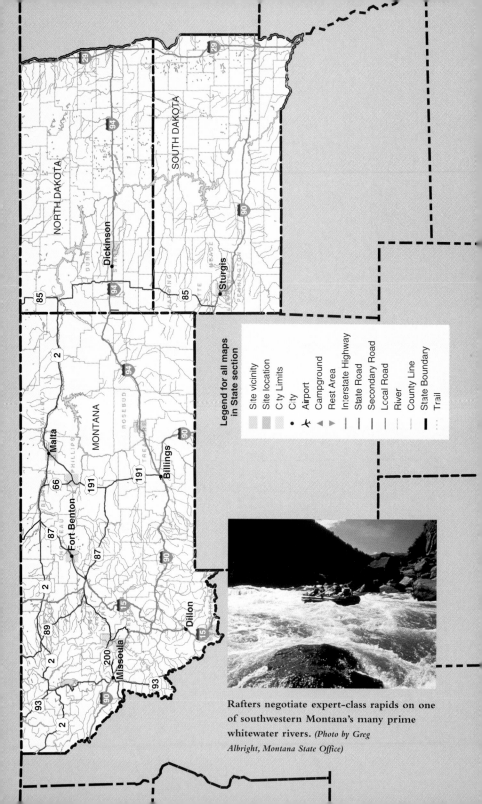

NORTH DAKOTA

SOUTH DAKOTA

MONTANA

29

29

94

90

Dickinson

Sturgis

85

94

85

2

94

Malta

66

87

191

191

Billings

90

Fort Benton

87

90

Dillon

15

15

2

89

200

Missoula

93

93

90

2

93

2

Legend for all maps in State section

	Site vicinity
	Site location
	City Limits
•	City
✈	Airport
◄	Campground
►	Rest Area
	Interstate Highway
	State Road
	Secondary Road
	Local Road
	River
	County Line
	State Boundary
	Trail

Rafters negotiate expert-class rapids on one of southwestern Montana's many prime whitewater rivers. *(Photo by Greg Albright, Montana State Office)*

Big Sheep Creek

Location
8 miles west of Dell, Montana

Description
This isolated, spectacular mountain valley is a narrow canyon with a good dirt road that often provides exceptional opportunities to view bighorn sheep and other wildlife.

Mailing Address
BLM - Dillon Resource Area
1005 Selway Drive
Dillon, MT 59725

Phone Number
(406) 683-2337

Fax Number
(406) 683-2229

Directions
From Dillon, take Interstate 15 about 40 miles south to Dell, then proceed south on the frontage road for 1.5 miles. Turn right onto Big Sheep Creek Road and follow it for about 4.5 miles.

Visitor Activitiess
Scenic drives, picnicking, hiking, wildlife viewing, plant viewing, and birdwatching.

Permits, Fees, Limitations
None

Accessibility
No special facilities are available.

Camping and Lodging
A campground is available along the Big Sheep Creek Back Country Byway. The nearest lodging is in Dillon.

Food and Supplies
Food and supplies are available in Dell.

Visitors traveling the dirt road through Big Sheep Creek's narrow valley have frequent opportunities for close-up viewing of bighorn sheep. *(Photo by Brian Hockett, Dillon Resource Area)*

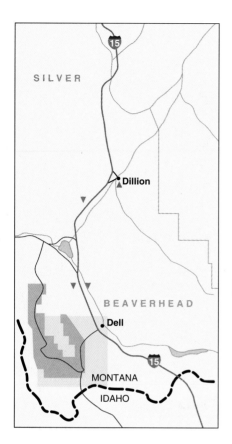

First Aid
The closest hospital and first aid are in Dillon.

Additional Information
Maps and additional information are available from BLM.

Sponsoring Partner

WILD SHEEP

Activity Codes

 - picnicking

Fort Meade Recreation Area

Location
Immediately east of Sturgis, South Dakota.

Description
The Fort Meade Recreation Area is composed of approximately 6,700 acres of forest and grasslands. The area is managed to protect, preserve, and enhance its cultural, historic, recreational, and wildlife values. Attractions include the Fort Meade Cavalry Post, the Old Fort Meade Cavalry Museum, the Fort Meade Post Cemetery, and the Centennial Trail.

Mailing Address
BLM - South Dakota Resource Area
310 Roundup Street
Belle Fourche, SD 57717

Phone Number	Fax Number
(605) 892-2526	(605) 892-4742

Directions
There are 2 entrances: one is 3 miles south of Sturgis at the Black Hills National Cemetery interchange (exit 34) on Interstate 90; the other is on State Highway 34, just east of Sturgis, at the entrance to Fort

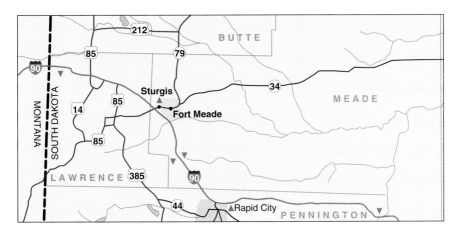

Meade Cavalry Post and Old Fort Meade Cavalry Museum.

Visitor Activities
Self-guided auto and walking tours, scenic drives, wildlife viewing, birdwatching, bow-hunting, hiking, and historic sites.

Permits, Fees, Limitations
A daily camping fee is charged. Motor vehicle use is restricted to maintained roads. Fires are allowed only in fire pits or grates.

Accessibility
Campgrounds are wheelchair-accessible.

Camping and Lodging
Six tent campsites and a 6-unit campground for horseback riders are available. Picnic facilities include 22 family picnic units and 3 group picnic units.

Food and Supplies
Food and supplies are available in Sturgis.

First Aid
The nearest hospital is in Sturgis.

Additional Information
The southern portion of this unit has a large population of Merriam's wild turkeys, which can be observed there at all times of the year. Hunting in this area is by archery only. Fort Meade has a mild climate with seasonal variations. Little snow accumulates during the winter months, but snowfall varies from year to year. Nearly 70 percent of the precipitation occurs during April, May and June.

Sponsoring Partner

Activity Codes

 - self-guided tours

Headstones in the Post Cemetery memorialize the lives of the cavalry soldiers who were once stationed at Fort Meade.
(Photo by Greg Albright, Montana State Office)

Garnet Range

Location
30 miles east of Missoula, Montana

Description
The 12-mile long Garnet Back Country Byway climbs 2,000 feet through the scenic Garnet Range to Garnet Ghost Town. Thanks to extensive preservation efforts, the 30 buildings in this historic town look much the same as they did in 1895.

Mailing Address
BLM - Garnet Resource Area
3255 Fort Missoula Road
Missoula, MT 59801

Phone Number   Fax Number
(406) 329-3914   (406) 549-1562

Directions
From Missoula, drive about 9 miles east on Interstate 90 and exit at State Highway 200. Continue traveling east on Highway 200 about 23 miles to the clearly marked turnoff to the Garnet Back Country Byway. This road will lead directly to the ghost town.

Another route is to take Interstate 90 to either the Bearmouth exit (32 miles east of Missoula) or Drummond exit (40 miles east of Missoula). Follow the old frontage road east (from the Bearmouth exit) or west (from the Drummond exit) to the clearly marked Bear Gulch Road turnoff. Take Bear Gulch Road 10 miles to Garnet Ghost Town.

Visitor Activities
Scenic drives, hiking, historical interpretation, wildlife viewing, plant viewing, birdwatching, snowmobiling, and cross-country skiing.

The buildings of Garnet, now a ghost town, greet today's visitors with much the same appearance as in the community's turn-of-the-century heyday. *(Courtesy BLM)*

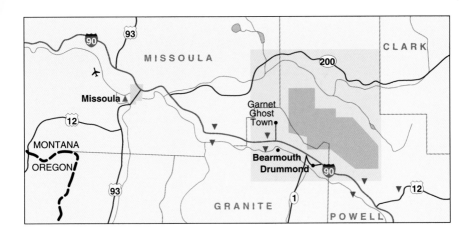

Permits, Fees, Limitations
Nightly rental fees are charged for two rustic cabins at Garnet Ghost Town. In the summer, there is a also a day-use fee at the Ghost Town.

Accessibility
Restrooms are wheelchair-accessible.

Camping and Lodging
During the winter, two rustic cabins at the ghost town can be rented for overnight stays. Contact BLM to make reservations. Other nearby lodging may be found at the Bearmouth Chalet, located at the Bearmouth exit off Interstate 90, and in the town of Drummond.

Food and Supplies
There are no commercial facilities at Garnet Ghost Town, but tour maps and limited sales items are available at the visitor center. The nearest food and supplies are in Drummond.

First Aid
The nearest hospital is in Missoula.

Additional Information
Travel on the Garnet Back Country Byway is limited to snowmobiles from January 1 through April 30. A network of trails called the Garnet National Winter Recreation Trail is accessible from Garnet Ghost Town. These 32 miles of trails are open from January 1 through April 30 for snowmobiling and cross-country skiing, with warming shelters provided along some of the trails. The visitor center at Garnet Ghost Town is open daily from June through September and on a limited basis the rest of the year. Maps and additional information are available from BLM.

Sponsoring Partner

SCENIC AMERICA

Activity Codes

 - ghost town, cross-country skiing, snowmobiling, historic interpretation

Little Rocky Mountains

Location
40 miles southwest of Malta, Montana

Description
This heavily-timbered, isolated mountain range rises abruptly from the surrounding plains, providing habitat for a unique mix of mountain and prairie wildlife. Many species found infrequently in eastern Montana are found here. Bighorn sheep can often be seen on the south side of Saddle Butte and Silver Peak, especially in winter.

Mailing Address
BLM - Phillips Resource Area
501 South Second Street East
HC 65 Box 5000
Malta, MT 59538-0047

Phone Number   Fax Number
(406) 654-1240   (406) 654-1241

Directions
From Malta, drive about 40 miles south on U.S. 191. Watch for a sign pointing west toward Zortman, and follow that road about 7 miles, turning at the Camp Creek Campground turnoff. Or, starting from Malta, drive about 55 miles south on U.S. 191 to its intersection with State Highway 66. Turn north onto Highway 66, and drive about 8 miles, watching for a sign pointing east to Landusky. Montana Gulch Campground is a short distance up this road.

Visitor Activities
Picnicking, hiking, scenic drives, wildlife viewing, birdwatching, and cross-country skiing.

Permits, Fees, Limitations
Camp Creek and Montana Gulch Campgrounds charge nightly fees.

Accessibility
None

Camping and Lodging
Camp Creek Campground is about 2 miles northeast of Zortman; Montana Gulch Campground is near Landusky. Limited lodging may be found in Zortman.

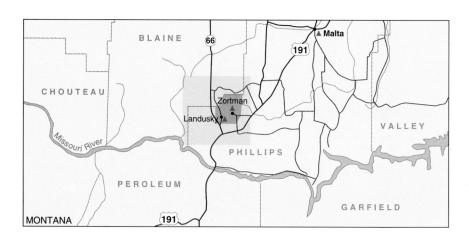

The tree-covered Little Rockies are typical of the isolated "island ranges" that dot the plains of eastern Montana. *(Courtesy BLM)*

Food and Supplies
Some facilities are available in Zortman; more are available in Malta.

First Aid
The closest hospital is in Malta.

Additional Information
Additional information and maps are available from the BLM office in Malta (open year-round) or the BLM office in Zortman (open June through August).

Sponsor

Activity Codes

 - picnicking, cross-country skiing

Lower Blackfoot River

Location
Less than 40 miles east of Missoula, Montana.

Description
The Blackfoot River is the subject of a best-selling 1976 book and a more recent popular movie, both of which carry the title, *A River Runs Through It*. The Blackfoot Valley provides habitat for a wide variety of plants and animals including grizzly bears, bighorn sheep, moose, elk, osprey, bald eagles, pileated woodpeckers, and neo-tropical migrant songbirds. Remnant populations of native bull trout and westslope cutthroat still exist, but are in jeopardy.

Mailing Address
BLM - Garnet Resource Area
3255 Fort Missoula Road
Missoula, MT 59804

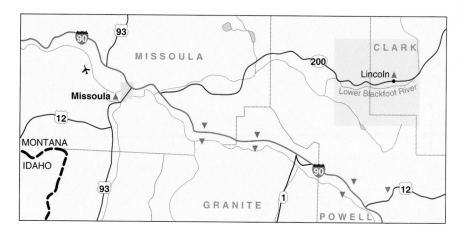

Phone Number
(406) 329-3914

Fax Number
(406) 549-1562

Directions
From Missoula, drive about 9 miles east on Interstate 90, exit at State Highway 200, and continue east. The highway crosses the river four times within 30 miles, and offers several access points.

Visitor Activities:
Wildlife viewing, rafting, boating, bird-watching, scenic drives, and fishing.

Permits, Fees, Limitations
Vary, depending on the particular site. Call BLM for details.

Accessibility
Varies, depending on the particular site. Call BLM for details.

Camping and Lodging
Several campgrounds and day-use areas are located along this stretch of Highway 200. The nearest lodging is in Missoula.

Food and Supplies
Food and supplies are available in Missoula.

First Aid
The nearest hospital and first aid is in Missoula.

Additional Information
Maps and additional information are available from BLM.

Sponsoring Partner

Activity Codes

Pompeys Pillar

Location
30 miles northeast of Billings, Montana

Description
Pompeys Pillar National Historic Landmark contains exceptional cultural, recreational and wildlife values. It represents the legacy of the early West and its development. At the Pillar, there is evidence of Native Americans, early explorers, fur trappers, the U.S. Cavalry, railroad development and early homesteaders, many of whom left their history embedded in this sandstone pillar. Captain William Clark, his guide, Sacagawea, her 18-month old son (nicknamed "Pompey") and a crew of 11 men stopped near the 200-foot-high rock outcropping on the return leg of the Lewis and Clark Expedition. On July 25, 1806, Clark carved his signature and the date in the rock and recorded doing so in his journal. The historic signature remains today, and visitors can walk on a boardwalk to see it.

Mailing Address
BLM - Billings Resource Area
810 East Main Street
Billings, MT 59105

Phone Number
(406) 238-1540

Fax Number
(406) 238-1565

Directions
From Billings, drive 30 miles east on Interstate 94 to the Pompeys Pillar Exit (#23). Signs clearly point the way to the site, which is only 0.5 mile off the Interstate.

Visitor Activities
Interpretive tours, wildlife viewing, birdwatching, picnicking, and hiking.

Permits, Fees, Limitations
A per-vehicle day-use fee is charged during the summer season. No fees are charged during the rest of the year, but in the off-season, the site is open to walk-in traffic only.

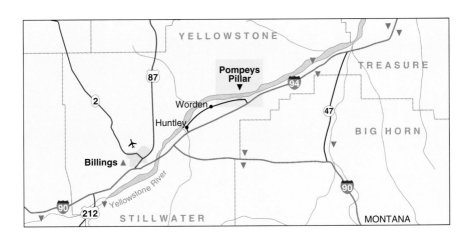

Accessibility
The visitor center, gift shop and restrooms are fully accessible.

Camping and Lodging
Recreational vehicle parking is available during the summer, but no overnight camping is permitted. The nearest lodging is in Billings.

Food and Supplies
There are several small towns west of Pompeys Pillar along Interstate 94 where food and supplies may be purchased. These include Ballantine, Worden and Huntley, all within 17 miles of Pompeys Pillar.

First Aid
The nearest hospital is in Billings.

Additional Information
The visitor center is open from 8 a.m. - 8 p.m. daily between Memorial Day and Labor Day, and 9 a.m. - 5 p.m. during September. The boardwalk and restrooms are open year-round. During the winter months, the site has walk-in access only (requires a hike of less than 1 mile in length, one way).

Sponsoring Partner

 SOCIETY *for* HISTORICAL ARCHAEOLOGY

Activity Codes

   - picnicking, interpretive tours

Schnell Ranch Recreation Area

Location
25 miles east of Dickinson, North Dakota

Description
The area is a 2,000-acre native prairie and woody draw that has been set aside for wildlife habitat, environmental education, and outdoor recreation.

Mailing Address
BLM - Dakotas District Office
2933 Third Avenue West
Dickinson, ND 58601

Phone Number
(701) 225-9148

Fax Number
(701) 227-8510

Directions
From Dickinson, drive about 25 miles east on Interstate 94. Take State Highway 8 north to Richardton. Take Old State Highway 10 west from Richardton for about one mile, then turn north on the County Road and drive about 0.5 mile to the property boundary. Signs direct you to the Recreation Area.

Visitor Activities:
Picnicking, wildlife viewing, birdwatching, cross-country skiing, hunting, fishing, mountain biking, horse adoptions, and horseback riding.

Permits, Fees, Limitations
Closed to motorized vehicles.

Accessibility
Restrooms are wheelchair-accessible.

Camping and Lodging
Primitive camping is allowed. Some future on-site facilities are planned.

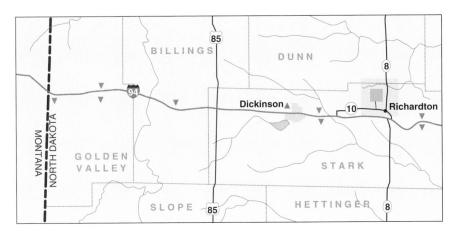

Food and Supplies
Supplies are available in Richardton.

First Aid
First aid is available in Richardton. The nearest hospital is in Dickinson.

Additional Information
The Schnell Ranch is the site of an annual wild horse adoption. The event coincides with the Taylor-Richardton Horse Fest, held every July. Call BLM for details on these events.

Sponsor

Activity Codes

 – horseback riding, wild horse adoptions, cross-country skiing, mountain biking, picnicking

The woody draws of South Dakota's Schnell Ranch provide protected habitat for a variety of wildlife. *(Photo by Don Rufledt, Dakotas District Office)*

South Phillips County

Location
Phillips County south of Malta, Montana

Description
This large area of rolling prairie with shrub/scrub is a nationally important breeding area for shortgrass bird species, such as mountain plover, burrowing owl, ferruginous hawk, Baird's sparrow, and Sprague's pipit. The area's prairie potholes attract more than 10,000 breeding ducks each year. Wildlife such as deer and antelope frequent the area. In addition, the area contains a concentration of prairie dog towns and is directly adjacent to a reintroduction site for the federally-listed, endangered black-footed ferret.

Mailing Address
BLM - Phillips Resource Area
501 South Second Street East
HC 65 Box 5000
Malta, MT 59538

A population of black-footed ferrets, an endangered species, is thriving on the plains of South Phillips County thanks to a federal reintroduction project. *(Courtesy BLM)*

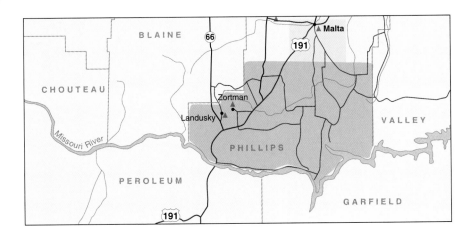

Phone Number   Fax Number
(406) 654-1240   (406) 654-1241

Directions
From Malta, drive south on U.S. Highway
191. Follow any of the major gravel roads
east off Highway 191.

Visitor Activities
Birdwatching, hiking, scenic drives, and
wildlife viewing.

Permits, Fees, Limitations
All vehicles must stay on designated roads.

Accessibility
None

Camping and Lodging
No camping facilities are available. Lodging is available in Malta.

Food and Supplies
No facilities are available on-site. The
nearest facilities are in Malta.

First Aid
The nearest hospital is located in Malta.

Additional Information
The area is open year-round, but travel
may be difficult during wet weather.
Land-status maps are available at the
Phillips Resource Area Office; please re-
spect the rights of private landowners.

Sponsoring Partners

Activity Codes

Upper Missouri National Wild and Scenic River and Missouri Breaks

Location
Central Montana

Description
This 149-mile section of the Missouri River is the only major portion that has been preserved in a natural and free-flowing state. It is a remarkable float trip for canoers and rafters, and is suitable for beginners. Along the way, habitats change from rolling grasslands to beautiful white cliffs to rugged badlands. Turkeys are common, and the chances of seeing bighorn sheep are very good, particularly after August of each year.

Mailing Addresses
BLM - Judith Resource Area
P.O. Box 1160
Airport Road
Lewistown, MT 59457-1160

BLM - Fort Benton Visitor Center
1718 Front Street
P.O. Box 1389
Fort Benton, MT 59442

Phone Numbers
Judith Resource Area: (406) 538-7461
Fort Benton Visitor Center:
(406) 622-5185

Fax Number
Judith Resource Area: (406) 538-7403

Directions
The most frequently used put-in/take-out points are:
• Fort Benton, about 40 miles northeast of Great Falls along U.S. Highway 87;
• Coal Banks Landing, about 12 miles southwest of Big Sandy (From Big Sandy, drive about 7 miles southwest on U.S. Highway 87, turning south onto a clearly marked graveled road. Continue following the signs to Coal Banks Landing.);
• Judith Landing, approximately 44 miles southeast of Big Sandy on County Road 236; and
• Kipp Recreation Area, where U.S. Highway 191 crosses the Missouri River.

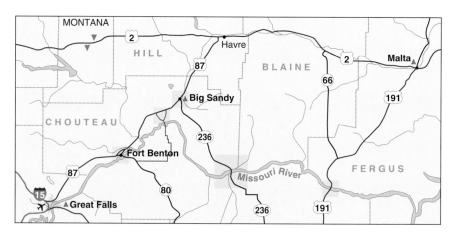

White cliffs reflect in the calm water of the Upper Missouri National Wild and Scenic River, whose banks provide habitat for wild turkey and bighorn sheep. *(Courtesy BLM)*

Visitor Activities
Canoeing, boating, fishing, hiking, picnicking, wildlife viewing, and birdwatching.

Permits, Fees, Limitations
There is a campsite fee per night at Kipp Recreation Area. For safety reasons, all floaters are asked to register at their put-in site.

Accessibility
None

Camping and Lodging
Camping is allowed on BLM land along the river. Kipp Recreation Area is the only one that charges a fee. Pit toilets are available at some sites; see Upper Missouri Wild and Scenic River, maps 1, 2, 3 & 4, (available at the BLM office and the BLM visitor center in Fort Benton) for exact locations.

Food and Supplies
The only stores along the way are in Fort Benton. Potable water is available at principal launch sites.

First Aid
The nearest hospitals are in Fort Benton, Havre (about 76 miles northeast of Fort Benton on U.S. Highway 87), and Malta (about 70 miles northeast of Kipp Recreation Area on U.S. Highway 191).

Additional Information
The Fort Benton Visitor Center is located on the town's Main Street, directly across from the put-in site. It offers books, maps, slide shows, and other displays about the river and its historical significance. Weather forecasts, safety information and detailed brochures about the river are also available here. It is open from Memorial Day through Labor Day each year. Please contact staff there or in the Judith Resource Area for more information in planning your float trip.

Sponsoring Partner

Activity Codes

 - canoeing, picnicking

Small bands of wild horses and burros roam freely on 97 herd management areas in Nevada. *(Courtesy Nevada State Office)*

Nevada

The beauty of Nevada may be the nation's best kept secret. The public lands range from the Sierra foothills in the west, across great open spaces, to piñon-juniper woodlands in the east. The geography of the state is characterized by broad valleys lined by mountain ranges. Scenic wonders are found throughout the state, from colored sandstone cliffs and desert bighorn sheep at Red Rock Canyon, near Las Vegas, to aspen trees and golden eagles at Blue Lakes and the Pine Forest north of Winnemucca. Historic sites also abound—from petroglyphs at Grimes Point/Hidden Cave, to the ghost town at Rhyolite.

With 48 million acres of public lands in Nevada, visitors stand a good chance of seeing public lands from any major highway and most rural roads. Those who travel in the spring, summer, and fall may choose to visit northern Nevada. The northern Great Basin is characterized by warm, even hot, dry days and cool nights. Visitors are often attracted in the fall and winter to southern Nevada where the northern Mojave Desert offers sunshine and pleasant temperatures. But, take a sweater as temperatures can drop to near freezing at night—especially in the higher elevations.

Off-road vehicle enthusiasts, hikers, campers, hunters, anglers, boaters, winter sports enthusiasts, and other recreationists will find easy access to the public lands. Photographers can find breathtaking views and spectacular scenes of wild, free-roaming horses and burros, wildlife, cattle, and sheep, which graze the rangelands. Nevada is a rockhound's delight. Garnet Hill recreation site near Ely is known for producing gem-quality garnets. Visitors are urged to obtain good maps, carry proper equipment and supplies, such as water, food, and shovels, and be aware of seasonal road conditions as towns with services may be miles away.

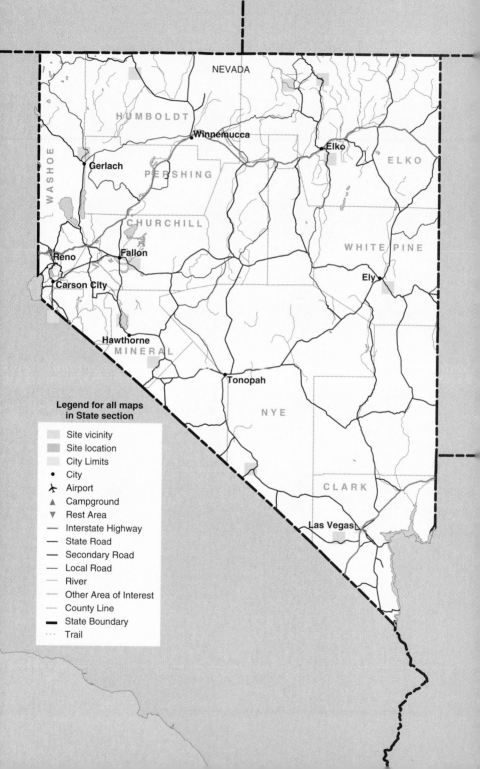

NEVADA

HUMBOLDT

Winnemucca

Gerlach

ELKO

Elko

WASHOE

PERSHING

CHURCHILL

WHITE PINE

Reno

Fallon

Carson City

Ely

Hawthorne

MINERAL

Tonopah

NYE

Legend for all maps in State section

	Site vicinity
	Site location
	City Limits
•	City
✈	Airport
▲	Campground
▼	Rest Area
—	Interstate Highway
—	State Road
—	Secondary Road
—	Local Road
—	River
—	Other Area of Interest
—	County Line
▬	State Boundary
···	Trail

CLARK

Las Vegas

Black Rock Desert Playa

Location
75 miles north of Wadsworth, Nevada

Description
Spectacular scenic opportunities abound in one of the largest and flattest alkaline playas in the United States. The Playa is a now-dry remnant of ancient Lake Lahontan; it is 44 miles long (oriented north-south), and averages 7 miles in width. Opportunities for solitude are considerable. A variety of interesting geologic features dominate the landscape. The near-pristine Applegate-Lassen section of the California National Historic Trail traverses the Playa.

Mailing Address
BLM - Winnemucca District Office
5100 East Winnemucca Boulevard
Winnemucca, NV 89445

Phone Number
(702) 623-1500

Fax Number
(702) 623-1503

Directions
From Reno, take Interstate 80 east to Wadsworth. Travel north for 75 miles on State Highway 447 to Gerlach. Drive 4 miles north to Playa West Access Point #1, or 6 miles north to Playa West Access Point #2.

Visitor Activities
Primitive camping, vehicle camping, hiking, scenic drives, mountain biking, photography, off-highway vehicle riding, and geologic and historic sightseeing.

Permits, Fees, Limitations
None

Accessibility
None

Camping and Lodging
Camping is primitive. A motel, restaurants and gas are available in Gerlach, the town immediately adjacent to the Playa.

Food and Supplies
Food and camping supplies are available in Reno and Gerlach.

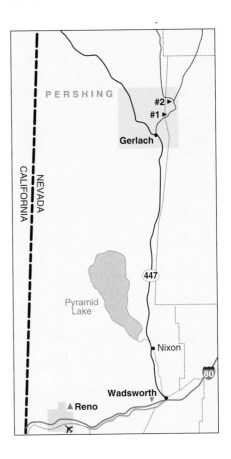

First Aid

First aid is not available in this isolated area. Be prepared for any emergency. Gerlach has a small clinic. The nearest hospital is located in Reno.

Additional Information

This high-desert location can experience temperature extremes in summer from 100°F at mid-day to nighttime chill. The best season to visit is from June to September. If you don't know the Playa, do not wander into this vast area alone! Roads are only passible in dry weather; when wet the Playa becomes an impassable sea of mud. Call BLM for current Playa conditions. Bring plenty of extra food and water. Even in summer, include some cool-weather clothing. Lip balm and sunscreen are also recommended.

Sponsor

Activity Codes

 - geologic sightseeing, mountain biking, photography, historic sightseeing

Ely Elk Viewing Area

Location

11 miles south of Ely, Nevada

Description

The largest herd of elk in Nevada can be observed feeding during the fall and spring seasons, both along the paved highway south of Ely and at the viewing area pull-out. Peak viewing times are October through November and March through April, with elk sometimes also seen in mid-winter. Other watchable wildlife species in the area include golden eagles, ravens, black-tailed jackrabbits and least chipmunks.

Mailing Address

BLM - Ely District Office
HC33 Box 33500
Ely, NV 89301-9408

Phone Number   Fax Number

(702) 289-1800   (702) 289-1910

Directions

From Ely, drive south on U.S. Highway 93. Elk can be seen on either side of the highway starting about 6 miles from town. Elk viewing signs along the highway designate the best viewing area.

Visitor Activities

Wildlife viewing and birdwatching.

Permits, Fees, Limitations

None

Accessibility

The facilities at the main parking area are wheelchair-accessible.

Camping and Lodging

The nearest developed facilities for camping are at the KOA of Ely, located 3 miles south of Ely on U.S. Highway 6/50/93. Numerous motels are also available in Ely.

Food and Supplies
No supplies are available on-site. Food and supplies may be purchased in Ely.

First Aid
There are a hospital with an emergency room and two clinics in Ely.

Additional Information
None

Sponsor

Activity Codes

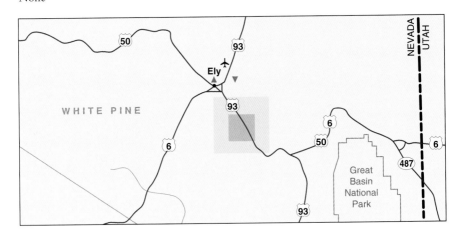

Grimes Point/Hidden Cave Archaeological Site

Location
50 miles east of Fallon, Nevada

Description
Grimes Point was first visited by Native Americans at least 8,000 years ago, and visitors can view examples of prehistoric rock art, called petroglyphs, as well as a storage cave. In addition to the self-guided interpretive trails at Grimes Point, there is a guided educational program to Hidden Cave for those interested in learning more about Great Basin prehistory.

Mailing Address
BLM - Carson City District Office
5665 Morgan Mill Road
Carson City, NV 89701

Phone Number   Fax Number
(702) 885-6000   (702) 885-6147

Directions
From Fallon, go east on U.S. Highway 50 approximately 10 miles until you see the archaeological site sign.

Visitor Activities
Hiking and interpretive programs.

Visitors can step out of the desert heat into the cool chamber of Hidden Cave to view 8,000-year-old Native American petroglyphs. *(Courtesy Nevada State Office)*

Permits, Fees, Limitations
No fees. Only day use is permitted.

Accessibility
Facilities near the highway at the Grimes Point Petroglyph Trail are accessible to wheelchairs. Hidden Cave is located on steep topography and is not accessible.

Camping and Lodging
There is no camping on-site. Lodging and restaurants are available in Fallon.

Food and Supplies
No supplies are available on-site. Food and supplies may be purchased in Fallon.

First Aid
First aid is not available on-site. A medical clinic is located in Fallon.

Additional Information
Summer temperatures are very high, exceeding 100°F on some days. Do not visit this area during the summer without taking water. Public tours to Hidden Cave are conducted from the Churchill County Museum (1050 S. Maine, Fallon) on the second and fourth Saturdays of the month. Call the Museum at (702) 423-3677 for information and reservations.

Sponsoring Partner

SAA
SOCIETY FOR AMERICAN ARCHAEOLOGY

Activity Codes

 - cave touring, interpretive programs

Indian Creek Recreation Area

Location
10 miles east of Markleeville, California

Description
Indian Creek Recreation Area is located
in a pine forest at an elevation of 6,000
feet. The area lies at the edge of the
scenic Sierra Nevada Mountains, approximately 20 miles southeast of Lake Tahoe.
The surrounding area ranges from high
mountains, rivers and streams in the west,
to Great Basin Desert with pinion pine
and sagebrush in the east. Recreational facilities include a 160-acre reservoir, a developed recreation site, and hiking trails.

Mailing Address
BLM - Carson City District Office
5665 Morgan Mill Road
Carson City, NV 89701

Phone Number   Fax Number
(702) 885-6000   (702) 885-6147

Directions
From Carson City, Nevada, take U.S.
Highway 395 south for 12 miles to State
Highway 88. Go south 15 miles on State
Highway 88 to Woodfords, California. At
Woodfords, turn south onto State High-
way 89 towards Markleeville, and go ap-
proximately 5 miles to the directional sign
for Indian Creek Reservoir.

Visitor Activities
Camping, mountain biking, hiking,
wildlife viewing, fishing, and rafting.

Permits, Fees, Limitations
Per-night fees are charged for overnight
camping. There are no day-use fees.

Accessibility
Recreational facilities are accessible to
wheelchairs, but only with difficulty and if
assistance is available. Access improvements
will be completed at the main bathroom
and shower facility by the summer of 1998.

Camping and Lodging
Camping is permitted in designated areas
on-site. The campground is open from
May through September, weather permitting. Reservations are required for the
group site.

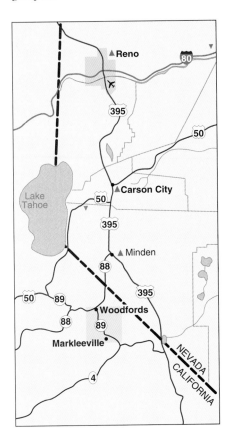

Food and Supplies
No supplies are available on-site. The nearest motel is in Markleeville.

First Aid
First aid is not available on-site. Emergency aid is available through the Alpine County Sheriff in Markleeville. The nearest hospital is located in Carson City.

Additional Information
This developed recreation area is popular during the summer. It is closed during the winter months.

Sponsor

Activity Codes

 - mountain biking

Marietta Wild Burro Range

Location
55 miles south of Hawthorne, Nevada

Description
Marietta is the nation's first formally recognized Wild Burro Range. The 68,000-acre site is home to about 85 burros. During the late 1800's, miners used burros as pack animals while prospecting for gold and silver in the Marietta Mining District. Some of these animals escaped or were released into the desert area surrounding Teels Marsh. The descendants of those burros now roam freely near the ruins of

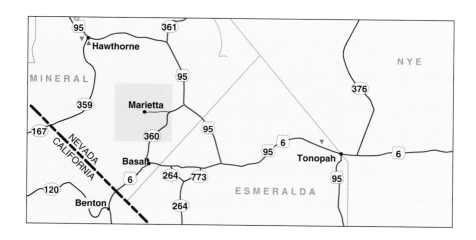

Ancestors of these photogenic wild burros served as pack animals for 19th-century gold and silver prospectors. *(Courtesy Nevada State Office)*

the historic Nevada mining town of Marietta, and through the marshlands. The Marietta herd is unique in Nevada, since this is one of the most northern burro populations of any size. Also, the animals themselves are larger than those encountered in areas to the south. In addition to up-close burro viewing, the range also offers opportunities for historical interpretation. The town of Marietta, which flourished when borax was in high demand, is now mostly old foundations and stone walls.

Mailing Address
BLM - Carson City District
5665 Morgan Mill Road
Carson City, NV 89701

Phone Number   Fax Number
(702) 885-6000   (702) 885-6147

Directions
From Hawthorne: Travel south on Interstate 95. Turn southwest onto State Highway 360 toward Benton, California. Turn west onto the maintained dirt country road to Marietta. From Tonopah: Travel north on Interstate 95 to the State High-

way 360 intersection. Turn west to the Marietta exit. From Benton: Travel north on State Highway 6. At Basalt, take State Highway 360 north. The road to Marietta will be a left turn as you drive north.

Visitor Activities
Burro viewing and historical site.

Permits, Fees, Limitations
No fees. Some of the property within Marietta is private; please respect boundaries. Since this is an old mining district, open mineshafts, shaky buildings, unstable rock ruins and rattlesnakes are common. Look before you step, touch or camp.

Accessibility
None

Camping and Lodging
There are no developed campsites. Dry camping is allowed for up to 14 days. The nearest lodging is in Tonopah and Hawthorne.

Food and Supplies
There are no supplies or services on site. The nearest supplies are available in Hawthorne, Tonopah and Benton.

First Aid
First aid is not available on site. The nearest hospital is in Hawthorne. There is a clinic in Tonopah.

Additional Information
There is no water available on-site. Nevada has 97 wild horse and burro herd management areas; locations of the individual herds vary with the season. For additional information, call BLM.

Sponsor

Activity Codes

North Wildhorse Recreation Area

Location
70 miles north of Elko, Nevada

Description
Wildhorse Reservoir is an important northeastern Nevada year-round fishery, which also offers excellent ice fishing in the winter (December through early March). Summers are mild, and boating, shore fishing, water skiing and wind surfing are popular activities.

Mailing Address
BLM - Elko District Office
3900 East Idaho Street
Elko, NV 89801

Phone Number
(702) 753-0200

Fax Number
(702) 753-0255

Directions
From Elko, (Interstate 80, Exit 301), travel north 70 miles on State Highway 225. The BLM North Wildhorse Campground is

The glistening waters of Wildhorse Reservoir provide visitors with year-round recreational opportunities in a stunning mountain setting. *(Courtesy Nevada State Office)*

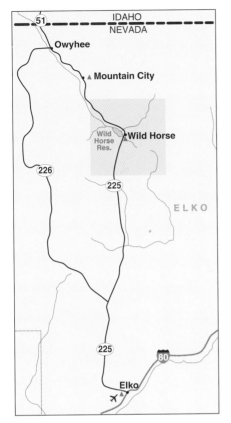

Camping and Lodging

There are 18 developed campsites. Three of these are group sites that can accommodate groups of 20-30 people. In addition to the BLM North Wildhorse Campground, both the Nevada State Parks and Bureau of Indian Affairs offer complete campgrounds and boat launch facilities.

The nearest lodging is available at Wild Horse Ranch and Resort, 3 miles south of the campgrounds. Lodging is also available at Mountain City (15 miles north) or Elko (70 miles south).

Food and Supplies

There are no services on-site. Food and supplies are available in Elko. Gas and groceries are also available at Mountain City and Elko. Limited supplies and a restaurant are available at Wild Horse Ranch and Resort.

First Aid

First aid is not available on-site. The nearest hospital is located in Elko. A medical clinic to handle emergencies is located at Owyhee, 25 miles north.

Additional Information

The BLM campground provides beautiful vistas of the reservoir and surrounding mountains. This area is only open from May to November, as the area's winter weather is very harsh.

Sponsor

along the northbound side of the highway. (State Park and Bureau of Indian Affairs campgrounds are on the southbound side of the highway, fronting on the reservoir.)

Visitor Activities

Camping, hiking, mountain biking, horseback riding, fishing, boating, scenic drives, snowmobiling, and cross-country skiing.

Permits, Fees, Limitations

Fees are charged for overnight camping from May 15 to November 15. There is no fee for day use. State Park and Bureau of Indian Affairs fees are slightly higher than BLM fees.

Accessibility

None

Activity Codes

 – mountain biking, cross-country skiing, horseback riding, snowmobiling

Pine Forest Recreation Area

Location
70 miles northwest of Winnemucca, Nevada

Description
There are three popular recreation sites within the Pine Forest Recreation Area: the Blue Lakes, Onion Reservoir and Knott Creek Reservoir. All three have superb scenery. The Blue Lakes are glacial in origin. Excellent opportunities for fishing, hunting, wildlife viewing, primitive camping, mountain biking, and photography exist at every turn.

Mailing Address
BLM - Winnemucca District Office
5100 East Winnemucca Boulevard
Winnemucca, NV 89445

Phone Number
(702) 623-1500

Fax Number
(702) 623-1503

Directions
From Winnemucca, drive 30 miles north on U.S. Highway 95, and then 50 miles west on State Highway 140. Turn left at Alta Creek Road. The Blue Lakes trailhead and the reservoirs are about 15 miles from Highway 140.

Visitor Activities:
Fishing, hiking, hunting, wildlife viewing, primitive camping, mountain biking, photography, and winter sports.

Permits, Fees, Limitations
None

Accessibility
None

Camping and Lodging
No fees. The nearest town is Denio Junction, 35 miles northeast. The town has a 12-room motel, gas station, restaurant, and bar.

Food and Supplies
Food and supplies are available in Winnemucca.

First Aid
First aid is not available in this isolated area. Be prepared for any emergency. The nearest hospital is located in Winnemucca.

Additional Information
Summer temperatures at this high-desert location can go from daytime highs in the

90's to nighttime chill. The best season to visit is from May to September. All roads into this remote area are dirt. Four-wheel-drive vehicles are highly recommended. The road to Knott Creek is extremely rough. Roads are only passible in dry weather, and are often snow-covered in winter. Call BLM to check on conditions. Bring extra food and water. Lip balm and sunscreen are also recommended.

Sponsor

Activity Codes

 - winter sports, mountain biking, photography

The interconnected Blue Lakes, nestled in a basin carved by a retreating glacier, provide excellent opportunities for fishing and wildlife viewing. *(Courtesy Nevada State Office)*

Red Rock Canyon
National Conservation Area

Location
20 miles west of Las Vegas, Nevada

Description
This is a beautiful area in which to experience the natural wonders of the Mohave Desert. The red- and cream-colored sandstone cliffs are awesome. Scramble across fossilized sand dunes, explore the recesses between the rocks, climb sheer rock walls, or just enjoy the scenic beauty along the road. Rock climbers dot the cliffs in this world-class climbing area. This area also features a 13-mile paved, scenic loop drive, visitor center, and day-use area.

Mailing Address
BLM - Las Vegas District Office
HCR 33, Box 5400
Las Vegas, NV 89124

Phone Number   Fax Number
(Red Rock Canyon Visitor Center)
(702) 363-1921   (702) 363-6779

Directions
From Las Vegas, travel west on Charleston Boulevard, which will become State Highway 159, to the Red Rock Canyon entrance.

Visitor Activities:
Mountain biking, rock climbing, hiking, wildlife viewing, horseback riding, geologic sightseeing, and scenic driving.

Permits, Fees, Limitations
There is a per-vehicle entrance fee, and a nightly fee is charged at the campground.

Accessibility
The visitor center has accessible restrooms, picnic tables and a TDD phone. The Willow Spring picnic area has accessible tables and one accessible restroom. The following pull-offs have accessible restrooms along the scenic loop: Sandstone Quarry, Willow Spring, and Pine Creek Canyon. Accessible campsites and restrooms are also located at Mile 13, at the new Red Rock Canyon Campground.

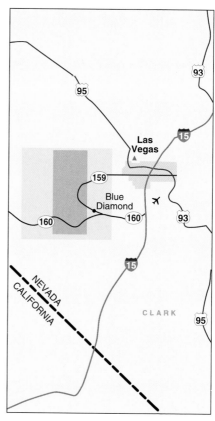

The colorful blocks of the Keystone Thrust Fault, towering 2,000 feet above the Mohave Desert floor, contain outstanding examples of rock art and prehistoric habitations. *(Courtesy Nevada State Office)*

Camping and Lodging

Camping is available on a first-come, first-served basis, with 22 car sites and 5 walk-in sites. The Oak Creek Campground will close sometime in 1998. The new Red Rock Canyon Campground is located at the Mile 13 turn-off, with access from West Charleston Boulevard.

Food and Supplies

No food or supplies are available on-site. Food and camping supplies may be purchased in Las Vegas.

First Aid

There is no first-aid station on-site. The nearest hospital is the University Medical Center, 15 miles east on Charleston Boulevard.

Additional Information

The most notable trail is the paved, one-way, 13-mile scenic loop drive.

Sponsoring Partner

SCENIC AMERICA   WILD SHEEP

Activity Codes

 - sightseeing, geologic sightseeing, mountain biking, rock climbing, horseback riding

Ryholite Historic Area

Location
4 miles southwest of Beatty, Nevada

Description
Historic ruins at this former gold-mining boomtown include the most photographed ghost-town building in the West—the Cook Bank Building—and Nevada's best-preserved "bottle house," constructed entirely of glass bottles. Death Valley Monument visitors frequently tour Rhyolite because it is along one of the major roads to that park.

Mailing Address
BLM - Tonopah Field Station
P.O. Box 911
Tonopah, NV 89049-0911

Phone Number
(702) 482-7800

Fax Number
(702) 482-7810

Directions
From Beatty, travel southwest on State Highway 374 approximately 2 miles. Turn right and proceed 2 miles to Rhyolite.

Visitor Activities
Historic sites, photography and hiking.

Permits, Fees, Limitations
No fees. The area is for day use only. There are no public facilities.

Accessibility
Limited to the paved road.

Camping and Lodging
No camping facilities are available. Lodging is available in Beatty.

Food and Supplies
No food or supplies are available on-site. Food and supplies are available in Beatty.

First Aid
There is no first aid available on site. A medical clinic is available in Beatty.

Additional Information
The area is open all year, but summer temperatures are very hot, exceeding

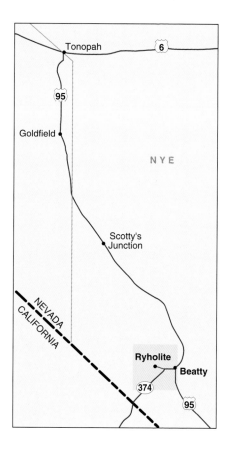

100°F most days from May through September. The best time to visit Rhyolite is during the winter months. Since the area is owned by multiple land owners, visitors are urged to respect private property rights and not climb on or near structures.

Sponsoring Partner

SOCIETY *for*
HISTORICAL
ARCHAEOLOGY

Activity Codes

 - photography

South Fork Owyhee River/ Owyhee River Canyon

Location
120 miles north of Elko, Nevada

Description
The South Fork Owyhee River flows north through the Owyhee desert, joining the river's East Fork in southwestern Idaho. River-running in rafts and kayaks through the steep-walled canyon is the most popular recreational activity from late March through early June.

Mailing Address
BLM - Elko District Office
3900 East Idaho Street
Elko, NV 89801

Phone Number   Fax Number
(702) 753-0200   (702) 753-0255

Directions
From Elko, travel 27 miles north on State Highway 225. Turn west onto State Highway 226 for 40 miles until the pavement ends. Then follow County Road 728 for 16 miles to the Petan Ranch. To launch a watercraft, you must first obtain permission at the Ranch.

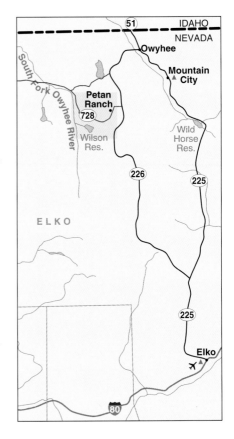

Visitor Activities
Hiking, fishing, hunting, and rafting.

Permits, Fees, Limitations
No fees, but permission is required to launch.

Accessibility
None

Camping and Lodging
BLM campgrounds are located at Wilson Reservoir. (Follow County Road 728 south 10 miles from the Ranch, then follow the signs to Wilson Reservoir another 12 miles.) The Bureau of Indian Affairs offers camping at Sheep Creek Reservoir. (Follow County Road 728 west 18 miles from Owyhee.) The nearest lodging is in Mountain City, 30 miles from the Ranch. (Follow County Road 728 north 18 miles to Owyhee, and then travel south on State Highway 225 for 12 miles.)

Food and Supplies
The nearest groceries and gas are available at Owyhee and Mountain City. Full services and camping supplies are available in Elko.

First Aid
First aid is available at the Owyhee Clinic.

Additional Information
This area is not accessible from winter through late spring or early summer, because of harsh winter weather. The canyon is remote, and vehicle access is limited at all times. The best floating opportunities are from early May through late June, when the river is at peak flow. The *Owyhee and Bruneau River System Boating Guide* is available for purchase from the BLM Boise (Idaho) Field Office, 3948 Development Avenue, Boise, ID 83705, Tel.: (208) 384-3300. Information regarding guided river trips with licensed outfitters is also available from BLM.

Sponsor

Activity Codes

Walker Lake Recreation Area

Location
75 miles south of Fallon, Nevada

Description
One of only two large natural lakes in Nevada, Walker Lake provides habitat for endangered Lahontan cutthroat trout. The 38,000-acre lake has a shoreline that varies from steep and rocky on the west side to sandy beaches on its east side. Regal Mt. Grant towers above the lake. Walker Lake is an oasis for migratory birds including the common loon. Snow geese, white pelicans, and several species of grebe are sometimes joined by brants, harlequin ducks, and oldsquaws. Snowy plovers feed along the shoreline and American avocets and black-necked stilts wade the shallows.

Mailing Address
BLM - Carson City District Office
5665 Morgan Mill Road
Carson City, NV 89701

Phone Number   Fax Number
(702) 885-6000   (702) 885-6147

Directions
From Fallon, take U.S. Highway 95 south for 75 miles. Walker Lake is located along the highway.

Visitor Activities
Camping, hiking, scenic viewing, fishing, and boating.

Permits, Fees, Limitations
None

Accessibility
Campsites at Sportsmans Beach are accessible to wheelchairs.

Camping and Lodging
Camping is permitted at designated sites, and along the lakeshore. Sportsmans Beach is a developed site on the west side of the lake on U.S. Highway 95. This area is accessible to large recreation trailers, and has tables, sun shelters and vault toilets. No drinking water or hookups are provided. Camping and exploring outside of developed sites require a four-wheel-drive vehicle. Motels and a casino are located in Hawthorne, Nevada, 12 miles south of Sportsmans Beach on U.S. Highway 95.

Food and Supplies
No supplies are available on-site. Food and supplies may be purchased in Hawthorne.

First Aid
First aid is not available on-site. A medical clinic is available in Hawthorne.

Additional Information
Summer temperatures can be very high.

Sponsor

Activity Codes

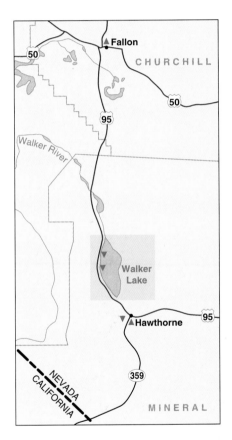

Piñon- and juniper-studded sandstone soars into a huge natural arch, just one example of New Mexico's vast array of spectacular high-desert landforms. *(Courtesy New Mexico State Office)*

New Mexico

Whether you're taking a whitewater river rafting trip down the Rio Grande or a leisurely drive through the Guadalupe Backcountry Byway, New Mexico holds true to its nickname, the Land of Enchantment. New Mexico's public lands encompass 12.8 million acres, or about 17 percent of the state. New Mexico is home to several 19th-century military forts as well as 250 caves. Visitors to New Mexico can experience landscapes found nowhere else in the world, such as the rugged lava flows of the Valley of Fires Recreation Area or the beautiful Rio Grande, portions of which are designated a Wild and Scenic River.

The varied geography showcases desert landscapes and sand dunes, mountain ranges, dry arroyos, wild caves, lava flows, multi-colored badland landscapes, and grass prairies. These striking landscapes have attracted the attention of Hollywood, providing settings for a number of major motion pictures. "Silverado," "Young Guns I and II," "Lonesome Dove," "Desperado," and "Earth 2," just to name a few, have all been filmed on public lands in New Mexico.

Public lands in New Mexico also are rich in major archaeological, cultural, and natural resources. The recent discovery of dinosaur bones and dinosaur skin impressions has put New Mexico on the map of world-class fossil sites.

Because of New Mexico's mild and varied climate, visitors may travel to scenic public land sites any time of the year. Although all of these areas are accessible, some are reached only by dirt roads. Visitors will be delighted by wildlife watching, birdwatching, diverse recreational opportunities, and much more on BLM's unique public lands in New Mexico's Land of Enchantment.

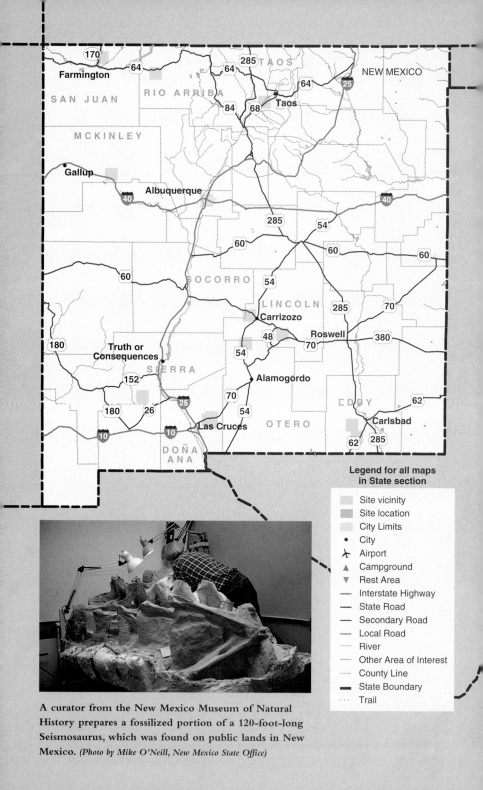

A curator from the New Mexico Museum of Natural History prepares a fossilized portion of a 120-foot-long Seismosaurus, which was found on public lands in New Mexico. *(Photo by Mike O'Neill, New Mexico State Office)*

Aguirre Spring Campground

Location
20 miles east of Las Cruces, New Mexico

Description
This campground is on the eastern slope of the Organ Mountains. Set in oak and juniper woodland and framed by jagged granite spires, it overlooks the Tularosa Basin and White Sands Missile Range.

Mailing Address
BLM - Mimbres Resource Area Office
1800 Marquess Street
Las Cruces, NM 88005

Phone Number
(505) 525-4300

Fax Number
(505) 525-4412

Directions
From Las Cruces, take Exit 5 off Interstate 25, turning east on U.S. Highway 70 for 14 miles. After traversing San Augustine Pass, turn south on the first paved road and go 6 miles to the campground. If traveling west on U.S. Highway 70, go 5 miles past the main-gate access road of the White Sands Missile Range, and turn south on the first paved road.

Visitor Activities
Hiking, picnicking, wildlife viewing, bird-watching, plant viewing, and technical climbing.

Permits, Fees, Limitations
There is a per-vehicle day-use fee. Annual visitor passes, good for one calendar year, are available from the Campground Host. The pass allows access to both Dripping Springs Natural Area and Aguirre Spring Campground.

Accessibility
Restrooms, picnic sites and group sites are wheelchair-accessible.

Camping and Lodging
Camping is available year-round on-site. Numerous hotels are available in Las Cruces.

Food and Supplies
Food and supplies are available in Las Cruces. Food and gas are available along U.S. Highway 70, 6 miles west of the campground access road.

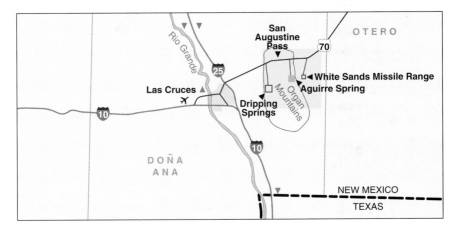

First Aid

First aid is available from the Campground Hosts, who reside on the campground access road, 3 miles south of Highway 70. The nearest hospital is in Las Cruces.

Additional Information

Two National Recreation Trails are accessible from the campground. The Pine Tree Trail is a 4-mile loop trail that begins and ends at the campground. The Baylor Pass Trail is a 6-mile trail that traverses the Organ Mountains from east to west.

The site is open year-round. Summers are hot, so bring water bottles. Drinking water and firewood are available from the Campground Hosts. Light jackets are fine in the spring and summer. Late afternoon and evening thunderstorms are common in July and August. Winters can be cold, so bring appropriate clothing. Pets must be leashed. Potential dangers in the area include rattlesnakes, mountain lions, and precipitous cliffs.

Sponsor

Activity Codes

- technical climbing, picnicking

Black River
Special Management Area

Location
25 miles southwest of Carlsbad, New Mexico

Description
BLM manages 1,200 acres along this oasis in the Chihuahuan Desert, including the springs that are the source of the river. Rare species of plants, fish, and reptiles make their home in and around the river. During migration seasons, the area teems with birds. This thriving riparian (streamside) community includes 15 plants and animals that rarely occur in New Mexico.

Mailing Address
BLM - Carlsbad Resource Area
620 East Greene
Carlsbad, NM 88220

Phone Number
(505) 887-6544

Fax Number
(505) 885-9264

Directions
From Carlsbad, take U.S. Highway 62/180 south about 25 miles and turn west onto County Road 418. Travel another 2 miles and turn left at the fork.

Visitor Activities
Hiking, wildlife viewing, fishing, and bird-watching.

Permits, Fees, Limitations
None

Accessibility
Some portions of the site are wheelchair-accessible.

Fed by springs, the tranquil Black River is an oasis in the Chihuahuan Desert, providing habitat for many rare species of plants and animals. *(Photo by Howard Parman, Roswell District Office)*

Camping and Lodging
Developed camping and lodging are available 5 miles north in White City.

Food and Supplies
Food and supplies are available in Carlsbad and White City.

First Aid
Emergency services are available at Columbia Hospital in Carlsbad.

Additional Information
None

Sponsor

Activity Codes

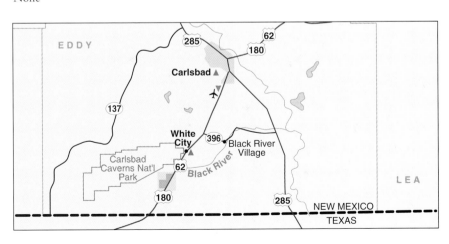

Casamero Chacoan Outlier

Location
20 miles west of Grants, New Mexico

Description
Casamero Pueblo was occupied by the Chacoan Anasazi between A.D. 1000 and 1125. It is an excellent example of a Chacoan outlier (an outlying community connected to Chaco Canyon by prehistoric roads), displaying many of the same cultural and architectural traits found at Chaco Canyon. Casamero was a community building that served a number of nearby farmsteads. It was used for social and religious activities aimed at uniting individual families into a cohesive community. Casamero (along with Chaco Cultural National Historical Park and 6 other outliers) is included on the World Heritage List.

Mailing Address
BLM - Albuquerque District Office
435 Montano NE
Albuquerque, NM 87107

Phone Number   Fax Number
(505) 761-8700   (505) 761-8911

Directions
From Grants, drive 15 miles west on Interstate 40. Take the Prewitt Exit, turn right and drive 0.25 mile north to old U.S. Highway 66. Turn right on Route 66 and drive 0.25 mile east to the intersection with County Road 19. Turn left and drive 4.5 miles north on the paved County Road to a small parking lot on the left (west) side of road. The ruin is visible 200 yards further west.

Visitor Activities
Heritage tourism, photography, hiking, and scenic drives.

Permits, Fees, Limitations
None

Accessibility
None

Camping and Lodging
The nearest lodging is available in Grants. For information on lodging and camping, contact the Grants Chamber of Commerce, 100 North Iron Ave., Grants, NM 87020, Tel.: (505) 287-4802.

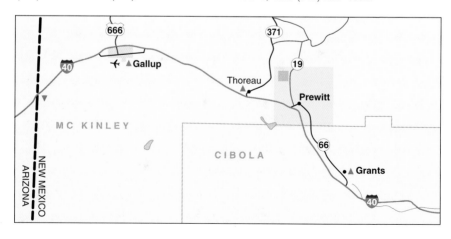

Food and Supplies
There is a convenience store at the intersection of Highway 66 and County Road 19, about 4.5 miles south of Casamero.

First Aid
The nearest medical facilities are in Grants.

Additional Information
The surrounding lands are private. Visitors should stay within the fenced parcel of public land.

Sponsoring Partner

SOCIETY FOR AMERICAN ARCHAEOLOGY

Activity Codes
 - photography

Dripping Springs Natural Area

Location
8 miles east of Las Cruces, New Mexico

Description
The Dripping Springs Natural Area lies on the west side of the Organ Mountains. Nestled at the base of towering gray granite spires and massive purple rhyolite cliffs, this area is home to rare plants and animals. Hiking trails, picnic areas, interpretive displays, and the A.B. Cox Visitor Center provide a diversity of outdoor recreational opportunities.

Mailing Address
BLM - Mimbres Resource Area
1800 Marquess Street
Las Cruces, NM 88005

Phone Numbers
(505) 525-4300 (BLM Office)
(505) 522-1219 (Visitor Center)

Fax Number
(505) 525-4412

Directions
In Las Cruces, take Exit 1 off Interstate 25, turning east on University Avenue.

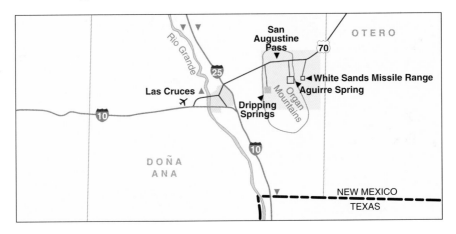

This street becomes Dripping Springs Road, which leads directly to the Dripping Springs Natural Area and the A.B. Cox Visitor Center.

Visitor Activities

Hiking, picnicking, wildlife viewing, bird-watching, plant viewing, historical and archaeological attractions, rappelling, and technical climbing.

Permits, Fees, Limitations

There is a per-vehicle day-use fee. Annual visitor passes, good for one calendar year, are available from the BLM Mimbres Resource Area and at the A.B. Cox Visitor Center. The pass allows access to both Dripping Springs Natural Area and Aguirre Spring Campground.

Accessibility

The visitor center, restrooms, picnic sites, and part of La Cueva Trail are wheelchair-accessible. La Cueva Trail extends northwest from the visitor center to La Cueva rock formation, 0.5 mile away.

Camping and Lodging

Overnight camping is not permitted within the Dripping Springs Natural Area. Camping is available at the Aguirre Spring Campground on the east side of the Organ Mountains. (Travel north on Baylor Canyon Road or Interstate 25 to U.S. Highway 70, then go east. Approximately 3.5 miles beyond the town of Organ, take Aguirre Spring Road south to the campground.) Numerous hotels are available in Las Cruces.

Food and Supplies

Food and supplies are available in Las Cruces.

First Aid

First aid is available at the visitor center. The nearest hospital is located on University Avenue in Las Cruces.

Additional Information

The area is open year-round. It can be very hot in the summer. Drinking water is available at the visitor center and at La Cueva Picnic Area; water supplies should be carried by all hikers. Light jackets are fine in spring and summer. Late afternoon and evening thunderstorms are common in July and August. Winter can be cold, so bring appropriate clothing. Pets are not allowed. Potential dangers in the area include rattlesnakes, mountain lions, and precipitous cliffs.

Sponsoring Partners

Activity Codes

 - rappelling, technical climbing, picnicking

Fort Stanton

Location
65 miles west of Roswell, New Mexico

Description
Populations of Merriam's wild turkey are found within the 26,000-acre Fort Stanton Special Management Area (SMA). Wild turkeys utilize piñon-juniper grassland habitat, riparian (streamside) areas along the Rio Bonito, and ponderosa pine draw bottoms. The Fort Stanton SMA contains the Rio Bonito Riparian Showcase, the first such area designated by BLM. Eight miles east is the historic village of Lincoln, scene of the Lincoln County War of the 1870's and birthplace of the legend of Billy the Kid. The Smokey Bear Museum is located in Capitan.

Mailing Address
BLM - Roswell Resource Area
2909 West Second Street
Roswell, NM 88201

Phone Number   Fax Number
(505) 627-0272   (505) 627-0276

Directions
From Roswell, travel 65 miles west on U.S. Highway 70 to the junction with State Highway 214, and turn north.

Or, from Ruidoso, travel north 7 miles on State Highway 48 to Alto. Turn east on State Highway 380 to State Highway 214, and travel south 10 miles to Fort Stanton.

Visitor Activities
Hiking, mountain biking, horseback riding, caving in Fort Stanton Cave, wildlife viewing, birdwatching, hunting, plant viewing, and scenic drives.

Supervised by professional cave specialists, Boy Scouts make their way through brush toward the mouth of Fort Stanton cave.
(Photo by Kitty Mulkey, New Mexico State Office)

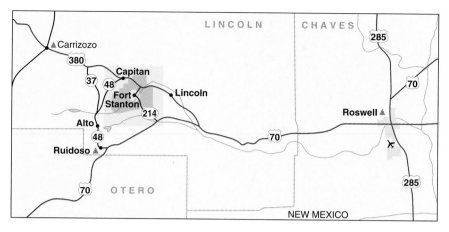

Permits, Fees, Limitations

A permit is required for entry into Fort Stanton Cave. Permits are available from April through October.

Accessibility

None

Camping and Lodging

The Fort Stanton SMA contains undeveloped camp sites. Recreational-vehicle campgrounds are located in Capitan and Ruidoso. A variety of lodging is also available in Lincoln, Capitan, Alto and Ruidoso.

Food and Supplies

Food and supplies are available in Ruidoso and Capitan.

First Aid

The nearest hospital is located in Ruidoso.

Additional Information

The Fort Stanton SMA is open year-round. The fort structure itself is managed by the State of New Mexico and is closed to visitors.

Sponsoring Partner

Activity Codes

 - caving, mountain biking, horseback riding

Glade Run Trail System

Location
Immediately north of the city of Farmington, New Mexico

Description
The approximately 27,400 acres of public land within the Glade Run Trail System encompass a wide variety of topography, from rolling hills to sandy arroyo bottoms to sandstone slickrock. Vegetation is sparse, primarily consisting of common grasses, rabbitbrush, sagebrush, and juniper and piñon. The area is widely used by a diverse range of recreationists. There are 42 miles of marked trails for motorized trailbike riders and mountain bikers. It is also the site of the Road Apple Rally, which is the oldest continuously held mountain bike race in the world. Portions of the marked trails are open to four-wheel-drive enthusiasts and all-terrain vehicles, and part is open to off-road vehicles.

Mailing Address
BLM - Farmington District Office
1235 La Plata Highway, Suite A
Farmington, NM 87401

Phone Number
(505) 599-8900

Fax Number
(505) 599-8998

Directions
In Farmington, follow signs to the San Juan Community College, then proceed north on College Boulevard past the Anasazi Amphitheater to the site. By 1999, trailhead parking also will be available at the north end of Foothills Boulevard.

Visitor Activities
Motorcycling, trailbiking, all-terrain-vehicle riding, off-road touring, mountain biking, hiking, and horseback riding.

Permits, Fees, Limitations
A free BLM permit is required for overnight camping. Any competitive or commercial use also requires a permit. Check with BLM for applicable fees and other requirements.

Accessibility
Much of the area is wheelchair-accessible, though it tends to be rough and sandy.

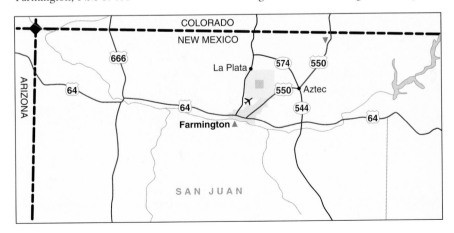

Casual bikers and competitors alike enjoy the biking challenges and scenic variety offered by Glade Run's 42-mile system of trails. *(Photo by Guadalupe Martinez, Farmington District Office)*

The single-track trails are too narrow for wheelchairs.

Camping and Lodging
A wide variety of lodging is available in Farmington.

Food and Supplies
Food and supplies are available in Farmington.

First Aid
There is no on-site first aid. The closest medical facilities are in Farmington.

Additional Information
No water is available at Glade Run. The trail system is used year-round; however, occasional snows may make routes temporarily impassable in winter. There is no water, nor are there any restroom facilities in the Glade.

Sponsoring Partner

Activity Codes

 - horseback riding, mountain biking, motorcycling, trailbiking, all-terrain-vehicle riding

Guadalupe Back Country Byway

Location
The beginning of the Byway is located 12 miles north of Carlsbad, New Mexico.

Description
For 30 miles, the Byway travels the transition from the cholla cactus of the Chihuahuan Desert to the pines of the Guadalupe Escarpment. Travelers can see mule deer, pronghorn antelope, gray fox, scaled quail, mourning dove, a variety of songbirds, and small mammals. Travelers can also learn about the multiple uses of public lands.

Geologically, the Byway is located along the Capitan Reef of the Permian Basin. The plains give way to steep limestone outcrops cut by dry arroyos. Beneath the surface are numerous caves, including Carlsbad Caverns and Lechugilla Cave within nearby Carlsbad Caverns National Park.

Mailing Address
BLM - Carlsbad Resource Area
620 East Greene
Carlsbad, NM 88220

Phone Number   Fax Number
(505) 887-6544   (505) 885-9264

Directions
From Carlsbad, take U.S. Highway 285 north about 12 miles and turn west on State Highway 137. There are signs on Highway 285 directing visitors to the Byway, and the Byway itself has signs marking the route.

Visitor Activities
Hiking, wildlife viewing, hunting, bird-watching, and caving.

Permits, Fees, Limitations
A BLM permit is required for caving.

Accessibility
None

Camping and Lodging
Developed camping and lodging are available 12 miles south in Carlsbad, and 20 miles north in Artesia. Approximately 27 miles past the Byway is the Dog Canyon Campground in Guadalupe National Park. Primitive camping is available on both BLM and National Forest lands.

Food and Supplies
Food and supplies are available in Carlsbad and Artesia.

First Aid
Emergency services are available at Columbia Hospital in Carlsbad.

Additional Information
Visitors may explore caves beneath BLM-managed lands by obtaining a permit from BLM.

Sponsor

Activity codes

 - caving

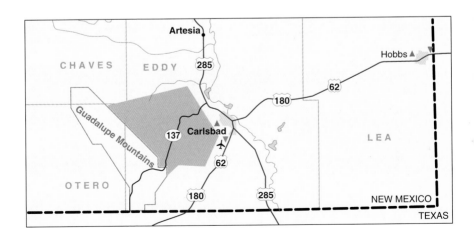

Laguna Seca Mesa

Location
55 miles east of Farmington, New Mexico

Description
Laguna Seca Mesa is characterized by mature ponderosa pine and Douglas fir trees in deep canyons. The upper slopes and ridges are dominated by piñon pine, juniper and Gambel's oak. BLM manages this 2,500-acre area for its varied and abundant wildlife. Species found here include mule deer, Rocky Mountain elk, black bear, Merriam's wild turkey, Abert's squirrel, mountain lion, Cooper's hawk, and a wide assortment of songbirds. Laguna Seca Mesa has also been designated as potential habitat for the Mexican spotted owl.

Mailing Address
BLM - Farmington District Office
1235 La Plata Highway
Farmington, NM 87401

Phone Number
(505) 599-8900

Fax Number
(505) 599-8998

Directions
From Gobernador, New Mexico, travel east on State Highway 64 for approximately 5 miles to Forest Service Road 314, and turn right (south). Travel 0.5 mile to the northern boundary of the Laguna Seca Management Area.

Visitor Activities
Hiking, wildlife viewing, hunting, and birdwatching.

Permits, Fees, Limitations
Camping in any one location is limited to 14 days.

Accessibility
None

Camping and Lodging
There are no developed campgrounds within the Laguna Seca Management Area. Cedar Springs Campground, located in the Carson National Forest, is about 2 miles to the east. Other camping facilities and lodging are located near Navajo

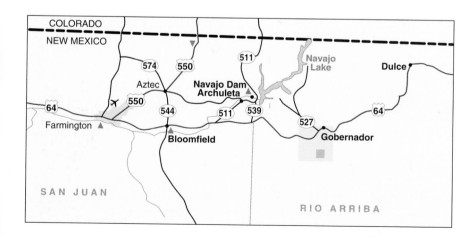

Reservoir at Archuleta, and at the Cottonwood Campground on the San Juan River. To get to Cottonwood, travel about 25 miles west on State Highway 64 to State Highway 539. Turn north onto State Highway 539 and go about 7 miles to State Highway 511. Go west on State Highway 511 for about 4 miles.

Food and Supplies
A variety of food and supplies are available in Bloomfield, with lesser selections at Dulce (30 miles east on Highway 64), Gobernador (5 miles west on Highway 64), Navajo Dam Marina, and Archuleta.

First Aid
The nearest hospital is in Farmington.

Additional Information
No drinking water is available in the Laguna Seca Management Area. Summer thunderstorms can make roads impassable.

Sponsoring Partner

Activity Codes

Lake Valley Historic Site

Location
15 miles south of Hillsboro, New Mexico

Description
Drive the scenic Lake Valley Back Country Byway, visit a historic schoolhouse, or take a self-guided walking tour through Lake Valley ghost town, an old mining town established in 1878. It was the site of the largest silver discovery ever made, and was at one time the transportation and commercial center of the local mining district. After the mining bust of 1893, the town's population declined. The community continued on as a supply center for surrounding sheep and cattle ranchers, until an 1895 fire destroyed half the town, causing the population to further dwindle.

Today, Lake Valley is listed on the State Register of Cultural Properties. Portions of the townsite, including several homes, a one-room schoolhouse, a chapel and coal depot, are located on BLM lands. Perma-

nent site caretakers and BLM staff are stabilizing the schoolhouse and chapel, performing archaeological surveys, and creating interpretive trails, signs, kiosks, and brochures. The schoolhouse is still used for community events.

Mailing Address
BLM - Caballo Resource Area
1800 Marquess Street
Las Cruces, NM 88005

A Back Country Byway kiosk overlooks a historic 1904 schoolhouse in Lake Valley ghost town, which is listed on New Mexico's Register of Cultural Properties. *(Photo by Russell Lummus, Las Cruces District Office)*

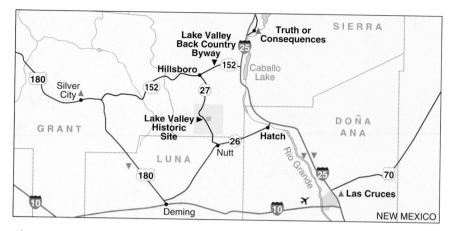

Phone Number
(505) 525-4300

Fax Number
(505) 525-4412

Directions

From Truth or Consequences, New Mexico, head south 12 miles on Interstate 25. Take the Hillsboro exit, then go west on State Highway 152 to Hillsboro. From Hillsboro, go 15 miles south on State Highway 27 to the townsite.

From Las Cruces, New Mexico, travel 41 miles north on Interstate 25 and exit at Hatch. Take State Highway 26 west, toward Deming, New Mexico, and go 19 miles to the town of Nutt. Turn north onto State Highway 27 and travel 12 miles to the Lake Valley townsite.

Visitor Activities

Scenic driving and historic sightseeing.

Permits, Fees, Limitations

There are no entrance fees, but donations are accepted. A permit is required to use the schoolhouse for organized events.

Accessibility

All sites are accessible to the hearing- and sight-impaired, but are not wheelchair-accessible.

Camping and Lodging

No picnic facilities, camping or lodging

are available at Lake Valley. The nearest lodging is available in Hillsboro and Hatch.

Food and Supplies

There are no supplies available at Lake Valley. Food and supplies are available in Hatch and Hillsboro.

First Aid

Emergency medical assistance is available through the Sheriff's Department in Hillsboro. The nearest hospital is in Truth or Consequences.

Additional Information

The site is open year-round. Schoolhouse hours are Friday through Tuesday 9-5, Wednesday and Thursday 9-3, and Sunday 11-5. This site is staffed by volunteers; hours sometimes vary with volunteer availability. Portable toilets are located near the schoolhouse.

Sponsoring Partner

 SOCIETY *for* **HISTORICAL ARCHAEOLOGY**

Activity Codes

  – historic sightseeing

Organ Mountains

Location
10 miles east of Las Cruces, New Mexico

Description
The Organ Mountains host diverse vegetation and habitat types. These range from desert grasslands to ponderosa pine and oak, and range in elevation from 5,000 feet to 9,000 feet. Approximately 80 species of mammals, 185 species of birds, and 60 species of reptiles and amphibians make their home within the range. The Organ Mountains have been designated as an Area of Critical Environmental Concern, contain 3 Wilderness Study Areas, and have been proposed as a National Conservation Area.

Mailing Address
BLM - Mimbres Resource Area
1800 Marquess
Las Cruces, NM 88005

Phone Number	Fax Number
(505) 525-4300	(505) 525-4412

Directions
From Interstate 25 in Las Cruces, take U.S. Highway 70 east approximately 10 miles to Baylor Canyon Road, which runs along the western base of the mountains for 6 miles.

Or, continue east on Highway 70. After traversing San Augustine Pass, turn south on the first paved road, and go 6 miles to the Aguirre Spring Campground.

Visitor Activities
Hiking, picnicking, hunting, birdwatching, wildlife viewing, photography, and rock climbing.

Permits, Fees, Limitations
There is a per-vehicle, day-use fee at the Aguirre Spring Campground and the Dripping Springs Natural Area. There is no fee for use of other portions of the mountains.

Accessibility
There are wheelchair-accessible facilities at both Aguirre Spring Campground and Dripping Springs Natural Area.

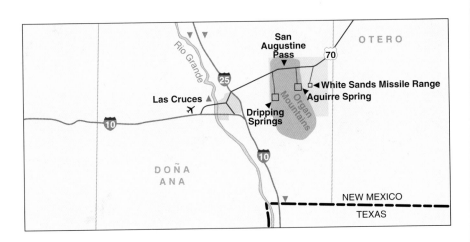

Camping and Lodging
Developed camping is available at Aguirre Spring Campground. Back-country areas in the mountains are open to primitive camping. Lodging is available in Las Cruces.

Food and Supplies
Food and supplies are available in Las Cruces.

First Aid
Emergency services are available through local law enforcement and search-and-rescue teams. The nearest hospital is in Las Cruces.

Additional Information
Much of the southeastern portion of the Organ Mountains is within the Ft. Bliss Military Reservation. This area is not open to the public; however, the boundary is not marked or signed in many locations. Potential dangers in the mountains include rattlesnakes, mountain lions, and precipitous cliffs.

Sponsor

Activity Codes

 - picnicking, rock climbing, photography

Orilla Verde Recreation Area

Location
1.5 miles west of Pilar, New Mexico

Description
Orilla Verde Recreation Area, nestled along the banks of the Rio Grande, offers visitors a wide variety of recreational opportunities. All facilities are located along the Rio Grande within the steep-walled Rio Grande Gorge. Because of the dramatic changes in elevation and the diversity of plant life, Orilla Verde draws many species of animals, including raptors (such as eagles and hawks), songbirds, waterfowl, beaver, cougar, ringtail, mule deer, and many more. Gentle waters with occasional small rapids flow through Orilla Verde, providing an ideal setting for many recreational activities.

Mailing Address
BLM - Taos Resource Area
226 Cruz Alta Road
Taos, NM 87571

Phone Number
(505) 758-8851

Fax Number
(505) 758-1620

Directions
From Española, New Mexico, take U.S. Highway 285 north, which will become State Highway 68. Take State Highway 68 approximately 23 miles (toward Taos) to the Village of Pilar. At the Village of Pilar, turn left on State Highway 570. Follow signs to Orilla Verde.

[Note: State Highway 570 has a posted speed limit of 25 mph; however, because of community safety concerns, BLM asks that speeds be kept to no higher than 15 mph on State Highway 570.]

Visitor Activities
Canoeing, kayaking, wildlife viewing, fishing, and non-whitewater rafting.

Permits, Fees, Limitations
There is a per-vehicle, day-use fee. An annual day-use pass, good for one calendar year, is available from the BLM Taos Resource Area Office or the BLM Rio Grande Gorge Visitor Center (located on the east side of State Highway 68, directly across from the Village of Pilar). There are nightly camping fees, with a maximum of 2 vehicles permitted per site. Call BLM for details.

Accessibility
All facilities at the BLM Rio Grande Gorge Visitor Center are wheelchair-accessible. There are also several wheelchair-accessible campsites at Orilla Verde Recreation area. Information on accessible campsites is available at the Visitor Center.

Camping and Lodging
There are campgrounds at the Orilla Verde Recreation Area (first come, first served), a KOA campground in Taos, and Forest Service campgrounds nearby. Lodging is available in Questa, Taos, Pilar, and Dixon. For further information on camping and lodging, contact or visit the Taos County Chamber of Commerce Visitor Center, Corner of State Highways 68 & 64, Taos, NM 87571, Tel.: (505) 758-3873.

Food and Supplies
Food and supplies are available in Taos, and in limited quantities in Pilar.

First Aid
First aid is available at the BLM Rio Grande Gorge Visitor Center. The nearest hospitals are located in Taos and Española.

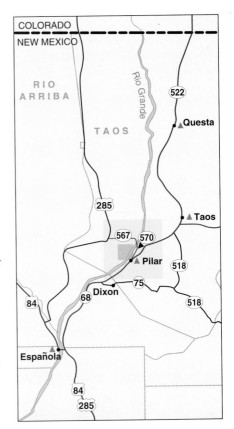

Just south of the Orilla Verde Recreation Area, whitewater rafters maneuver through the challenging "rock garden" rapids of the Rio Grande's "BLM Racecourse" segment. *(Photo by M'Lee Beazley, Albuquerque District Office)*

Additional Information

The climate is semi-arid, with thunderstorms common in July and August, and snow possible from October through March. The weather is unpredictable; visitors should bring warm clothing. La Vista Verde Trail is the only developed hiking trail within Orilla Verde Recreation Area. The Visitor Center is open from May 1 through early September.

Sponsoring Partners

Activity Codes

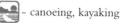 - canoeing, kayaking

Three Rivers Petroglyph Site

Location
17 miles north of Tularosa, New Mexico

Description
The Three Rivers Petroglyphs are outstanding examples of prehistoric Jornada Mogollon rock art. The basaltic ridge rising above the Three Rivers Valley contains over 21,000 petroglyphs, including masks, sunbursts, wildlife, handprints, and geometric designs. The number and concentration of petroglyphs make this one of the largest and most interesting rock art sites in the Southwest. A rugged 0.5-mile trail begins at the visitor shelter and links many of the most interesting petroglyphs. Another short trail begins on the east side of the picnic area and leads to a partially excavated prehistoric village.

Mailing Address
BLM - Caballo Resource Area Office
1800 Marquess Street
Las Cruces, NM 88005

Phone Number
(505) 525-4300

Fax Number
(505) 525-4412

Directions
From Tularosa, take U.S. Highway 54 north for 17 miles. Turn right (east) onto County Road B30, and travel 5 miles on the paved road, following the signs.

Visitor Activities
Hiking, viewing pertroglyphs, visiting the Prehistoric Pithouse Village, and picnicking.

Permits, Fees, Limitations
There is a day-use vehicle fee. Pets and smoking are not allowed on trails. Charcoal grills are available, but campfires are not permitted.

Accessibility
There are two wheelchair-accessible toilets and an accessible picnic shelter, with accessible trails leading to them. There are also wheelchair-accessible trails to the visitor shelter and up to the base of the main petroglyph hill, where a spotting scope enhances viewing.

Camping and Lodging
The site offers 7 shelters with tables, barbecue grills, trash cans, restrooms, and water. Camping is permitted on-site. The nearest lodging is in Alamogordo, 30 miles south on State Highway 54.

At Three Rivers, the prehistoric Jornada Mogollon people carved over 21,000 petro-glyphs, such as this representation of a fish. *(Photo by Russell Lummus, Las Cruces District)*

Food and Supplies

The Three Rivers Trading Post at the entry to County Road B30 offers limited food and supplies. A variety of food and supplies can be found in the towns of Tularosa and Carrizozo (28 miles north on State Highway 54).

First Aid

Medical emergency assistance is available through the Sheriff's Department in Tularosa. The closest hospital is in Alamogordo.

Additional Information

The site is open to the public year-round. Rugged trails, extreme temperatures, and poisonous snakes may be encountered. If you are planning to hike, wear sturdy shoes or boots, and carry water and sunscreen with you.

Sponsor

Activity Codes

   – picnicking, viewing petroglyphs, visiting prehistoric village

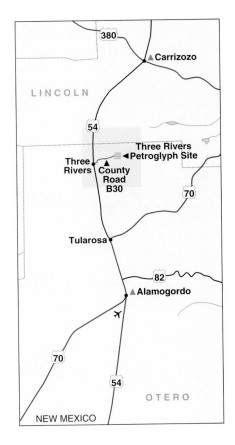

Valley of Fires Recreation Area

Location
4 miles west of Carrizozo, New Mexico

Description
The Valley of Fires Recreation Area is adjacent to the Malpais Lava Flow, a BLM Wilderness Study Area. The lava flow is between 1,500 and 2,000 years old, making it the youngest such flow in the continental United States. It extends from Little Black Peak south into the Tularosa Basin for 44 miles. The flow is between 4 and 6 miles wide and the lava is 160 feet deep at its thickest point. A surprising number and variety of plants and animals thrive in the rugged landscape of the flow.

Mailing Address
BLM - Valley of Fires Recreation Area
P. O. Box 871
Carrizozo, NM 88301

Phone Number
(505) 648-2241

Fax Number
(505) 648-2241

Directions
From Alamogordo, New Mexico, travel 58 miles north on U.S. Highway 54 to Carrizozo. From Carrizozo, travel 4 miles west on State Highway 380 to Valley of Fires.

Or, from Interstate 25, exit at San Antonio and travel 62 miles east on Highway 380 to Valley of Fires.

Visitor Activities
Hiking, wildlife viewing, birdwatching, plant viewing, and a self-guided nature trail.

Permits, Fees, Limitations
There is a day-use fee.

Accessibility
Two camp sites and the restrooms area are wheelchair-accessible, as is approximately one-third of the Malpais Nature Trail.

Camping and Lodging
Valley of Fires has 30 developed campsites with drinking water, picnic tables and grills available. Some sites have 30-amp electrical service. Tent-camping sites are also available. Recreational-vehicle campgrounds are located in Capitan and Ruidoso. A variety of lodging is also available

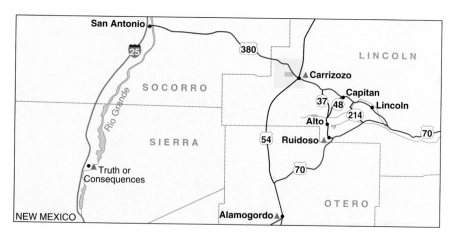

in Carrizozo, Lincoln, Capitan, Alto, and Ruidoso.

Food and Supplies
Food and supplies are available in Carrizozo, Ruidoso, and Capitan.

First Aid
The nearest hospital is located in Ruidoso.

Additional Information
Valley of Fires is open year-round. White Sands National Monument, the National Space Exploration Hall of Fame in Alamogordo, and the historic village of Lincoln are all nearby.

Sponsor

Activity Codes

 - self-guided nature trail

Wild Rivers Recreation Area

Location
The area is located approximately 42 miles northwest of Taos, New Mexico.

Description
The Rio Grande Gorge is a rugged, steep-walled canyon that cuts into the volcanic plateaus of north-central New Mexico. The Wild Rivers Recreation Area provides splendid views into this 800-foot-deep gorge. Most visitor facilities are located along the rim, but several trails provide access to the river and to facilities located within the gorge.

Mailing Address
BLM - Taos Resource Area
226 Cruz Alta Road
Taos, NM 87571

Phone Number
(505) 758-8851

Fax Number
(505) 758-1620

Directions
From Taos, follow State Highway 68 north 7 miles to its end. Continue straight (north) on State Highway 522 approximately 20 miles to Questa. Travel 3 miles past the stoplight in Questa to reach State Highway 378. Turn left onto Highway 378, and follow signs approximately 12 miles west to Wild Rivers Recreation Area. The BLM Wild Rivers Visitor Center is located within the Recreation Area; follow the signs as you enter the gate.

Visitor Activities
Hiking, fishing, wildlife viewing, hunting, birdwatching, plant viewing, scenic drives, and mountain biking.

Permits, Fees, Limitations
There are day-use and camping fees. Annual day-use passes, good for 1 calendar year, are also available. There is a maximum of 2 vehicles permitted per camp site. Walk-in river campsites are available for a reduced rate.

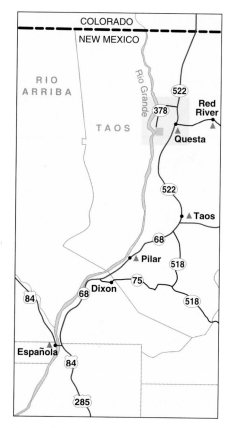

Accessibility

The BLM Wild Rivers Visitor Center, restrooms, a few trails and some campsites are wheelchair-accessible.

Camping and Lodging

There are BLM campgrounds in or adjacent to the gorge at Wild Rivers Recreation Area. There are also a KOA campground in Taos, and U.S. Forest Service campgrounds nearby. Lodging is available in Questa, Taos, and Red River. For further information on camping and lodging,

contact or visit the Taos County Chamber of Commerce Visitor Center, Corner of State Highways 68 & 64, Taos, NM, 87571, Tel.: (505) 758-3873.

Food and Supplies

Food and supplies are available in Taos and in limited quantity in Questa and Red River.

First Aid

First aid is available at the BLM Wild Rivers Visitor Center. First aid is also available in Questa and Taos. There is a hospital in Taos.

Additional Information

Facilities are at elevations ranging from 7,200-7,800 feet. The climate is semi-arid, with thunderstorms common in July and August. Snow is likely to occur from November through March. The area is open year-round, but winter access may be difficult. The weather is unpredictable. Visitors should anticipate changeable weather conditions and bring warm clothing. The BLM Wild Rivers Visitor Center is open daily from 9 a.m. to 5 p.m., Memorial Day through Labor Day.

Sponsoring Partner

Activity Codes

 - mountain biking

The Rio Grande cuts through the high plains of northern New Mexico at Wild Rivers, where an 800-foot-deep volcanic canyon attracts rugged recreationists as well as raptors, elk and beaver. *(Photo by M'Lee Beazley, Albuquerque District Office)*

A horse-drawn wagon crosses the sandy hummocks of Washington's Juniper Dunes Wilderness Area. *(Courtesy BLM)*

Oregon & Washington

From the sculpted Owyhee Canyonlands of eastern Oregon to the Pacific Coast tidepools of Yaquina Head Outstanding Natural Area, public lands in Oregon and Washington provide a variety of climates, beautiful natural landscapes, important wildlife habitats, and outstanding recreational opportunities. Public lands make up about 25 percent of the State of Oregon. Additionally, the State of Washington has over 300 thousand acres of public land.

From the Cascade Mountains eastward is high desert. Sagebrush, prairie grasses, and juniper provide cover and forage for a variety of wildlife, birds, and livestock. Recreational opportunities include rafting the white waters of the Deschutes River or hiking the Oregon High Desert Trail across the Steens Mountain.

To the west of the Cascades are 2.2 million acres of deciduous and evergreen forests. These lands provide habitat for a variety of fish and wildlife, numerous recreational opportunities, and a variety of forest products such as timber, ferns, mushrooms, and bear grass. During the spring and summer, an abundance of wildflowers can be found in the Table Rock Wilderness Area. Throughout most of the year, Roosevelt elk can be seen at the Dean Creek Elk Viewing Area near Reedsport.

Two outstanding interpretive facilities managed by the Bureau of Land Management in Oregon are the National Historic Oregon Trail Interpretive Center near Baker City and the Yaquina Head Interpretive Center near Newport.

Whether inspired by the vastness of the desert, the mystery of the forest, or the wonder of ocean tidepools, visitors to public lands in Oregon and Washington will experience an unforgettable glimpse of our spectacular natural world.

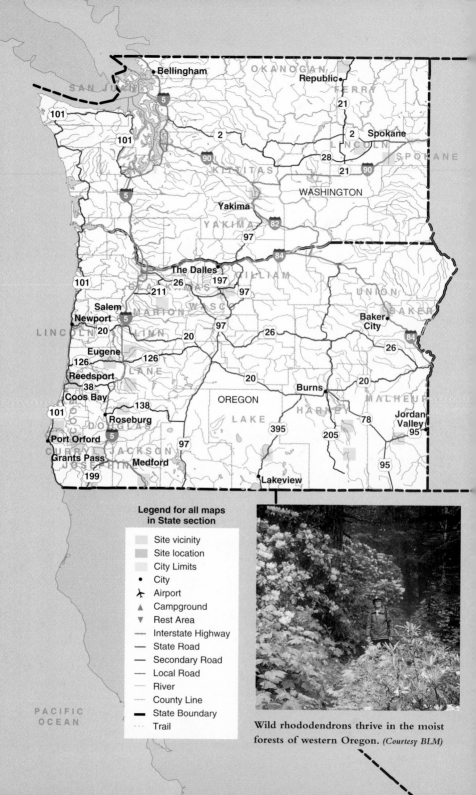

**Legend for all maps
in State section**

	Site vicinity
	Site location
	City Limits
•	City
✈	Airport
▲	Campground
▼	Rest Area
—	Interstate Highway
—	State Road
—	Secondary Road
—	Local Road
—	River
—	County Line
—	State Boundary
···	Trail

Wild rhododendrons thrive in the moist
forests of western Oregon. *(Courtesy BLM)*

PACIFIC
OCEAN

Cape Blanco Lighthouse

Location
10 miles northwest of Port Orford, Oregon

Description
Cape Blanco Lighthouse is the oldest standing lighthouse on the westernmost point of the Oregon coast. It was commissioned in 1870 to aid shipping of products of the gold-mining and lumber industries. Bring binoculars and a camera to view and photograph some of the roughest and most scenic portions of the Oregon coastline.

Mailing Address
BLM – Coos Bay District Office
1300 Airport Lane
North Bend, OR 97459

Phone Number   Fax Number
(541) 756-0100   (541) 756-9303

Directions
From Port Orford, go 5 miles north on U.S. Highway 101 to Cape Blanco Highway, then 5 miles west to the site.

Visitor Activities
Historic interpretation and photography.

The Cape Blanco Lighthouse, commissioned in 1870, stands guard on one of the roughest and most beautiful portions of Oregon's coastline. *(Courtesy BLM)*

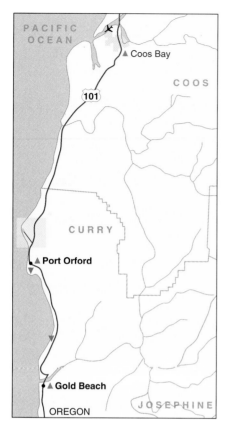

PACIFIC
OCEAN

▲ Coos Bay

COOS

101

CURRY

▲ Port Orford

▲ Gold Beach

OREGON

JOSEPHINE

Permits, Fees, Limitations

There are no required fees, but donations are accepted.

Accessibility

The visitor center and associated restrooms are wheelchair-accessible. The lighthouse is not.

Camping and Lodging

Camping is available at the Cape Blanco State Park within walking distance of the site. Lodging is available in Port Orford.

Food and Supplies

Food, supplies, and restaurants are available in Port Orford.

First Aid

Volunteer site hosts are trained in basic first aid. The nearest hospital is in Gold Beach, Oregon, 25 miles south of Port Orford, off U.S. Highway 101.

Additional Information

There is a visitor center with information on the lighthouse and area history. Lighthouse tours (5 persons per group) are offered from April 1 through October 30. Visitor hours are 10 a.m. to 4 p.m., Thursday through Monday; the center is closed Tuesday and Wednesday. Photography is encouraged. The weather at the lighthouse is very unpredictable, but usually windy and cool.

Sponsoring Partner

NATIONAL
GEOGRAPHIC
SOCIETY

Activity Codes

  - photography, historic interpretation

Channeled Scablands

Location
Numerous locations in Lincoln County, Washington

Description
The Channeled Scablands of Lincoln County are home to geologic features not found anywhere else in the world. Catastrophic floods raced through the area during the last Ice Age, carving channels through the mostly flat land. Today, rolling hills of cropland and sagebrush steppe habitat are interspersed with canyons of carved basalt columns. A completely unique world exists within those canyon walls. Creeks and lakes support grasslands and trees. Wildlife and wildflowers thrive. Remnants of early Native American settlements and pioneer homesteads speak of the first inhabitants.

Mailing Address
BLM - Spokane District Office
1103 N. Fancher Road
Spokane, WA 99212

Phone Number   Fax Number
(509) 536-1200   (509) 536-1275

Directions
From Spokane, take U.S. Highway 2 west 30 miles to Davenport. Or, from Seattle take Interstate 90 east, then State Highway 21 north for 19 miles.

Visitor Activities
Picnicking, hiking, mountain biking, horseback riding, fishing, hunting, wildlife viewing, birdwatching, and wildflower viewing.

Permits, Fees, Limitations
None

Accessibility
There are wheelchair-accessible composting toilets at the Twin Lakes site, 15 miles west of Harrington on Coffee Pot Road. The Watchable Wildlife trail at Wilson Creek, 4.5 miles west of Almira on Lewis Bridge County Road, is wheelchair-accessible.

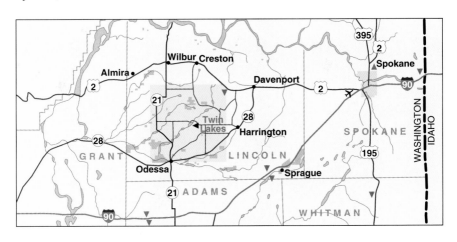

Camping and Lodging

All public lands in Lincoln County are open to camping, but there are no developed campsites. Recreational vehicle parking and lodging are available in the communities of Davenport, Odessa, Wilbur, Harrington, and Sprague.

Food and Supplies

No supplies are available on-site. Purchase supplies in Davenport, Odessa, Wilbur, Harrington, Creston, Almira, or Sprague.

First Aid

First aid is not available on-site. The nearest hospitals are located in Davenport and Odessa. Enhanced 911 service is available countywide.

Additional Information

Lincoln County is sparsely populated and contains rough terrain. No drinking water is provided on the public lands; visitors should bring their own, especially during the summer, when temperatures can climb above 90°F. Visitors may encounter rattlesnakes and poison ivy. On public lands, vehicles are limited to designated roads and trails, and campfires must be self-contained. To get to specific sites, visitors can obtain a free recreation map of the Channeled Scablands from BLM.

Sponsoring Partner

Activity Codes

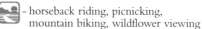 - horseback riding, picnicking, mountain biking, wildflower viewing

Dean Creek Elk Viewing Area

Location
3 miles east of Reedsport, Oregon

Description
The Dean Creek Elk Viewing Area is a mosaic of pastures, woodlands, and wetlands, providing a variety of wildlife viewing experiences. A herd of 60 to 100 Roosevelt elk are year-round residents, and visitors can also view numerous birds in the area, including waterfowl. Each of 2 viewing areas provides parking, an interpretive center, viewing scopes, and restrooms. The area is contiguous with the scenic Umpqua River.

Mailing Address
BLM - Coos Bay District Office
1300 Airport Lane
North Bend, OR 97459

Phone Number	Fax Number
(541) 756-0100	(541) 756-9303

Directions
From Reedsport, go 3 miles east on State Highway 38. The Viewing Area begins at that point and extends for an additional 3 miles along the highway.

Visitor Activities
Wildlife viewing and birdwatching.

Resident Roosevelt elk roam freely in the pastures, woodlands, and wetlands of the Dean Creek Elk Viewing Area. *(Photo by Will B. Golden, Coos Bay District Office)*

Permits, Fees, Limitations

There are no fees; hunting, overnight camping/parking, and hiking are not permitted.

Accessibility

The area is fully wheelchair-accessible.

Camping and Lodging

There is no camping permitted on-site. Camping is available at the Umpqua Lighthouse State Park, 5 miles south of Reedsport on U.S. Highway 101, and at

BLM's Loon Lake Recreation Area. To reach Loon Lake, travel about 7 miles east on State Highway 38, and then 6 miles south on Loon Lake Road. Reedport offers several motels and recreational vehicle parks.

Food and Supplies

There are no food or supplies available on-site. Groceries and restaurants are available in Reedsport.

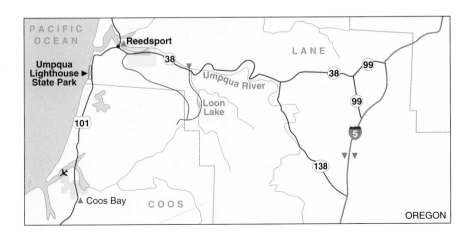

First Aid
There is no first aid on-site. The nearest hospital is in Reedsport.

Additional Information
Elk roam the area freely, and their numbers fluctuate with the seasons. During the summer, the best times to view elk are the early morning and before dusk. During the other 3 seasons, the chances of seeing elk are better during the day. Daytime temperatures tend to be cool or cold, even during the summer, and the area is generally windy. Dean Creek is managed to provide optimum viewing opportunities.

Pastures are mowed, plowed and/or fertilized to improve their nutrition and palatability for the elk. Portions of the wetlands have been enhanced to provide more standing water and islands for waterfowl.

Sponsoring Partner

Activity Codes

Diamond Craters Outstanding Natural Area

Location
55 miles south of Burns, Oregon

Description
This is a fascinating area that contains hundreds of pristine volcanic features. Geologists maintain that the area has some of the best and most diverse examples of basaltic volcanism in the United States. Features include blast craters, small calderas, unusual lava flow formations, a water-filled crater (maar), and unusual plant communities.

Mailing Address
BLM - Andrews Resource Area
HC74-12533 Highway 20, West
Hines, OR 97738

Phone Number
(541) 573-4400

Fax Number
(541) 573-4411

Directions
From Burns, take State Highway 205 south approximately 41 miles to the Dia-

mond turn-off. Travel east 7 miles to Diamond Craters junction, turn left on Lava Beds Road, and follow signs 2 miles north to Diamond Craters.

Visitor Activities
Hiking, picnicking, photography, geological interpretation, scenic drives, birdwatching, and wildflower viewing.

Permits, Fees, Limitations
No permits or fees are required. Vehicle access is permitted on designated roads only. No removal of rock materials, plants, or animals is permitted.

Accessibility
None

Camping and Lodging
There are no facilities on-site. Year-round camping (36 sites) is available at BLM's Page Springs campground near Frenchglen, 23 miles south on State Highway 205. No services are available from Octo-

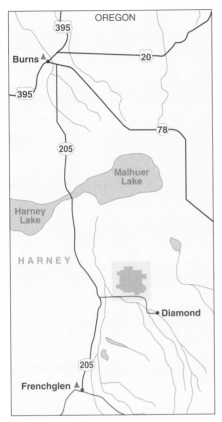

ber through April. In season, a fee is charged, which includes some amenities (toilets, water, picnic tables, fire rings, parking pads, but no waste water disposal). Lodging is available in Diamond (8 miles southeast on the County road), Frenchglen, and Burns (55 miles north on State Highway 205).

Food and Supplies

Supplies are available in Diamond, Frenchglen, and Burns.

First Aid

There is no first aid available on-site. The nearest hospital is in Burns.

Additional Information

The area is open all year; however, winter weather can restrict travel. This is an isolated area of rocky terrain, inhabited by rattlesnakes and ticks. The best times to visit are May through June and September through October. The weather is very hot and dry in July through August. There are no facilities of any kind on-site. Wildflowers are in bloom from May through August.

Sponsor

Activity Codes

    – geologic interpretation, photography, picnicking, wildflower viewing

Little Red Cone is one of many well-preserved volcanic features that highlight the landscape at Diamond Craters. *(Photo by Mark Armstrong, Burns District Office)*

Folsom Farm Site

Location
8 miles northeast of Sprague, Washington

Description
Folsom Farm consists of an early 1900's homestead overlooking Smick Meadows, a renovated marsh. From a scenic overlook, visitors can observe wildlife, including nesting waterfowl, deer, raptors, amphibians, and other animals.

Mailing Address
BLM - Spokane District Office
1103 North Fancher
Spokane, WA 99212

Phone Number
(509) 536-1200

Fax Number
(509) 536-1275

Directions
From Interstate 90, take exit 254. Proceed south 2.25 miles to Scroggie Road. Turn east, and proceed 0.75 mile to the entrance.

Visitor Activities:
Hiking, picnicking, wildlife viewing, historic site, birdwatching, hunting, fishing, and horseback riding.

Permits, Fees, Limitations
No fees or permits. Motor vehicle use is limited to the parking lot and access road. There are no restroom facilities on-site.

Accessibility
Existing trails are wheelchair-accessible. In addition, plans call for the development of a boardwalk to an observation point overlooking the Smick Meadows.

Camping and Lodging
Adjacent BLM lands are open to primitive camping. Fishtrap Resort, 0.25 mile east of the Folsom Farm entrance on Scroggie Road, has facilities for recreational vehicles.

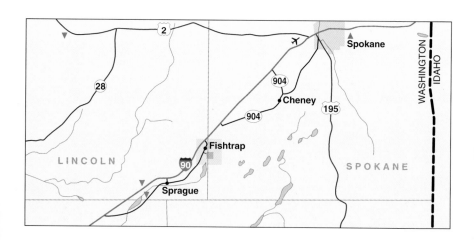

Food and Supplies
Food and supplies can be purchased in Sprague or at the Fishtrap Resort.

First Aid
There is no first aid available on-site. The closest medical facility is located in Cheney, 25 miles north via Interstate 90 and State Highway 904.

Additional Information
Support facilities are limited to a parking lot, picnic area, hiking trail, and scenic overlook.

Sponsoring Partner

SOCIETY *for*
HISTORICAL
ARCHAEOLOGY

Activity Codes

 - horseback riding, picnicking

Galice-Hellgate Back Country Byway

Location
The east end of the Byway is located 4 miles east of Merlin, Oregon. The west end of the Byway is located 58 miles east of Gold Beach, Oregon.

Description
The Galice-Hellgate National Back Country Byway is a 39-mile-long scenic motor route starting from Interstate 5 near Merlin ("Gateway to the Rogue") and progressing along the Rogue National Wild and Scenic River. The Byway travels past majestic vistas of a deep and rocky river canyon, densely wooded hillsides, and whitewater rapids. Motorists progress into the Siskiyou Mountains along one portion of the route, climbing up and away from the river and topping out into a high altitude forest environment offering spectacular views of nearby mountains and stands of Douglas fir. This portion of the route

eventually takes travelers to Gold Beach and the Oregon coast.

Mailing Address
BLM - Medford District Office
3040 Biddle Road
Medford, OR 97504

Phone Number   **Fax Number**
(541) 770-2200   (541) 770-2400

Directions
On Interstate 5, 2 miles north of Grants Pass, take the Merlin exit (#61). Travel west on the Merlin Galice Road 9 miles through the town of Merlin until you reach the river canyon. Continuing on the Merlin-Galice Road takes you to the Rand Visitor Center, where you can obtain written information about the area. Near the community of Galice, a side route off the Byway leads to the Oregon coast. The side route is 8 miles long and is

called the Galice Access Road (#34-8-36). To reach the coast, travel another 58 miles to the end of the Byway, on narrow, winding mountain roads. The Galice Access Road leads you to the Bear Camp Road (#FS 23). When you reach the Rogue River again near Agness, proceed on road #FS 33 to the coast.

The Byway affords stunning views of the Rogue River's rocky canyon and whitewater rapids, against a backdrop of the fir-studded Siskiyou Mountains. *(Courtesy BLM)*

Visitor Activities
Sightseeing, boating, swimming, power-boat rides, wildlife viewing, fishing, hunting, and hiking.

Permits, Fees, Limitations
No fees. Travelers wishing to boat down the adjacent Rogue River wild section must obtain a permit from the Rand Visitor Center from May 15 through the end of October.

Accessibility
There are numerous wheelchair-accessible overlooks and 1 major accessible campground (Indian Mary Park) with full facilities.

Camping and Lodging
Grants Pass, just 6 miles southeast of the Byway's eastern terminus, offers a variety of lodging and camping opportunities. Indian Mary Park is located along the Byway route, on the Rogue River, 11 miles northwest of Interstate 5.

Food and Supplies
Food and supplies are available in Grants Pass, Merlin, and Galice. Grants Pass is located approximately 2 miles south of the Byway just off Interstate 5. Merlin is the gateway community to the Byway, located approximately 4 miles northwest of the Interstate 5 exit, where the Byway begins. The historic community of Galice is located 11 miles northwest of Merlin along the Byway, just past the junction to the coastal route.

First Aid
Ambulance service is available throughout the route; however, as travelers progress into the more remote portions of the Byway, telephone availability diminishes. The nearest hospitals are in Grants Pass; these are located in the northwest part of town.

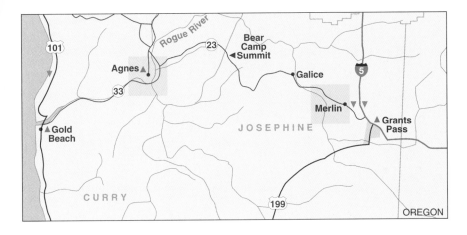

Additional Information

For the most part, the Byway is a well maintained, 2-lane country road; however, visitors progressing into the Siskiyou Mountains will find the road to be narrower, requiring very careful driving. In winter months, this mountainous portion of the Byway is generally closed by snow accumulations. The best time of year to visit the area is from May through October.

Sponsoring Partner

Activity Codes

 - sightseeing, swimming, powerboat rides

Graves Creek to Marial
Back Country Byway

Location
8 miles north of Galice, Oregon

Description
When you enter this gateway to the back country, you'll feel the cool mist surrounding Rainie Falls. A strenuous hike along the historic Rogue River or the Mule Creek Canyon Trails offers visitors an invigorating challenge.

Mailing Address
BLM - Medford District Office
3040 Biddle Road
Medford, OR 97504

Phone Number	Fax Number
(541) 770-2200	(541) 770-2400

Directions
From Galice, head north on Galice Road 8 miles to the Graves Creek Bridge. The

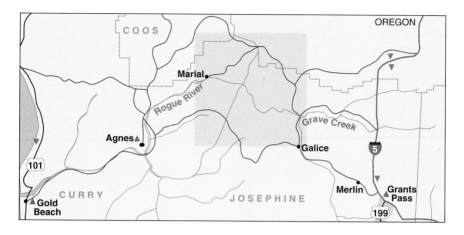

Byway route starts here; follow the Back Country Byway signs, or the following directions:

Cross the Graves Creek Bridge and bear left uphill on paved BLM Road #34-8-1 for 5 miles. At the junction with Whisky Creek Road (#33-8-26), bear right and continue on #34-8-1 (sign reads "Marial 28 Miles") for 3 miles. At the junction with BLM Road #33-8-13 (on the right), bear left and continue on #34-8-1 for 8 miles. At the junction with BLM Road #32-8-31, bear left and continue on a paved road for 5 miles to the junction with BLM Road #32-8-9.2. Bear left and continue on #32-8-31 for 1 mile to Anaktuvuk Saddle Junction. Turn left on BLM road #32-9-14.2 for 3 miles to Marble Gap Junction. Continue ahead (pavement will end) for another 3 miles to Fourmile Saddle junction. Bear left and stay on #32-9-14.2 for another 9 miles to the Rogue River Ranch.

[Note: these directions are identical to those for the Rogue River Ranch.]

Visitor Activities
Sightseeing, scenic drives, boating, swimming, wildlife viewing, birdwatching, plant viewing, historical interpretation, and hiking.

Permits, Fees, Limitations
No fees. Boating on the Rogue River requires a permit, which can be obtained at the Rand Visitor Center near Galice, at the eastern terminus of the route.

Accessibility
The Rogue River Ranch main museum building has ramps for wheelchair access. In other areas, wheelchair-assisted visitors will require help from others.

Camping and Lodging
There is a BLM primitive campground approximately 0.5 mile from the Rogue River Ranch. There are no fees. Drinking water is not available.

Food and Supplies
All food and supplies should be obtained prior to beginning the trip. There are no gas stations in the area. Travelers should fill their tanks when they purchase their supplies in Grants Pass or Merlin.

First Aid
This is a remote site without phone service or medical care. During the peak-use

season of May through September, care-takers are on duty at the site and can provide first-aid supplies and radio communication. The nearest hospital is in Grants Pass. (From Galice, travel east approximately 20 miles on the Merlin-Galice Road to Interstate 5. Grants Pass is 2 miles south on Interstate 5.)

Additional Information
This site is extremely remote, with no visitor services. Travelers should expect to arrive well prepared for a long trip on mostly 1-lane dirt roads, which are well-maintained and passable by passenger vehicles. Access to the area is often impossible during the winter months because of

snow accumulations. The best time of year to visit the site is from May through September.

Sponsoring Partner

SCENIC AMERICA

Activity Codes

 - swimming, sightseeing, historical interpretation

Lake Abert and Abert Rim

Location
25 miles north of Lakeview, Oregon

Description
Lake Abert is the third-largest saline body of water in North America. Brine shrimp in the lake provide the food supply for a number of bird species.

Mailing Address
BLM - Lakeview District Office
P.O. Box 151
U. S. Highway 395 South
Lakeview, OR 97630

Phone Number   Fax Number
(541) 947-2177   (541) 947-2143

Directions
From Lakeview, drive 25 miles north on U.S. Highway 395 through Valley Falls.

Continue north 3 miles. The highway parallels the lake for the next 18 miles.

Visitor Activities
Wildlife viewing, hunting, geologic sightseeing, and hiking.

Permits, Fees, Limitations
None

Accessibility
The watchable-wildlife site is wheelchair-accessible. The rim itself and surrounding terrain are extremely steep, and consequently are not wheelchair-accessible.

Camping and Lodging
Developed campgrounds are available near Lakeview. Motel lodging is available in Lakeview and Paisley, 20 miles north of Lakeview on State Highway 31.

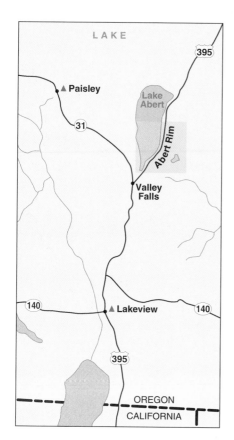

Food and Supplies
There are a small store and gas station at Valley Falls.

First Aid
The nearest hospital is located in Lakeview.

Additional Information
Restroom facilities are not available at Abert Lake. Hang-glider pilots launch south of the rim and can often be seen flying in the area during the summer months.

Sponsor

Activity Codes

 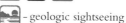 - geologic sightseeing

Little Vulcan Mountain

Location
6 miles west of Curlew, Washington

Description
This area consists of 600 acres of public land. The combination of elevation, aspect, and rock outcroppings within this vegetative community provides the unique qualities that create bighorn sheep habitat. This habitat is critical for the continued existence of the local herd. The BLM lands contain the best winter range and es-

cape cover, as well as half of the lambing area. Other wildlife at the site include deer and bear.

Mailing Address
BLM - Spokane District Office
1103 North Fancher
Spokane, WA 99212

Phone Number   Fax Number
(509) 536-1200   (509) 536-1275

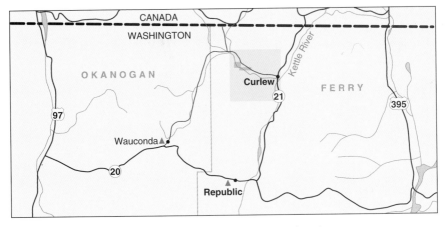

Directions
Take State Highway 21 to Curlew. Turn west on East Kettle River Road, and travel 6 miles to Little Vulcan Mountain.

Visitor Activities
Hunting, hiking, birdwatching, and wildlife viewing.

Permits, Fees, Limitations
None

Accessibility
None

Camping and Lodging
Primitive camping is permitted on the public land. Lodging is available in Curlew and Republic, 21 miles south of Curlew on State Highway 21.

Food and Supplies
There are no food or services available on-site. Supplies can be purchased in Curlew.

First Aid
The closest first aid is available in Curlew. The nearest hospital is located in Republic.

Little Vulcan Mountain provides winter range, escape cover, and lambing areas for a thriving local herd of bighorn sheep. *(Courtesy BLM)*

Additional Information
Because of the critical nature of the habitat, visitors should refrain from entering the area during the spring lambing period (April 1 through July 15). Temperatures range from 90°F and higher in the summer, to below 0°F in the winter. Please respect the rights of private property owners and other recreationists.

Sponsor

Activity Codes

Lower Deschutes River

Location
The Lower Deschutes Wild and Scenic River stretches 100 miles from the Pelton reregulating dam, downstream to the river's confluence with the Columbia River. Nearby towns include Maupin, Warm Springs, Madras, and The Dalles.

Description
This popular whitewater river offers day-long and overnight float trips, as well as blue-ribbon trout and steelhead fishing. About half of the river's length is on public land. The Warm Springs Indian Reservation stretches along the west bank for about 30 miles.

Mailing Address
BLM - Prineville District Office
3050 NE 3rd Street
P.O. Box 550
Prineville, OR 97754

Phone Number
(541) 416-6700

Fax Number
(541) 416-6798

Directions
River access is available in Maupin from U.S. Highway 197 (crosses the river at this point, and intersects the Deschutes River Access Road). Access is also available in The Dalles from U.S. Highway 30/Interstate 84 (crosses the river at Deschutes State Park).

Visitor Activities
Hiking, fishing, hunting, boating, rafting, wildlife viewing, birdwatching, scenic drives, plant viewing, and historical/archaeological attractions.

Permits, Fees, Limitations
Nightly fees are charged for campsites. Group sites are available at the campgrounds along the Deschutes River Access Road. Picnic areas are free-use. Drinking water is available only at the Beavertail and Macks Canyon campgrounds.

Accessibility
Most sites along the Deschutes River Access Road are wheelchair-accessible and have accessible vault toilets. The campgrounds have some sites that are wheelchair accessible.

Camping and Lodging
There are about 20 drive-in campgrounds and 5 picnic areas along the river. Camping is available year-round at all camp-

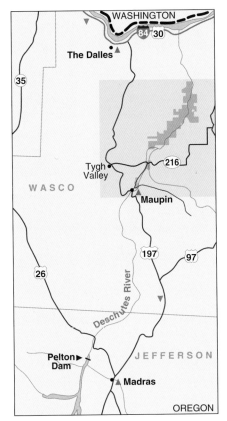

grounds. Facilities include picnic tables, vault toilets, garbage dumpsters, sink-water sumps, a boat ramp and an interpretive display. Wood and charcoal fires are not permitted from June 1 to October 15.

Food and Supplies

There are no food or supplies on-site. The nearest supplies are available in Maupin, 29 miles south on the Deschutes River Access Road.

First Aid

No first-aid facilities are available on-site; however, many BLM personnel have first-aid skills. Maupin has an ambulance service. The nearest hospitals are located in Madras and The Dalles.

Additional Information

Boaters are required to obtain a "boater pass" from the Oregon Department of Parks and Recreation in order to float the river (Tel.: (541) 687-5333). There is also a per-person daily charge. Check with the Oregon Department of Fish and Wildlife for current fishing regulations on the Deschutes River (Tel.: (541) 440-3353). The Deschutes River is managed jointly by BLM, the State of Oregon, and the Confederated Tribes of the Warm Springs Reservation.

Sponsoring Partner

Activity Codes

Macks Canyon Site

Location
29 miles north of Maupin, Oregon

Description
The Macks Canyon archaeological site is a large, prehistoric village locale overlooking the Deschutes River in north-central Oregon. The site is characterized by shallow, circular, semi-subterranean house depressions, surface artifacts, and riverine shell deposits. Limited excavations conducted in the late 1960's indicate that the site was the location of a winter village occupied by Sahaptin-speaking people of the Columbia Plateau. Although the main period of occupation appears to have occurred within the last 2,000 years, the site may have been occupied as early as 5,000 BC. A campground is situated at the end of the Access Road along the east bank of the Lower Deschutes River. The area is popular with boaters and fishermen. The route to Macks Canyon is also a National Back Country Byway.

Mailing Address
BLM - Prineville District Office
3050 NE 3rd Street
P.O. Box 550
Prineville, OR 97754

Phone Number
(541) 416-6700

Fax Number
(541) 416-6798

Directions
Macks Canyon can be accessed from U.S. Highway 197 in Maupin by following the Deschutes River Access Road along the east bank of the river. The Access Road can also be reached from State Highway 216 near Sherars Falls (where the highway crosses the Deschutes River).

Visitor Activities
Hiking, fishing, boating, rafting, wildlife viewing, birdwatching, plant viewing, and historical/archaeological attractions.

Permits, Fees, Limitations
A nightly fee is charged for camping.

Accessibility
The site features wheelchair-accessible restrooms and campsites.

Camping and Lodging
Eighteen campsites are available all year on a first-come, first-served basis. Facilities

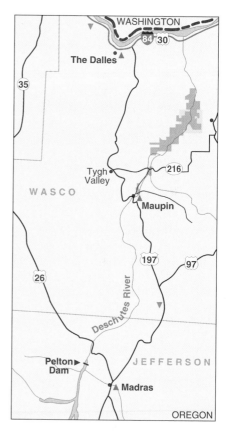

and services include drinking water, picnic tables, vault toilets, garbage dumpsters, sink-water sumps, a boat ramp, and an interpretive display. No wood or charcoal fires are permitted from June 1 to October 15.

Food and Supplies
There are no food or supplies on-site. Supplies are available in Maupin, 29 miles south on the Deschutes River Access Road.

First Aid
No first-aid facilities are available on-site; however, many BLM personnel have first-aid skills. Maupin has an ambulance service. The nearest hospitals are in Madras and The Dalles.

Additional Information
The Macks Canyon Site was placed on the National Register of Historic Places in 1975. An informational sign briefly relates the history of the area to visitors.

Sponsoring Partner

SAA
SOCIETY FOR AMERICAN ARCHAEOLOGY

Activity Codes

National Historic Oregon Trail Interpretive Center

Location
5 miles east of Baker City, Oregon

Description
Using life-size displays, and multi-media and living-history presentations, this Center dramatically tells the story of the hopes, dreams, joys, and heartaches of Oregon Trail-era pioneers. A visit to the Center provides a unique opportunity to walk through a wagon train, join a group of emigrants as they cross the frontier, and experience history come to life.

Mailing Address
BLM - Baker Resource Area
P.O. Box 987
Baker City, OR 97814

Phone Number
(541) 523-1843

Fax Number
(541) 523-1834

Directions
From Baker City, go east on State Highway 84 for 5 miles. Turn at the National Historic Oregon Trail Interpretive Center sign.

Visitor Activities
Interpretive exhibits and hiking.

Permits, Fees, Limitations
Fees vary during the year. Call the Center at (541) 523-1845 for information. The Center is open daily from 9 a.m. to 6 p.m., April through October, and 9 a.m. to 4 p.m., November through March, except Christmas Day and New Year's Day.

Accessibility
The Center is fully wheelchair-accessible.

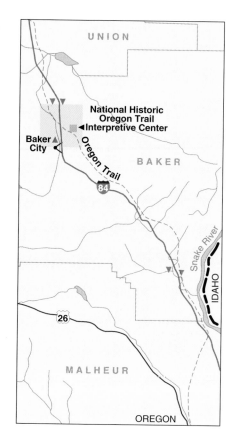

Baker
City

National Historic
Oregon Trail
◀Interpretive Center

UNION

BAKER

Oregon Trail

84

Snake River

IDAHO

26

MALHEUR

OREGON

Camping and Lodging

Motels are available in Baker City. There are also 2 recreational vehicle parks in Baker City. There are no full-service campgrounds within 15 miles of the site.

Food and Supplies

Vending machines are located on-site. A wide range of supplies and services is available in Baker City.

First Aid

First aid is available on-site at the Center. The nearest hospital is in Baker City.

Additional Information

None

Sponsor

Activity Codes

 - interpretive exhibits

New River Area of Critical Environmental Concern

Location
8 miles south of Bandon, Oregon

Description
The New River Area currently covers 1,168 acres designated as an Area of Critical Environmental Concern (ACEC), and is managed to maintain biodiversity and quality habitat for native communities of plants, birds, animals, and fish. Varied ecosystems include meadows, deflation plains, forests, estuaries, open sand dunes, brackish and fresh waters, and wetlands. The wide range of ecosystems in the ACEC is used by a variety of avian species, including the bald eagle, peregrine falcon, brown pelican, shorebirds, neotropical birds, and wintering waterfowl.

Mailing Address
BLM - Coos Bay District Office
1300 Airport Lane
North Bend, OR 97459

Phone Number
(541) 756-0100

Fax Number
(541) 756-9303

Directions
From Bandon, travel approximately 8 miles south on U.S. Highway 101, and make a left turn onto Croft Road. Follow Croft Road 1.5 miles to the administrative site at Storm Ranch.

Visitor Activities
Birdwatching, wildflower identification, hiking, and fishing.

Permits, Fees, Limitations
There are no fees at the site. There is no hunting permitted, with the exception of waterfowl hunting in designated areas. Also prohibited are overnight camping/parking, collection of any plants, animals or other special forest products, and collection of any cultural or historical items.

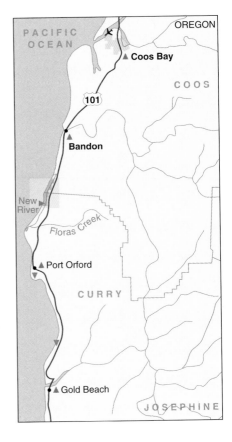

Accessibility

There is minimal wheelchair access; accessible nature experience is available only at Storm Ranch. The rest of the ACEC is not wheelchair-accessible. An accessible administrative building and restrooms are available at the Storm Ranch. No other sites have accessible facilities.

Camping and Lodging

Lodging is available in Bandon. Camping is available at Boice Cope County Park at Floras Lake, (approximately 9 miles south of New River on U.S. Highway 101), and at Bullards Beach State Park (2 miles north of Bandon on U.S. Highway 101, across the Coquille River).

Food and Supplies

There are no supplies or food available on-site. Groceries and restaurants are located in Bandon.

First Aid

There is no first aid on-site unless site hosts are on duty. A medical center is located in Bandon. The nearest hospital is in Coos Bay, approximately 35 miles north of the site on U.S. Highway 101.

Additional Information

The weather in this area is unpredictable. Expect cool and windy conditions year-round, and anticipate rain from mid-October to mid-May. Overall, the best time to visit is June through early October. To better enjoy your experience, you may wish to bring binoculars or a spotting scope, as well as plant, animal, and avian identification guides. Call the Oregon Department of Fish and Wildlife for details on hunting seasons (Tel.: (541) 440-3353). The area is open all year for day use only.

Sponsoring Partners

Activity Codes

- wildflower identification

North Umpqua Wild and Scenic River Corridor

Location
Begins 23 miles east of Roseburg, Oregon, and extends 34 miles to Soda Springs, Oregon

Description
Within this beautiful corridor, there are world-class fly-fishing opportunities, exhilarating whitewater for rafters and kayakers, picture postcard scenery, a recently renovated 31-unit BLM campground, and a hiking and biking trail, which follows the river for the entire length of the corridor and beyond. The western portion of the corridor (about 8 river miles, or 11 trail miles) is administered by BLM's Roseburg District; the remaining area is within the Umpqua National Forest, administered by the U.S. Forest Service (USFS). Beyond the corridor lies majestic Crater Lake, managed by the National Park Service.

Mailing Address
BLM - Roseburg District Office
777 Northwest Garden Valley Blvd.
Roseburg, OR 97470

Phone Number
(541) 440-4930

Fax Number
(541) 440-4948

Directions
From Roseburg, travel 23 miles east on State Highway 138, through Glide, to Swiftwater Recreation Site. Here, Rock Creek joins the North Umpqua River and the Wild and Scenic River begins.

Visitor Activities
Scenic drives, sightseeing, fishing, whitewater rafting, kayaking, hiking, mountain biking, wildlife viewing, birdwatching, photography, and picnicking.

Permits, Fees, Limitations
A nightly fee is charged for camping at Susan Creek Campground, 29.5 miles east of Roseburg on State Highway 138. Voluntary donations are accepted for showers. There is a 14-day limit. Dogs must be leashed and all pets must be controlled. Commercial river outfitters are required to have a special recreation use permit.

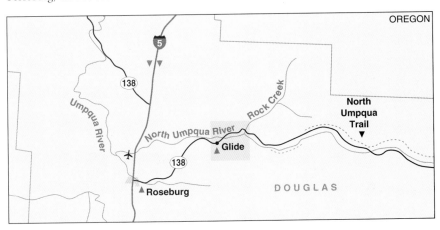

Accessibility

Many facilities and trails are wheelchair-accessible. The first 0.25 mile of the North Umpqua Trail is accessible all the way to Deadline Falls Watchable Wildlife Site, where anadromous fish may be viewed jumping falls during the summer months. Several day-use areas, trails, and campgrounds are also accessible. Contact BLM for a full list.

Camping and Lodging

The Susan Creek Campground is open from May through October. This 31-unit campground is set under the canopy of a mature forest along the banks of the North Umpqua Wild and Scenic River.

Additional campgrounds upriver are managed by USFS, including Bogus Creek, Canton Creek, Island, Apple Creek, Horseshoe Bend, Eagle Rock, and Boulder Flat Campgrounds. Cabins are also available for rent on private lands within the corridor.

Food and Supplies

Convenience stores are located along Highway 138, near or within the corridor. A broader selection of groceries and other items is available at stores in Glide, approximately 6 miles west of the beginning of the corridor on Highway 138. Full services and complete supplies are available in Roseburg.

First Aid

The Glide Rural Fire Department/Ambulance Service responds to 911 calls. Two hospitals are located in Roseburg. There are no first-aid stations within the corridor.

Additional Information

Barrier-free trails wind through the forest and provide views of migrating fish and soaring osprey searching for food. A 0.5-mile trail follows the river to a picnic area. From there, a 1-mile hike leads to Susan Creek Falls. Another 0.25 mile up the trail are the Susan Creek Indian Mounds, which are believed to be Native American vision sites. The difficulty of rapids of the North Umpqua River for rafts and kayaks is dependent primarily on water flow levels. Most rapids increase in difficulty with higher water; however, several rapids on the North Umpqua become more difficult as the water level decreases because of rock exposures and the currents around them. Non-government river publications are available at local bookstores.

Mountain biking should not be attempted during wet conditions because rutting can result in severe trail damage. Watch for and avoid poison oak, which can be identified by its cluster of three oak leaves and red berries. Do not drink from open water sources, such as springs, streams, and ponds.

The best time to observe fish jumping at Deadline Falls is between June and September. Within the corridor, only fly fishing is permitted. For more information about fishing regulations, licenses, etc., contact the Oregon Department of Fish and Wildlife at (541) 440-3353.

Sponsor

Activity Codes

 - mountain biking, photography, sightseeing, picnicking

Owyhee National Wild and Scenic River/Owyhee Canyonlands

Location
The main river access is in Rome, Oregon.

Description
This wild river corridor flows through southeastern Oregon from the Idaho/Oregon state line to Owyhee Reservoir. (It excludes the Rome Valley, which is a ranching and agricultural area.) Explore this National Wild and Scenic River by floating some of its 120 miles through rugged, spectacular canyonlands and ash flows. The river was included in the National Wild and Scenic River System in 1984 because of its outstanding scenic, recreational, geologic, wildlife, and cultural values.

Mailing Address
BLM - Vale District Office
100 Oregon Street
Vale, OR 97918.

Phone Number
(541) 473-3144

Fax Number
(541) 473-6213

Directions
From Jordan Valley, take U.S. Highway 95 southwest 32 miles. The Rome Launch Site is located just before Highway 95 crosses the river, on the south side of the road.

Visitor Activities
River floating, geologic sightseeing, wildlife viewing, and birdwatching.

Permits, Fees, Limitations
Trip registration by all river floaters is required. Also required are a firepan and a portable toilet system. Float group size is limited to 15 people above Rome, and 20 people below Rome.

Accessibility
None

Camping and Lodging
Camping is available at BLM's Rome Launch site, at the privately-owned Rome Recreational Vehicle Park and Cafe, and at BLM's Antelope Reservoir Campground

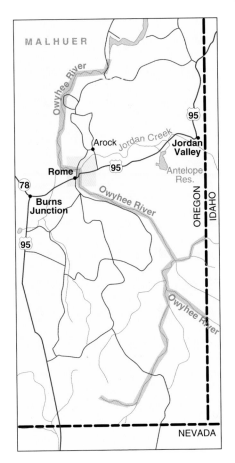

Food and Supplies
Gas, food, and limited supplies are available in Rome and Burns Junction. Jordan Valley has gas, food, groceries, and a small medical clinic.

First Aid
The nearest hospitals are in Ontario, Oregon, (approximately 120 miles north via Highway 95 to U.S. Highways 20/26) and Caldwell, Idaho (100 miles north via Highway 95 and Idaho State Highway 55).

Additional Information
Floating the river requires a high degree of technical skill. River flows are seasonal, with peak-flow times usually occurring in early spring. The river has several sections to float: the lower section is from Rome downstream; the middle section is from Three Forks to Rome; and the upper section is all of the river above Three Forks, including segments in Idaho and Nevada. Call BLM for details.

The river canyon is extremely remote and visitors should come well-prepared for emergencies. Historic Birch Creek Ranch, managed by BLM, is 50 miles downstream from Rome, and provides a unique view of early Basque ranch life. It is accessible by four-wheel-drive or high-clearance vehicle.

Sponsoring Partner

The Owyhee River's spectacular canyon cuts through ancient volcanic ash flows in southeastern Oregon. *(Courtesy BLM)*

(22 miles northeast of Rome on Highway 95). Lodging, including recreational vehicle facilities, are available in Rome, Jordan Valley, and Burns Junction (15 miles southwest of Rome on Highway 95).

Activity Codes

-geologic sightseeing

Pacific Crest National Scenic Trail - Siskiyou/Cascades Segment

Location
14 miles south of Ashland, Oregon

Description
BLM manages approximately 40 miles of this National Trail. The Siskiyou/Cascades segment of the Trail passes interesting attractions such as Pilot Rock, an ancient volcanic plug used as a landmark by pioneers, much like Devils Tower in Wyoming. The Trail passes Hobart Peak and Hobart Lake, and crosses through some old-growth forests.

Mailing Address
BLM - Medford District Office
3040 Biddle Road
Medford, OR 97504

Phone Number   Fax Number
(541) 770-2200   (541) 770-2400

Directions
The BLM-managed portion of the Trail begins approximately 5 miles west of the Siskiyou summit.

Trailhead locations are at Mt. Ashland Road, 5 miles west of Siskiyou summit, at Interstate 5, exit 6; Callahan's Restaurant, at Interstate 5, exit 6; and Greensprings summit, mile 17 of State Highway 66.

Visitor Activities
Hiking, hunting, rock-climbing, scenic drives, and geologic sightseeing.

Permits, Fees, Limitations
None

Accessibility
None

Camping and Lodging
Developed camp sites, including hot showers, are available at the BLM Hyatt Lake campground from May through September. Hyatt Lake campground is 18 miles east of Ashland on Highway 66.

Food and Supplies
Food and supplies are available at the Greensprings Inn, located on Highway 66, 16 miles east of Ashland.

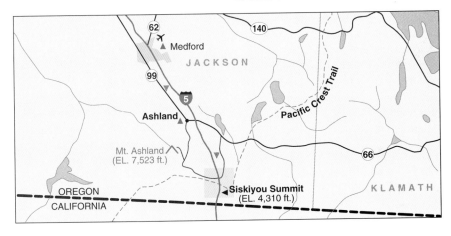

First Aid
The nearest hospital is located in Ashland, an average of 20 miles from the trail. No first aid is available on-site.

Additional Information
Sections of the Trail pass through private property, some of which has been recently logged. BLM has a 100-foot easement on each side of the trail through this private property. Please respect private property owners' rights.

Sponsoring Partner

American Hiking Society

Activity Codes

- geologic sightseeing, rock-climbing

Rogue River Ranch

Location
45 miles northwest of Galice, Oregon

Description
The Rogue River Ranch is on the National Register of Historic Places and is nestled in the heart of the Rogue River's wild section. Once a major Native American habitation site, the area has enjoyed a rich human history of over 9,000 years. After Europeans arrived, the site evolved into a small gold-mining community, with up to 100 residents trying to scratch a living from the gold-bearing gravel bars of the mighty Rogue River. The ranch structures remaining today represent the center of the old community, which had a trading post with upstairs lodging, a blacksmith's shop, and numerous outbuildings that filled the early residents' social and commercial needs.

Mailing Address
BLM - Medford District Office
3040 Biddle Road
Medford, OR 97504

Phone Number
(541) 770-2200

Fax Number
(541) 770-2400

Directions
From Galice, head north on Galice Road 8 miles to the Graves Creek Bridge. Cross the Graves Creek Bridge and bear left uphill on paved BLM Road #34-8-1 for 5 miles. At the junction with Whisky Creek Road (#33-8-26), bear right and continue on #34-8-1 (sign reads "Marial 28 Miles") for 3 miles. At the junction with BLM Road #33 8-13 (on the right), bear left and continue on #34-8-1 for 8 miles. At the junction with BLM Road #32-8-31, bear left and continue on a paved road for 5 miles to the junction with BLM Road #32-8-9.2. Bear left and continue on #32-8-31 for 1 mile to Anaktuvuk Saddle Junction. Turn left on BLM road #32-9-14.2 for 3 miles to Marble Gap Junction. Continue ahead (pavement will end) for another 3 miles to Fourmile Saddle Junction. Bear left and stay on #32-9-14.2 for another 9 miles to the Rogue River Ranch.

Nestled in the heart of the Rogue River's wild section, the Ranch is a welcome stopping place for day visitors. *(Photo by B. Brown, Medford District Office)*

[Note: these directions are identical to those for the Graves Creek to Marial Back Country Byway.]

Rand Visitor Center is 3 miles northwest of Galice, on the route to the Ranch. Information and brochures about the ranch can be obtained from the visitor center.

Visitor Activities

Sightseeing, boating, swimming, wildlife viewing, birdwatching, plant viewing, historical interpretation, scenic drives, and hiking.

Permits, Fees, Limitations

Permits are not required for vehicle access or foot travel at the site; however, boating on the nearby Rogue River does require a permit, obtainable at the Rand Visitor Center.

Accessibility

The main museum building is wheelchair-accessible. Other areas will require assisted access.

Camping and Lodging

There is a BLM primitive campground approximately 0.5 mile from the historic site. It is a no-charge site with a primitive toilet and no water. There is a lodge 1 mile west of the ranch. Two other lodges along the river can be reached by driving 2 miles west from the Ranch and then hiking 4 miles west on the Rogue River Trail. Call ahead for reservations with the lodges, as they are popular and in remote locations. Primitive camping is allowed on surrounding public lands. Other lodging and camping can be found off Interstate 5, 45 to 75 miles to the east, in Galice, Glendale, Merlin, and Grants Pass.

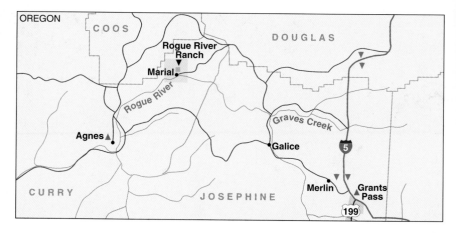

Food and Supplies

All food and supplies should be obtained prior to beginning the trip. There are no gas stations in the area. Supplies and gas are available in Galice, Glendale, Merlin, and Grants Pass.

First Aid

This is a remote site with no phone service or medical facilities. During the peak-use season of May through September, caretakers are on duty at the site and can provide first-aid supplies and radio communication. The 2 nearest hospitals are in Grants Pass; both are located in the northwest part of town.

Additional Information

This site is extremely remote, with no visitor services. All food and supplies should be obtained prior to beginning the trip. There are no gas stations in the area. Trav-

elers should expect to come well-prepared for a long trip on mostly one-lane, winding, mountain dirt roads. Roads are maintained and are passable by passenger vehicles. Access to the area is often impossible during the winter months because of snow accumulations. The best time of the year to visit the site is from May through September.

Sponsoring Partners

Activity Codes

 – swimming, sightseeing, historical interpretation

Rough and Ready Flat Area of Critical Environmental Concern

Location
6 miles south of Cave Junction, Oregon

Description
This is a unique botanical area along Rough and Ready Creek. It harbors a multitude of rare or special-status plants endemic to the serpentine soils of the Siskiyou Mountains. The area has been a popular wildflower-watching spot for decades, and plant species are actively evolving here. The impetus to protect the area was provided by the Illinois Valley Garden Club in 1937.

Mailing Address
BLM - Medford District Office
3040 Biddle Road
Medford, OR 97504

Phone Number
(541) 770-2200

Fax Number
(541) 770-2400

Directions
From Cave Junction, travel 4.5 miles south on U.S. Highway 199. Park at the turnout on the right, just before the highway crosses Rough and Ready Creek. A botanical wayside sign designates the area.

Visitor Activities
Wildflower viewing, hiking, biking, nature study, and environmental educational.

Permits, Fees, Limitations
No fees. No off-highway vehicle use is allowed.

Accessibility
There are currently no wheelchair-accessible facilities, but a road system through flat terrain has been proposed for use as an accessible interpretive trail.

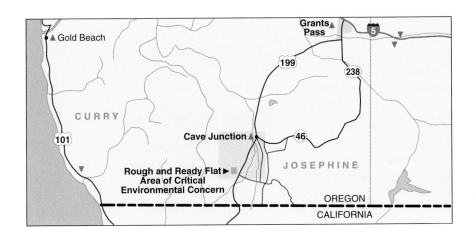

Camping and Lodging

Lodging is available in Cave Junction. Several recreational vehicle campgrounds are located near Cave Junction, and two U.S. Forest Service campgrounds are located on State Highway 46 (Caves Highway) between Cave Junction and the Oregon Caves National Monument. Campgrounds are only open in the summer months.

Food and Supplies

Food and supplies are available in Cave Junction.

First Aid

There is no first aid available on-site. A clinic is located in Cave Junction. The closest hospital is in Grants Pass, approximately 30 miles north on U.S. Highway 199.

Additional Information

No facilities are available on-site. An interagency visitor center is located in Cave Junction; this is the best source for information on the area.

Sponsoring Partner

Activity Codes

 - biking, nature study, environmental educations, wildflower viewing

Row River Trail

Location

3 miles east of Cottage Grove, Oregon

Description

This 14-mile trail follows the route of the now abandoned Oregon Pacific & Eastern Railroad line, along the scenic shore of the Row River and Dorena Reservoir. Several quaint, covered bridges are located nearby, as is the historic Bohemia Mining area.

Mailing Address

BLM - Eugene District Office
2890 Chad Drive
Eugene, OR 97408

Phone Number	Fax Number
(541) 683-6600	(541) 638-6981

Directions

From Interstate 5, take the Cottage Grove exit, and turn east onto Row River Road. Travel for 3.5 miles. The trail intersects the road at the Currin Covered Bridge, and it parallels the road along Dorena Reservoir.

Visitor Activities

Picnicking, hiking, biking, horseback riding, wildlife viewing, and photography.

Permits, Fees, Limitations

None

Accessibility

When fully developed, the trail will be paved to allow wheelchair access.

Camping and Lodging

No camping is allowed on the trail. Designated campgrounds are located nearby at Schwarz Park, Baker Bay, and Sharps Creek.

Food and Supplies

No food or water is available on the trail. Several general stores are located in Cottage Grove, Dorena (across Row River Road from the trail), and Culp Creek (0.25 mile east on Row River Road).

First Aid

No first aid is available along the trail. BLM Rangers or Lane County Sheriff's Deputies may be on patrol in the area to provide assistance. The nearest hospital is located in Cottage Grove.

Additional Information

The trail is located in a forest environment. Visitors can expect warm, dry conditions in the summer, and cool, damp conditions in the spring, fall, and winter. Travel to the site is on 2-lane, rural roads, which often have heavy truck traffic. Parking and restroom facilities are located at 2- to 3-mile intervals, adjacent to the trail. When finally developed, the trail will be partially paved and provide trailhead and interpretive facilities.

Sponsor

Activity Codes

 - biking, horseback riding, photography, picnicking

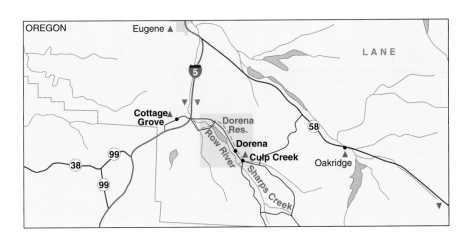

Shotgun Creek Recreation Site

Location
3 miles northeast of Marcola, Oregon

Description
This day-use site is in the foothills of the Cascade Mountains. Twenty acres are developed, and 240 acres retain the natural characteristics typical of the region's temperate coniferous rainforest. Historical highlights of the surrounding area include evidence of the early native Kalapuya people, traces of pioneer homesteaders, and reminders of the colorful days of logging and timber booms.

Mailing Address
BLM - Eugene District Office
2890 Chad Drive
Eugene, OR 97408

Phone Number	Fax Number
(541) 683-6600	(541) 683-6981

Directions
From Interstate 105 in Springfield, take the 42nd Street exit, and turn onto Marcola Road heading north. Travel 3 miles past the town of Marcola, and turn left onto Shotgun Creek Road. Proceed about 1.5 miles to the site.

Visitor Activities
Picnicking, hiking, swimming, ballsports, playground activities, wildlife viewing, and photography.

Permits, Fees, Limitations
No fees, except for rental of group shelters.

Accessibility
All the high-use areas of the site are wheelchair accessible. Trails within developed areas are paved, and some playground equipment is designed for people with special needs.

Camping and Lodging
No camping is allowed on-site, nor are any developed camp sites located nearby. Lodging is available in Springfield, 15 miles away on the Marcola Road.

Food and Supplies
No food is available on-site. The nearest store is located in Marcola.

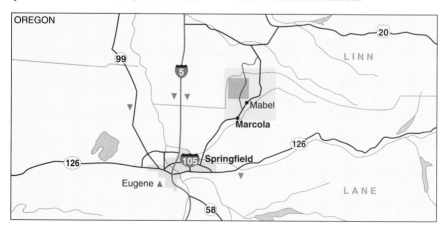

First Aid
Basic first aid is available on-site from BLM employees. First-aid supplies and radio/telephone units are available for emergencies. The nearest hospital is located in Springfield.

Additional Information
The Shotgun Creek Recreation Site is located in a forested environment. Visitors can expect warm, dry conditions in summer and cool, damp conditions in spring, fall and winter. Travel to the site is on 2-lane, rural roads, which often have heavy truck traffic. The 2 large group shelters, with amenities, are ideal for reunions, office parties, school outings and weddings.

Sponsor

Activity Codes

- swimming, photography, ballsports, playground activities

Steens Mountain, East Rim Overlook

Location
25 miles east of Frenchglen, Oregon

Description
Rising 9,700 feet above sea level, Steens Mountain is the highest peak in the northern Great Basin desert. The East Rim Overlook provides a stunning view of this rugged country. The 66-mile Steens Mountain Loop Road offers visitors a chance to see bighorn sheep, as well as prairie falcons, American Kestrels, and other birds of prey.

Mailing Address
BLM - Burns District Office
HC-74-12533, HWY 20 West
Burns, OR 97738

Phone Number	Fax Number
(541) 573-4400	(541) 573-4411

Directions
From Burns, drive south 60 miles on State Highway 205 to Frenchglen. From there, follow signs to Steens Mountain Loop Road and turn left. The East Rim Overlook is at the 25-mile mark.

Visitor Activities
Scenic drives, nature study, sightseeing, hiking, wildlife viewing, and photography.

Permits, Fees, Limitations
None

Accessibility
None

Camping and Lodging
BLM camp sites are available at Jackman Park, Fish Lake, and Page Springs, which are located along the Steens Mountain

Loop Road (north segment), 5 miles, 7 miles, and 22 miles west of the East Rim Viewpoint, respectively. Another BLM campground (South Steens) is located 9 miles southwest of the East Rim viewpoint along the Steens Mountain Loop Road (south segment).

Food and Supplies
Frenchglen and Burns have the closest food and supplies.

First Aid
The nearest hospital is in Burns. No closer first aid is available.

Big Indian Gorge is one of several spectacular glacial canyons at Steens Mountain. *(Photo by Mark Armstrong, Burns District Office)*

Additional Information
Steens Mountain Loop Road is closed during the winter and usually does not re-open until June or July.

Sponsoring Partner

WILD SHEEP

Activity Codes

- photography, nature study, sightseeing

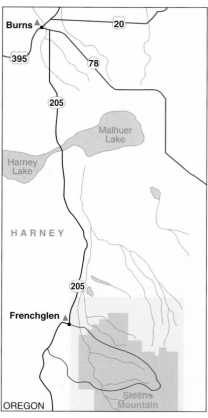

Table Rock Wilderness

Location
19 miles southeast of Molalla, Oregon

Description
Table Rock Wilderness was designated a part of the National Wilderness System in 1984. It is the last large area—6,028 acres—of pristine forest land in the Molalla River drainage. Its steep, rugged terrain, towering basalt cliffs, spectacular vistas, brilliant wildflowers, diverse wildlife, and unique history combine to create a distinctive wilderness experience.

Mailing Address
BLM - Salem District Office
1717 Fabry Road SE
Salem, OR 97306

Phone Number
(503) 375-5646

Fax Number
(503) 375-5622

Directions
From Interstate 5, take the Woodburn exit. Travel east on State Highway 211 to Molalla. East of Molalla, follow signs to Feyer Park. Turn right on South Dickie Prairie Road and travel about 6 miles south to the bridge at Glen Avonn, where the name of the road changes to South Molalla Road. Cross the bridge, and travel south another 12 miles on South Molalla Road to the junction of Middle Fork and Copper Creeks Roads. A right turn leads to the Old Bridge Trailhead, immediately across the bridge. A left turn leads to the Table Rock Trailhead.

Visitor Activities
Hiking, photography, and wildlife viewing.

Permits, Fees, Limitations
No motorized vehicles or bicycles are permitted.

Accessibility
None

Camping and Lodging
Along the Molalla River, there are several primitive camping sites with no facilities. In Molalla, the Feyer Park Campground (with full facilities) and a motel are available.

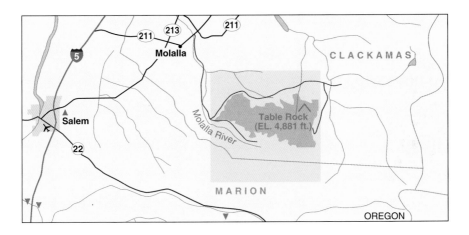

Food and Supplies
Grocery and sporting goods stores are located in Molalla.

First Aid
The nearest medical clinic is in Molalla.

Additional Information
Contact BLM for a brochure, which includes a map.

Sponsoring Partner

AMERICA
OUTDOORS

Activity Codes
 - photography

Turn Point Island

Location
The western tip of Stuart Island, San Juan Islands, Washington

Description
The Turn Point location combines areas of grassy bluffs and coastal forest with the historical buildings of the Turn Point Lighthouse Station. While the buildings are closed to the public at this time, Turn Point remains a beautiful spot in which to picnic, whale-watch, and explore the past.

Mailing Address
BLM - Wenatchee Resource Area
915 Walla Walla
Wenatchee, WA 98801

Phone Number   Fax Number
(509) 665-2100   (509) 665-2121

Directions
Stuart Island lies in the northwestern corner of the San Juan Islands, and is without commercial ferry service. Access is by pri-

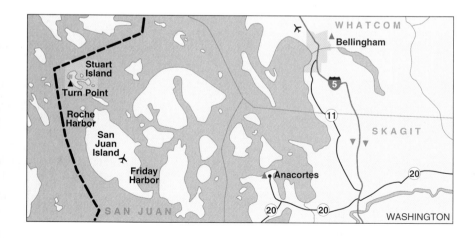

vate boat or airplane. From Prevost Harbor on the southwestern end of Stuart Island, follow the gravel road west 0.75 mile to its end at Turn Point Island.

Visitor Activities
Hiking, picnicking, historical education, and plant viewing.

Permits, Fees, Limitations
None. Site use is limited by the lack of public transportation to Stuart Island.

Accessibility
A wheelchair-accessible outhouse is located on site.

Camping and Lodging
Turn Point is a day-use site only. Public camping facilities are available at Reid Harbor State Park on the west end of Stuart Island.

Food and Supplies
No supplies are available on-site. Supplies may be purchased at Roche Harbor and Friday Harbor on San Juan Island.

First Aid
First aid is not available on-site. There is a hospital located at Friday Harbor on San Juan Island.

Additional Information
The best time to visit Turn Point is in the summer. Visitors should bring water, food, hiking shoes, binoculars, and a jacket to guard against changing weather. Weather ranges from warm, dry summers to cold, wet, stormy winters. At times, storms might prevent entry onto, or exit from, the island. The lighthouse facility is set high on a bluff; avoid getting too close to hazardous cliffs.

Sponsoring Partner

Activity Codes

 - picnicking, historical education

West Eugene Wetlands

Location
15 miles west of Eugene, Oregon

Description
The West Eugene Wetlands is a 600-acre cooperative venture between the BLM's Eugene District, the City of Eugene, and The Nature Conservancy to protect and restore wetland ecosystems in the southern Willamette Valley of Oregon. The Wetlands, with a projected final acquisition area of 1,500 acres, have protected many

important endangered-species habitats. The project serves an urban area of more than 200,000 people. While providing visitors scenic views of native wetland plants, birds and animals, the West Eugene Wetlands has been recognized as a national model for wetlands planning.

Mailing Address
BLM - Eugene District Office
2890 Chad Drive
Eugene, OR 97408

Phone Number   Fax Number
(541) 683-6600   (541) 683-6981

Directions
From Eugene, travel 5 miles west on State
Highway 126.

Visitor Activities
Photography, hiking, birdwatching, and
guided tours.

Permits, Fees, Limitations
None

Accessibility
Two viewing platforms are wheelchair-accessible.

Camping and Lodging
There is no overnight camping on-site.
Campgrounds are located at Richardson
Park on Fern Ridge Reservoir (5 miles
west on State Highway 126, then 5 miles

north on Territorial Road). Motel accommodations are available 5 miles east on
West 11th Avenue in Eugene.

Food and Supplies
Food and supplies are available in Eugene.

First Aid
The nearest hospitals and clinics are located in Eugene.

Additional Information
Contact BLM about guided tours.

Sponsoring Partner

Activity Codes

  – photography,
guided tours

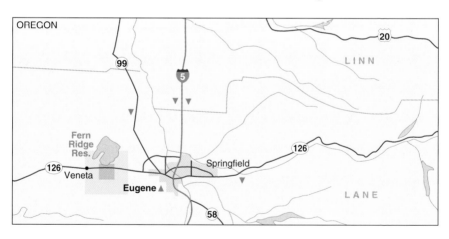

Yakima River Canyon

Location
5 miles south of Ellensburg, Washington

Description
The Yakima River flows through 25 scenic miles of massive basalt cliffs and rolling desert hills. The river is part of a thriving sagebrush-steppe ecosystem, with birds of prey and bighorn sheep sharing the high cliffs, and high-quality "catch and release" trout fishing in the river itself. The Canyon is also popular for many other recreational activities.

Mailing Address
BLM - Wenatchee Resource Area
915 Walla Walla
Wenatchee, WA 98801

Phone Number
(509) 665-2100

Fax Number
(509) 665-2121

Directions
From Ellensburg, travel south 5 miles on State Highway 821 to the entrance of the Yakima River Canyon. Squaw Creek Recreation Site is located 12 miles beyond that point, and Roza Recreation Site is located 5 miles further still.

Visitor Activities
"Catch & release fishing," hunting (bird and big game), river floating, picnicking, hiking, plant and wildlife viewing, boating, and swimming.

Permits, Fees, Limitations
Day-use fees are charged.

Accessibility
There are wheelchair-accessible outhouses at Roza and Squaw Creek. All 3 recreation sites (Squaw Creek, Roza and

The Yakima River winds through basalt cliffs and desert hills, part of a unique ecosystem that attracts an unusual diversity of animal life. *(Courtesy BLM)*

Umtanum) are flat, and Squaw Creek has asphalt-hardened, wheelchair-accessible camping spots.

Camping and Lodging

Squaw Creek and Roza permit camping in designated sites. The camping stay limit is 7 days total at BLM areas within the Canyon. Other nearby lodging includes a private campground in the Canyon, and other camping facilities and motels in Ellensburg, Yakima and Selah (10 miles south of Roza on State Highway 821).

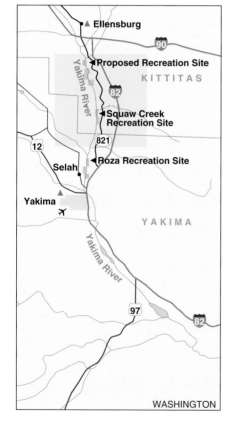

Food and Supplies

No food or supplies are available on-site. Purchase these in Ellensburg or Selah, at either end of the Canyon.

First Aid

BLM recreation technicians have general first-aid qualifications and cell phones for emergencies. Hospital and first-aid facilities are located in Ellensburg and Yakima (approximately 14 miles south of the Roza Recreation Site). Emergency medical services serve the Yakima River Canyon.

Additional Information

Spring, fall, and winter are good times to view wildlife and enjoy the solitude of the Canyon, while summer brings large crowds to enjoy water activities. Some motorized boat activities are permitted in the Roza Dam pool, which extends for 1.5 miles north to the Roza Recreation Site. Bring water, food, binoculars, and appropriate clothing. Temperatures range from 100°F and higher in the summer, to below 0°F in the winter. Please respect the rights of private property owners and other recreationists.

Sponsor

Activity Codes

- swimming, picnicking

Yaquina Head
Outstanding Natural Area

Location
3 miles north of Newport, Oregon

Description
Jutting into the Pacific Ocean, this harsh, unforgiving environment hosts many forms of life. Harbor seals and whales are visible offshore year-round. In spring and summer, thousands of seabirds flock to the near-shore islands to breed and raise their young. At low tide, you can observe pools filled with intertidal life. Oregon's tallest and second-oldest lighthouse has illuminated this promontory since 1873. Archaeologists have also discovered evidence of Native American visits to the site. Yaquina Head is managed by BLM to protect its scenic, scientific, educational and recreational values.

Mailing Address
BLM - Yaquina Head
Outstanding Natural Area
P.O. Box 936
Newport, OR 97365

Phone Number   Fax Number
(541) 574-3100   (541) 574-3141

Directions
From Newport, drive north on U.S. Highway 101 for 3 miles. Look for the Yaquina Head sign. Turn left on Lighthouse Drive.

Visitor Activities
Tidepool study, wildlife viewing, and summer lighthouse tours.

Permits, Fees, Limitations
Fees vary. Please call BLM for information.

Accessibility
There are wheelchair-accessible trails through tidepools, around the outside of the lighthouse, and at wildlife-viewing decks.

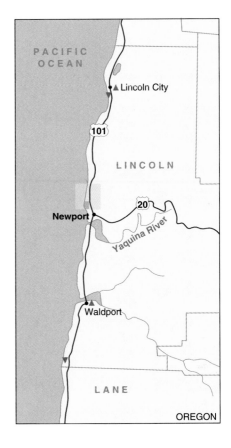

Camping and Lodging

Newport has several hotels and motels, and the central Oregon coast includes state parks with camping facilities.

Food and Supplies

Newport has several large grocery stores and a department store.

First Aid

The nearest hospital is located in Newport.

Additional Information

This day-use area is open daily from dawn to dusk. Remember to bring a telephoto lens to take close-up pictures of whales, seals and birds from one of the nation's closest mainland viewpoints of seabird nesting colonies. Come explore the world's first artificially-constructed, wheelchair accessible tidepools, which were once an old quarry site. Round out the experience with a visit to the lighthouse interpretive center.

Sponsoring Partners

Activity Codes

 - tidepool study, lighthouse tours

Utah's rugged Gray Canyon, named for the color of its walls, was once called "Coal Canyon" and then "Lignite Canyon" by early visitors. *(Photo by Kelly Rigby, Utah State Office)*

Utah

Utah's public lands contain some of the most spectacular scenery in the world, from the snow capped peaks of remote mountain ranges to the colorful red-rock canyons of the Colorado Plateau. There are over 22 million acres of public lands in Utah, representing about 42 percent of the state. These lands are located mostly in western and southeastern Utah. The terrain is varied, ranging from rolling uplands in the Uintah Basin to sprawling lowlands in the Mojave Desert.

Utah's public lands offer unparalleled recreational opportunities, including mountain biking, desert backpacking, and whitewater rafting on the Green, San Juan, and Colorado Rivers. Visitors can also explore a number of significant archaeological and historical sites in Utah, including those along a 165-mile segment of the Pony Express Trail. The John Jarvie Historic Site provides visitors with a flavor of the Wild West, having hidden such famous outlaws as Butch Cassidy and the Sundance Kid. Aspiring paleontologists may find their special experience at the Cleveland-Lloyd Dinosaur Quarry, an active operation from which 18,000 bones have been excavated so far.

The nation's newest national monument is located on public lands in Utah. Located in the stunningly beautiful red-rock country of south central Utah, the Grand Staircase-Escalante National Monument is a dramatic, multi-hued landscape that encompasses 1.7 million acres. Rich in natural and human history, the area boasts a unique combination of archaeological, historical, paleontological, geological, and biological resources. One of the last places to be mapped, this national monument in south central Utah is definitely worth the trip for those with a sense of adventure and a little time to explore.

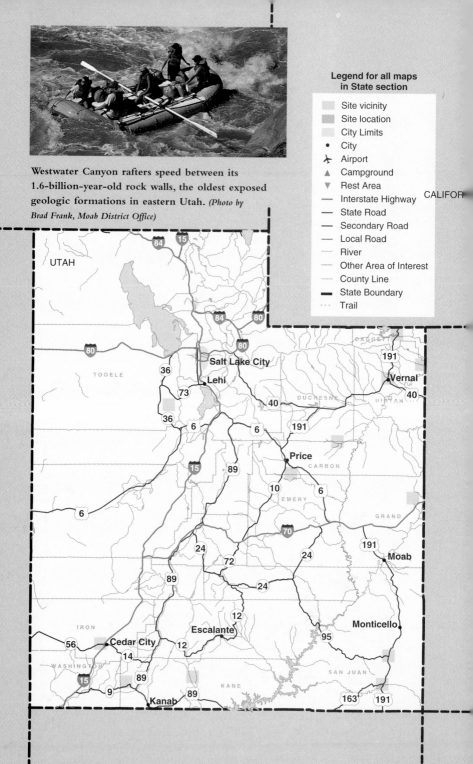

Westwater Canyon rafters speed between its
1.6-billion-year-old rock walls, the oldest exposed
geologic formations in eastern Utah. *(Photo by
Brad Frank, Moab District Office)*

CALIFOR

UTAH

TOOELE

Salt Lake City
Lehi
36
73
36
6
6
6
6

DUCHESNE
191
Vernal
40
40
UINTAH

191
Price
CARBON
10
6
EMERY
GRAND

70
24
24
191
Moab
72
89
24

IRON
12
Escalante
95
Monticello
56
Cedar City
12
14
89
KANE
SAN JUAN
9
15
89
89
Kanab
163
191

WASHINGTON

Book Cliffs Area

Location
50 miles south of Vernal, Utah

Description
This area contains 455,000 acres of diverse ecosystems in a very remote setting, and maintains a "frontier mystique." There is an abundance of wildlife species for viewing, including deer, elk, black bear, blue and sage grouse, numerous hawks, antelope, mountain lion, small mammals, birds, reptiles, and amphibians. The Book Cliffs Area begins in the northern desert shrub zone at about 5,500 feet in elevation and rises southward to about 8,500 feet in the aspen and fir zones. The vista is broken by deep valleys, many containing perennial streams.

Mailing Address
BLM – Vernal District Office
170 South 500 East
Vernal, UT 84078

Phone Number
(801) 781-4400

Fax Number
(801) 781-4410

Directions
Stop at the Vernal District office to obtain a map, directions, and information on road conditions. Many gravel roads are unmarked.

Visitor Activities
Wildlife viewing, photography, hiking, birdwatching, fishing, hunting, plant viewing, scenic driving, and horse packing.

Visitors can experience a "frontier mystique" at the remote Book Cliffs Area, whose vistas present a spectrum of landscapes, from desert to lush hills, deep valleys to clifftop overlooks. *(Photo by Jerry Sintz, Utah State Office)*

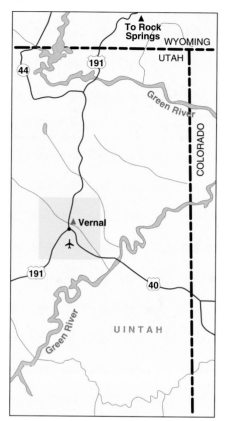

Permits, Fees, Limitations

There are no fees or permits required. Some areas are closed to the public, and the entire area is closed in winter because of heavy snow. Check with the Utah Division of Wildlife Resources for information on hunting and fishing license requirements. The Utah Division of Wildlife Resources may be contacted at 152 East 100 North, Vernal, Utah 84078, phone (801) 789-3103.

Camping and Lodging

There are no developed facilities in the area. Only primitive camping is available in the spring, summer, and fall. Commercial camping and motel accommodations are available Roosevelt and Vernal.

Food and Supplies

Gas, food and supplies are available in Vernal, Utah, and Green River, Wyoming.

First Aid

There is no first aid on-site. The nearest hospitals are in Vernal, Utah, and Grand Junction, Colorado.

Additional Information

This is a very remote area accessed by gravel and dirt roads. Some roads are impassable when wet. This is rugged country: a high-clearance or four-wheel-drive vehicle is recommended. Carry extra water and food, and make sure your vehicle has a full tank of gas.

Sponsoring Partner

Activity Codes

 - photography

Cleveland-Lloyd Dinosaur Quarry

Location
30 miles south of Price, Utah

Description
The Cleveland-Lloyd Dinosaur Quarry was initially excavated by scientists in 1931, following reports by local cowboys and sheepherders, who found fossil bones in the area. Since that date, at least 18,000 fossil bones have been taken from the quarry, representing at least 70 different animals. Over 60 cast and original skeletons have been assembled from these bones and are on display across the United States and around the world. The fossil dinosaurs excavated from the quarry are from the Jurassic Morrison Formation, and allosaurus skeletons have been found in particular abundance. The quarry is open seasonally for visitation, with exhibit buildings, interpretive displays, picnic facilities, and a self-guided nature trail. The Cleveland-Lloyd Dinosaur Quarry is a National Natural Landmark.

Mailing Address
BLM - Price Field Office
P.O. Box 7004
125 South 600 West
Price, UT 84501

Phone Number   Fax Number
(801) 636-3600   (801) 636-3657

Directions
From Price, drive south about 30 miles on State Highway 10. Turn left onto State Highway 155, and follow the signs to Elmo, Utah. Just past Elmo, turn right onto a graded dirt road and follow the signs 12 miles through the Desert Lake Waterfowl Reserve and on to the Cleveland-Lloyd Dinosaur Quarry. You may wish to stop at the BLM office in Price to pick up a map beforehand. The road to the quarry is well-signed, but there are a number of turns.

Visitor Activities
Fossil viewing, interpretive exhibits, wildlife viewing, and hiking.

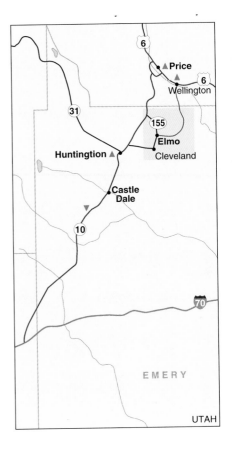

Permits, Fees, Limitations

There are no fees for a visit to the Cleveland-Lloyd Dinosaur Quarry, but donations are accepted.

Accessibility

The restrooms at the quarry are not wheelchair-accessible. Because the path to the exhibit buildings may be difficult for disabled persons to traverse, vehicles are allowed down the path to provide access for these visitors. The buildings are wheelchair-accessible.

Camping and Lodging

There are no BLM-operated camping facilities near the Cleveland-Lloyd Dinosaur Quarry, although most of the surrounding public lands are open to camping. The closest state campground is in Huntington, located near Highway 10 south of Price. Motel accommodations are available in Price, Huntington, and Castle Dale. Castle Dale is on State Highway 10, 32 miles south of Price.

Food and Supplies

Food, gas, and supplies are available in Price, Huntington, and Castle Dale.

First Aid

Medical services are available in Price and in Castle Dale. The nearest hospital is in Price.

This exhibit building maintains thousands of prehistoric animal bones, from which more than 60 cast and original skeletons have been assembled for display across the United States. *(Photo by Jerry Sintz, Utah State Office)*

Additional Information

Hours may vary, and a phone call to BLM in advance of your trip is recommended. The quarry is usually open from 9 a.m. to 5 p.m. weekends from Easter through Memorial Day. From Memorial Day through Labor Day, the quarry is open 7 days a week from 9 a.m. to 5 p.m. The quarry is closed at all other times.

There are a visitor center, bathroom facilities, and an area for picnicking near the parking lot. A dirt trail leads to the quarry and exhibit buildings. There is a self-guided Rock Walk Nature Trail.

The Cleveland-Lloyd Dinosaur Quarry, although staffed in season, is still relatively remote. Travelers should be prepared with adequate gas, food, and water for the trip. Graded dirt roads to the quarry are maintained, but may become unstable during wet weather. Winter conditions are often very cold, and heavy snowstorms may occur.

The Prehistoric Museum of the College of Eastern Utah currently staffs and operates the quarry under a cooperative agreement with BLM. Located at 155 East Main Street, Price, Utah 84501, the Prehistoric Museum offers additional exhibits and displays, including a wall-mounted dinosaur skeleton. Call the museum at (801) 637-5060 for further information.

Sponsor

Activity Codes

 - fossil viewing, interpretive exhibits

Desolation and Gray Canyons

Location
42 miles south of Myton, Utah

Description
The 84 miles of the Green River that run through Desolation and Gray Canyons provide a premiere wilderness river trip through Utah's deepest canyons. The river traveler encounters approximately 60 Class II and III rapids. In addition to river-running, there are wonderful opportunities for camping, archaeologic and geologic interpretation, wildlife watching, hiking, and exploring.

Mailing Address
BLM - Price Resource Area
125 South 600 West
Price, UT 84501

Phone Number
(801) 636-3622

Fax Number
(801) 636-3657

Directions
To get to Sand Wash (the put-in point), travel west from Myton 1 mile on U.S. Highway 40. Turn south onto 5550 West Street or Wells Draw Road, and follow signs approximately 40 miles to Sand Wash. You can also fly from the town of Green River to an airstrip on a mesa top above Sand Wash.

Visitor Activities
Whitewater rafting, kayaking, hiking, swimming, camping, wildlife viewing, archaeological and historical site viewing, fishing, and hunting.

A visitor contemplates a deceptively placid stretch of the Green River, whose 84 miles in Desolation and Gray Canyons boast 60 Class II and III rapids. *(Photo by Kelly Rigby, Utah State Office)*

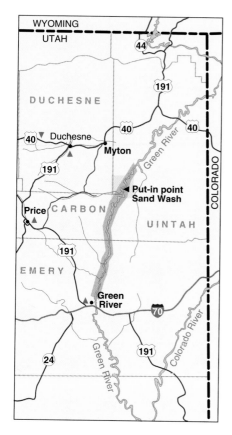

Camping and Lodging

No camping is allowed within 0.5 mile of the mouth of Rock Creek. There are 90 campsites along the river corridor; occupation is on a first-come, first-served basis. No visitor is obligated to share a campsite with other groups; however, in an emergency, this is considered common courtesy. All sites are undeveloped. Lodging is available in Price, Utah, and Green River, Utah.

Accessibility

There are no wheelchair-accessible sites along the river corridor. The Swasey Take-out has an accessible campsite and toilet facilities. The Sand Wash Contact Station has an accessible screen house and toilet facilities. Go across the river (Green River) and go past Powell Museum to Hastings Road. Turn left and Swasey Take-out is about 8 miles from the turn. To get to Sand Wash take Highway 40, mile marker 105, and street sign 5550 West. Four miles after the pavement ends, take the only right, and the rest is 30 miles of dirt road.

Food and Supplies

Shuttles, outfitters, gasoline, equipment rentals, and food are available in Price, Utah, and Green River, Utah.

First Aid

Boaters are required to carry a major first-aid kit on all trips. No first aid is available on-site. The nearest hospital is in Price, Utah.

Additional Information

The area is remote and not serviced by roads or communication facilities. Therefore, visitors are dependent upon self-rescue in emergencies. Class III boating skills are recommended. Open canoes are not advised. The character of individual rapids

Permits, Fees, Limitations

Advance reservations and BLM permits to conduct private river trips are limited and required year-round. The permit system is run by lottery system from April 1 to September 30; otherwise, it is first-come, first-served by written application to BLM. Applications for the lottery are accepted from January 1 to January 31. Permit and equipment checks are conducted by the ranger at the boat ramp prior to your scheduled launch. Trips are limited to 1 trip per person per year. Check with the Utah Division of Wildlife Resources for hunting and fishing license requirements (Tel.: (801) 636-0260).

fluctuates greatly with changing river flows; flash floods from side canyons can create new rapids or change existing ones. Scouting those rapids that are not clearly visible from upstream is recommended.

There are several boat take-out points. The best is just below Swasey Rapid at Milepost 12. Should you choose to extend your trip past this point, be aware that there is a low-head dam that blocks the river 3 miles below Swasey Rapid. This dam forms a Class IV drop, which must be scouted. The lands below this point are all private, and permission of the landowners should be obtained in advance of entering this section of the canyon.

The water in the canyon has not been tested and should be treated before drinking. Better yet, carry in your own water.

Sponsoring Partner

Activity Codes

-kayaking, swimming

Grand Staircase-Escalante National Monument

Location
South-central Utah

Description
On September 18, 1996, President Clinton signed a proclamation creating the Grand Staircase-Escalante National Monument on the Colorado Plateau, in the pristine and spectacular Canyonlands of south-central Utah, west of the Colorado River.

The Grand Staircase-Escalante National Monument's 1.7 million acres of vast and austere landscape embraces a spectacular array of scientific and historic resources. This high, rugged, and remote region, where bold plateaus and multi-hued cliffs run for distances that defy human perspective, was the last place in the continental United States to be mapped. Even today, this unspoiled natural area remains a frontier, a quality that greatly enhances the Monument's value.

Mailing Address
BLM – Grand Staircase-Escalante National Monument, Planning Team
337 South Main, Suite 10
Cedar City, UT 84720

Phone Number
(801) 865-5100

Fax Number
(801) 865-5170

Directions
Located in south-central Utah, the Monument is near the towns of Kanab, Boulder, Tropic, and Escalante. Scenic Highway 12 runs along the northern portion of the Monument, and State Highway 89 is located on the southern boundary. Lake Powell lies directly east of the Monument.

Visitor Activities
Hiking, scenic drives, horseback riding, wildlife viewing, birdwatching, photography, plant viewing, mountain biking, and popular-movie location.

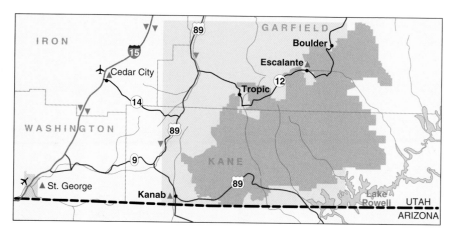

Permits/Fees Limitations

No fees at present. A 3-year planning effort will be completed in October 1999; fees and permits for various uses may be required in the future. Permits are required for commercial users such as guides, outfitters and large group events. Each has an entrance fee, and no-cost permits are required for back-country overnight use.

The Grand Staircase-Escalante National Monument contains some of the most remote country in the nation. Visitors are cautioned to be very careful, whether riding in a vehicle or hiking. No services are available on-site. Roads can become impassable when wet.

Accessibility

Highway 12 and the Burr Trail within the Monument are paved and wheelchair-accessible. Other roads are improved or unimproved gravel, so are less accessible.

Camping and Lodging

Lodging is available in nearby communities such as Kanab, Escalante, Boulder and Tropic. Kodachrome Basin State Park and Escalante Petrified Forest State Park Campgrounds are located adjacent to the

Monument. Primitive camping is available within the Monument.

Food and Supplies

No services are available within the Monument. Services are available in the nearby communities of Kanab, Tropic, Escalante, and Boulder.

First Aid

No first aid is available within the Monument. The nearest hospitals are located in Page (Arizona), Panguitch, and Kanab. Limited medical services are available in Escalante.

Additional Information

It is recommended that visitors check with BLM before visiting the Monument.

Sponsor

Activity Codes

 -photography, horseback riding, mountain biking

Green River

Location
50 miles north of Vernal, Utah.

Description
The Green River flows east from Flaming Gorge Dam toward the Utah/Colorado state line. Along its shores, cottonwood bottoms provide habitat for wildlife. The cold, clear water is a blue-ribbon trout fishery and provides for various types of water recreation. Along the way, stop at the historic Jarvie Ranch to glimpse what frontier life was like, and take time to picnic or camp.

Mailing Address
BLM - Vernal District Office
170 South 500 East
Vernal, UT 84078

Phone Number	Fax Number
(801) 781-4400	(801) 781-4410

Directions
From Vernal, travel north for 45 miles on U.S. Highway 191. The launch point at Little Hole is at the end of a 5-mile paved road that turns off U.S. Highway 191, 0.3 mile east of Dutch John. The John Jarvie Historic Site is 16 miles downriver in Brown's Park.

Visitor Activities
Fishing, camping, rafting, hiking, wildlife viewing, swimming, canoeing, kayaking, exploring historic sites, and hunting.

Permits, Fees, Limitations
Permits are required for commercial floating only. Motors are not allowed. Fishing is limited to artificial bait only. All fish be-
tween 13 and 20 inches in length must be released. You may keep two fish under 13 inches and one fish over 20 inches. Check with the Utah State Division of Wildlife Resources for fishing and hunting license requirements (Tel.: (801) 789-3103).

Accessibility
Indian Crossing Campground has wheelchair-accessible toilets and 2 accessible picnic sites. John Jarvie Historic Ranch has a wheelchair-accessible picnic site and acces-

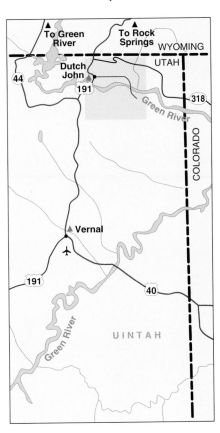

sible toilets. Bridge Hollow campground has wheelchair-accessible toilets.

Camping and Lodging

From the put-in point at Little Hole, any of 28 float camps can be accessed. Two campgrounds, Bridge Hollow and Indian Crossing, are each located 0.25 mile from the John Jarvie Historic Site. They are fee sites, and both have potable water. Swallow Canyon raft ramp is the last takeout from BLM-managed waters (a distance of 20 miles downriver from Little Hole). Lodging is available in Green River and Rock Springs, Wyoming; Maybell, Colorado; and Vernal, Manila, and Dutch John, Utah. To reach Rock Springs from Brown's Park, follow signs to U.S. Highway 191 and proceed north to Rock Springs. It is a distance of approximately 80 miles. To reach Vernal from Brown's Park, follow signs to U.S. Highway 191 and proceed south through Dutch John. It is a distance of 65 miles.

Food and Supplies

Gas, food, and supplies are available in Green River and Rock Springs, Wyoming; Maybell, Colorado; and Vernal, Manila, and Dutch John, Utah. Gas, food, and phone services are available at the Brown's Park Store in Colorado. Fishing gear, boat rentals, etc., are available in Dutch John and Manila, Utah, and in Green River, Wyoming. The Brown's Park Store is in Colorado, approximately 20 miles east of the John Jarvie Historic Site, just off Highway 318. Follow the signs.

First Aid

The nearest hospitals are in Rock Springs, Wyoming, and Vernal, Utah. Emergency medical technicians and an ambulance are available in Dutch John, Utah.

Additional Information

There are 10 Class II rapids between the Flaming Gorge Dam and Little Hole. There is 1 Class III rapid: Red Creek Rapid is between Little Hole and the Jarvie Historic Ranch. Fishing is usually best during the evening, when the level of the river is dropping. Life jackets must be worn. Extra gas for land vehicles should be carried for travel in the area.

Sponsoring Partners

Activity Codes

 - swimming, canoeing, kayaking

Brilliant skies illuminate vegetation lining the tranquil Green River as it flows through Brown's Park near the Flaming Gorge Reservoir. *(Photo by Frank Jensen, Moab District Office)*

John Jarvie Historic Site

Location
75 miles northeast of Vernal, Utah

Description
Experience a bit of the Wild West at the John Jarvie Historic Site in Brown's Park, a small mountain valley in the remote northeast corner of Utah. Originally used by mountain men and trappers for shelter in the early 19th century, Brown's Park was settled in 1880 by Jarvie, who operated a Green River ferry as well as a store and a post office. In addition to being a common stopping place for travelers, the area became known as an outlaw hideout frequented by Butch Cassidy and the Sundance Kid, Matt Warner, Isom Dart, and Ann Bassett, Queen of the Rustlers. Today, several historic structures are maintained by BLM, and the facility is open to the public.

Mailing Address
BLM - Vernal Field Office
170 South 500 East
Vernal, UT 84078

Phone Numbers
(801) 781-4400
(801) 885-3307 (John Jarvie Park Ranger)

Fax Number
(801) 781-4410

Directions
From Vernal (via Crouse Canyon), go north on Vernal Avenue to Fifth North, then east for 25 miles on Fifth North to Diamond Mountain and the signed turnoff to Brown's Park. Travel 16 miles north on an infrequently maintained dirt road to Brown's Park. There is a fork in the road at the bottom of Crouse Canyon, providing 2 travel options:

1) West (left) side of fork (jeep trail) - After approximately 10 miles, you will cross Taylor Flats, which is a sparse arrangement of cabins. After passing the cabin area, you will drop down to the Green River and cross the steel bridge. Turn left (west) and travel 0.5 mile to the historic site.

2) East (right) side of fork - Travel about 4 miles to the Utah/Colorado line, and another 1 mile to the Swinging Bridge. Cross the bridge (and it does swing!), and then proceed north about 4 miles to the paved state highway. Turn west (left) and proceed 8 miles to the historic sign turnoff. Proceed west 1 mile (upriver) to the historic site.

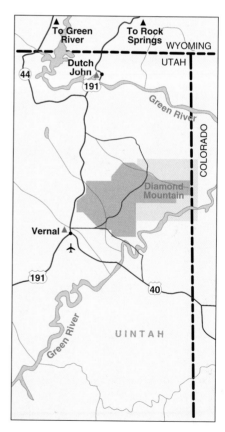

Visitor Activities

Camping, river rafting, and touring the historic buildings and property.

Permits, Fees, Limitations

Fees are charged for camping.

Accessibility

The parking area, restrooms, and some paths and structures at the John Jarvie Historic Site are wheelchair-accessible; however, the store and some other structures are not. The restrooms at both Bridge Hollow and Indian Crossing Campgrounds are wheelchair-accessible.

Camping and Lodging

Bridge Hollow Campground, operated by BLM near the John Jarvie site, charges a per-vehicle, per-night fee. Check with BLM for details. This facility has water and toilets and is open year-round. Indian Crossing Campground is being refurbished, and no fees are charged at this time. Also near John Jarvie, Indian Crossing is open year-round and features water, toilets, picnic tables and grills. Lodging is available in Green River and Rock Springs, Wyoming; Maybell, Colorado;

and in the towns of Vernal, Manila, and Dutch John, Utah. To reach Vernal from the historic site, follow signs to U.S. Highway 191 and proceed south through Dutch John. It is a distance of 65 miles. To reach Rock Springs from the historic site, follow signs to U.S. Highway 191 and proceed south to Rock Springs. It is a distance of approximately 80 miles.

Food and Supplies

Food and supplies are available in the towns of Green River and Rock Springs, Wyoming; Maybell, Colorado; and Dutch John, Manila, and Vernal, Utah. In addition, gas, food, and supplies, as well as telephone service, are available at the Brown's Park Store in Colorado. (Brown's Park extends into Colorado.)

First Aid

The nearest hospitals are in Vernal and Rock Springs. Emergency medical technicians and an ambulance are available at Dutch John.

Additional Information

Visitors should be aware that John Jarvie Historic Site is in a remote location with

Visitors can view 19th-century regional artifacts at this faithful replica of the original 1881 John Jarvie General Store. *(Photo by Garth Portillo, Utah State Office)*

an infrequently maintained dirt access road; trips should be planned accordingly. The site is open for tours from May through October each year. There is a resident Park Ranger. Ramps for launching river rafts are located along the river in Brown's Park. A permit is required for commercial rafts. Visitors should purchase gas, food and supplies for the entire trip prior to leaving the last town en route to the area. Carrying extra gas, tire chains, a shovel, and adequate food and water is recommended.

Sponsoring Partner

SOCIETY *for*
HISTORICAL
ARCHAEOLOGY

Activity Codes

Mule Canyon Ruin

Location
20 miles west of Blanding, Utah.

Description
Mule Canyon Ruin is a classic ancestral Puebloan (previously called Anasazi) archaeological site that has been stabilized and interpreted for the public. The site, displaying a kiva, small tower, and a room block, provides a close-up, convenient and casual view into the past without the crowds associated with some of the more prominent Four Corners ruins and monuments.

Mailing Address
BLM - San Juan Field Office
435 North Main
Monticello, UT 84535

Phone Number   Fax Number
(801) 587-1500   (801) 587-1518

Directions
From Blanding, travel south 3 miles on U.S. Highway 191. Turn west on State Highway 95. Drive approximately 20 miles through breathtaking country, crossing Comb Ridge and Comb Wash. The turnoff into the Mule Canyon Ruin parking area is well-marked on the highway.

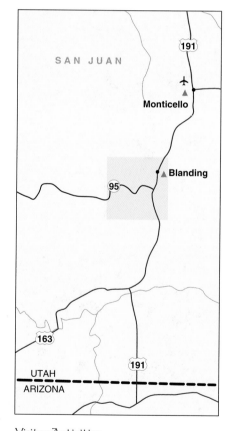

Visitor Activities
Scenic drives, hiking, biking, and historic archaeological ruins.

The Mule Canyon archaeological site offers visitors an opportunity to view a stabilized and interpreted Four Corners Anasazi ruin. *(Photo by Jerry Sintz, Utah State Office)*

Permits, Fees, Limitations
None

Accessibility
The ruin is wheelchair-accessible along a paved trail with a smooth gradient. At this time, however, the toilet facilities at the ruins are not wheelchair-accessible. The Comb Wash campground, about 14 miles away, has wheelchair-accessible vault toilets.

Camping and Lodging
Motel accommodations are available in Hanksville (100 miles southwest on State Highway 95), Bluff (25 miles south on U.S. Highway 191), Blanding, and Monticello. The closest BLM Campground is at Comb Wash, 14 miles west on Highway 95 between Mule Canyon Ruin and Blanding. The Comb Wash campground is primitive, with no water; however, vault toilets are available.

Food and Supplies
Food, supplies, and gas are available in Blanding.

First Aid
Emergency care is available in Blanding. The nearest hospital is located in Monticello.

Additional Information
State Highway 95 is open year-round, although roads may have snow or ice immediately after winter storms and may be difficult to access. The site is used primarily as a roadside rest and as an opportunity to view the ruins. There is a parking area

with restrooms and a paved trail to the ruin. A ramada covers the kiva to protect the structure from harsh weather; the site is interpreted with panels. No services are provided, and no water is available. The region is exceptionally popular from spring through fall each year. Travelers are encouraged to contact BLM or the Utah Travel Council for additional information.

Sponsoring Partner

SOCIETY FOR AMERICAN ARCHAEOLOGY

Activity Codes

 - biking, ruins

North Fork Virgin River Merriam's Turkey Viewing Area

Location
30 miles northeast of Springdale, Utah

Description
The North Fork Virgin River Merriam's Turkey Viewing Area consists of a stream that runs through small meadows interspersed with forest. Streamside vegetation is composed of cottonwood and willows, while uplands are primarily piñon-juniper and Gambel oak stands with scattered ponderosa pines.

Merriam's turkey are present in the general area year-round but are most commonly observed from May through August in meadows along the Virgin River. This area is within the Zion Turkey Unit, a spring gobbler turkey unit.

Mailing Address
BLM - Kanab Field Office
318 North 100 East
Kanab, Utah 84741

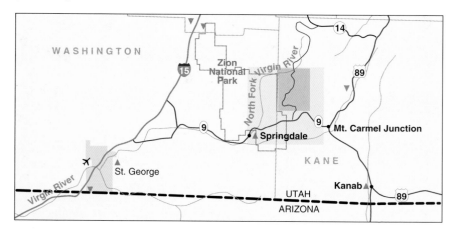

Phone Number
(801) 644-2672

Fax Number
(801) 644-2694

Directions
From Springdale, take State Route 9
through Zion National Park. Exit Zion at
the park's east entrance. Travel 2.5 miles
and turn north onto North Fork Road.
There are 8-10 miles of BLM land along
this road, and public lands are posted.

Visitor Activities
Wildlife viewing and hunting.

Permits, Fees, Limitations
No permits or fees are required. Hunters
are required to have a permit to hunt
turkeys in this and all other units in Utah.
Check with the Utah Division of Wildlife
Resources for current hunting license requirements (Tel.: (801) 538-4700).

Accessibility
There are no facilities on-site. Turkeys can
be observed from the roadside.

Camping and Lodging
The nearest campgrounds are at Navajo
Lake, located 25 miles north on State

Route 14 in the Dixie National Forest.
This U.S. Forest Service campground is
open during the summer only. Lodging is
available in Springdale.

Food and Supplies
Food and supplies are available in Mt.
Carmel Junction and Springdale.

First Aid
No first aid is available on-site. The nearest hospital is in Kanab, 25 miles southeast
on U.S. Highway 89.

Additional Information
The area is accessible from May through
September, but the North Fork road can
be impassable in wet weather and is closed
in the winter by snow accumulations.

Sponsor

Activity Codes

Pony Express National Historic Trail

Location
The eastern terminus of the Trail is located at Stagecoach Inn State Park, Fairfield, Utah, 55 miles southwest of downtown Salt Lake City. The western terminus
of the trail is located at Ibapah, Utah, 60
miles south of Wendover, Nevada.

Description
A trip down the Pony Express Trail is a
celebration of the beautiful desert setting

through which the route winds. It is an
opportunity to enjoy and explore the ro-
mance, vastness, history, and solitude of
America's outback. From Fairfield to Ibapah, the legendary road snakes south and
west across the Bonneville Basin of west-
central Utah. With 14 station sites, markers or ruins, spaced every 6 to 13 miles
along its course, the trail crosses broad valleys, ascends mountain passes, and serves as
the main street to small, isolated settle-

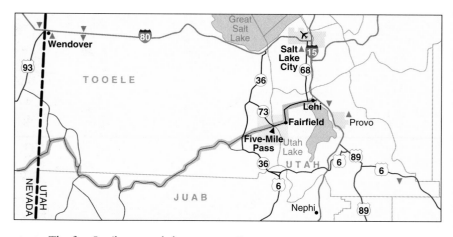

ments. The first 5 miles are asphalt, as are the last 2, but in between lie 126 miles of what the pioneers called "Piute Hell." The trail crosses hundreds of square miles — 2 million acres — of topographical extremes that showcase distant alpine forests, accessible desert hot springs, and a lifestyle reminiscent of America's Old West, now all but vanished. The exact route taken by the Pony Express riders is unknown. As historian John Husar describes the evolution of the trail: "Although a road winds from stop to stop, there's no guarantee that it actually was the trail. What kind of a path could be carved by two daily horses over 18 months? The riders were only kids who followed whims, avoiding dust, skirting patches of alkali mud, changing routes to avoid boredom. Sometimes they'd circle a rocky point; sometimes they'd climb a hill. Each kid found his most comfortable way."

Mailing Address
BLM - Salt Lake District Office
2370 South 2300 West
Salt Lake City, UT 84119

Phone Number   Fax Number
(801) 977-4300   (801) 977-4397

Directions
(To Fairfield): From downtown Salt Lake City, travel south on Interstate 15 approximately 30 miles to Lehi. Get off at exit 282 (Lehi), and proceed west on State Highway 73 (Lehi's main thoroughfare). Continue 5 miles west through Lehi to the junction of State Highways 68 and 73, then approximately 20 more miles west on Highway 73 to Fairfield and the Stagecoach Inn State Park. The Pony Express Trail Kiosk is in the southwest corner of the park grounds. To get to the trail's eastern end, continue west from Fairfield another five miles to the Five Mile Pass turnoff and the start of the Pony Express Trail dirt road. A large sign points the way west.

Visitor Activities
Scenic drives, camping, biking, hiking, photography, wildlife viewing, and viewing historic remains.

Permits, Fees, Limitations
There is a per-vehicle, per-night fee charged for camping at the Simpsons Springs Campground. Contact BLM for details. There is no charge for picnicking or for day use at the campground.

The restored structure of Simpson Springs Station, named for 1858 mail-route explorer Captain J.H. Simpson, is still considered a dependable desert watering hole on the historic Pony Express Trail. *(Photo by Jerry Sintz, Utah State Office)*

Accessibility

The vault toilet at the Pony Express Trail Kiosk site and the 3 vault toilets at the Simpson Springs Campground, 100 miles southwest of Salt Lake City, are all wheelchair-accessible.

Camping and Lodging

There are motels along Interstate 15, within 20 miles of the Pony Express Trail's eastern terminus (Fairfield). There are no motels at the western terminus (Ibapah). The closest motels to that terminus are in Wendover, Nevada, 60 miles north of Ibapah. To get to Wendover from Ibapah, take the unnumbered, unnamed paved road north 32 miles to State Highway Alternate [A] 93, and then travel an additional 26 miles north on Highway A93 to Wendover, Nevada.

Food and Supplies

Food and supplies are available at either end of the Pony Express Trail, in Lehi and in Wendover. Along the trail, gas and snacks are available at Vernon, 5 miles south of the intersection of the Pony Express Trail with State Highway 36, and occasionally in Ibapah. Travelers are encouraged to be prepared for a long drive with no services between Vernon and Wendover.

First Aid

There is no first-aid facility between Lehi and Wendover. There are first-aid-qualified government staff along the trail, but there is no facility. Hospitals are located in Tooele, 35 miles north of Vernon, and approximately 110 miles east of Wendover; in Salt Lake City, 120 miles east of Wendover; and in American Fork, one mile north of Lehi. There is also a medical clinic in Wendover. Air Med and Life Flight fly out of Salt Lake City in cases of emergency.

Additional Information

A portion of this route is paved; however, the greater length of the route is graded or graveled dirt road until pavement is reached again at Ibapah. The desert environment can be harsh. Extreme summer and winter weather is possible, with summer temperatures in excess of 100°F. Winter weather is often extremely cold, with snow and ice common. Spring and fall are typically more moderate. Plan ahead and be prepared. Road conditions vary with weather, and the road surface may be muddy and unstable in wet weather. Travelers are advised to carry adequate fuel, water, food, 2 spare tires (if possible), and other supplies for the entire trip. There is no place along the trail where a visitor can have a tire repaired. Visitors are also encouraged to carry at least a Utah State Highway Map. Those planning to camp on BLM-managed lands at undeveloped locations along the trail should have BLM 1:100,000-scale maps showing land ownership.

There are many sites of interest along the trail. Stagecoach Inn State Park in Fairfield is open from Easter through October. The original adobe structure is still standing here. Camp Floyd, established in 1858, is adjacent to Stagecoach Inn. This historic military installation once housed 3,000 troops. Simpson Springs Station is a restored structure closely resembling the original (circa 1860) station that was located on that site. There is no staff, but the Simpson Springs Campground is open year-round— it is the only campground on the Pony Express Trail.

Sponsoring Partner

SCENIC AMERICA

Activity Codes

-photography, biking

San Juan River

Location
3 miles west of Bluff, Utah

Description
There is something for everyone on this remote river in Utah's high-desert country. Bighorn sheep can be viewed along the river's south side, so remember to bring your binoculars. You can choose to run the upper 26-mile section from Sand Island to Mexican Hat, or the 58-mile section from Mexican Hat to Clay Hills Crossing. Or you can run the total length of 84 miles. You can also start your trip from Montezuma Creek upstream of Sand Island.

Mailing Address
BLM - San Juan Resource Area
P.O. Box 7
Monticello, UT 84532

Phone Number   Fax Number
(801) 587-1544   (801) 587-1518

Directions
From Bluff, travel 3 miles west along the Trail of the Ancients, U.S. Highway 191.

Visitor Activities

Rafting, sightseeing, geologic viewing, hiking, camping, archaeology, and wildlife viewing.

Permits, Fees, Limitations

A BLM permit is required to float any section of the San Juan River downstream of Montezuma Creek. A fee is charged for permits to float from Sand Island to Clay Hills Crossing from April 1 through October 31. The 17-mile portion of the river from Montezuma Creek to Sand Island also requires a permit, but there is no fee charged for this section. Check with BLM for details. The longitudinal center of the river marks the border of the Navajo Nation. Everything south of that, from Mon-

tezuma Creek to Clay Hills Crossing, is Navajo land. A Navajo permit is needed to camp and hike on this land. For permit information, call or write Navajo Parks and Recreation Department, P.O. Box 9000, Window Rock, AZ 86515, Tel.: (520) 871-6647, Fax: (520) 872-6637. Allow at least 30 days for the permit to be issued.

Accessibility

Wheelchair-accessible toilets are located at the Sand Island campground and at Mexican Hat.

Camping and Lodging

Although there are plenty of campsites on the upper portion of the river (Sand Island to Mexican Hat), share your campsite intentions with other river parties. If your group is small, leave the larger campsites for bigger groups. Campsites on the lower 58 miles of the river are limited, and it is necessary to register for 9 of the most frequently used sites from Slickhorn Gulch (mile 66) downstream. The register is in a metal box on the downstream side of Mendenhall Loop, 3.5 miles below the Mexican Hat bridge. At the 5 Slickhorn Gulch sites and the Grand Gulch campsite, only a 1-night stay is allowed from April 1 through October 31. Trimble Camp (mile 71.7), Oljeto Wash (mile 75.6), and Steer Gulch (mile 77.5) may be reserved for only 1 night from April 1 to July 10. There are other campsites available that are not on the register. Please use these sites if your group size allows. The registration system operates on a first-come, first-served basis, and you may not register ahead for other parties nor register for more than 1 campsite on any night.

Food and Supplies

Food and supplies may be purchased in nearby Bluff. Information about outfitter

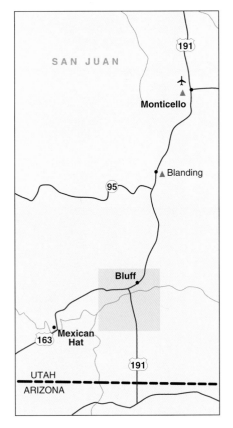

services, accommodations, and shuttles is available from the San Juan County Travel Council, 117 South Main Street, Monticello, UT 84535, Tel.: 1-800-574-4386 or (801) 587-3235.

First Aid

The nearest hospital is in Monticello, Utah, 50 miles north on US Highway 191.

Additional Information

The river corridor is quite remote, especially the lower 58 miles. Novice river-runners should always be accompanied by those who are more experienced. Life jackets are required. Although the river has been controlled by the Navajo Dam in New Mexico since 1963, its level can change rapidly as a result of thunderstorms and flash floods. Always tie your boat securely when stopping. The river moves surprisingly fast, and has some Class II and III rapids. Clay Hills Crossing is the last river takeout because there is a waterfall 3 miles downstream of this point. Water temperatures vary between 41° F in April to 67° F in July.

Bring drinking water. There are no reliable, potable sources of drinking water on the San Juan. During the summer, a gallon per person per day is recommended.

Pets are not allowed below Mexican Hat. If you must travel with your pet on the upper section, please leash it so it does not disturb wildlife or other boaters. Pack out all pet waste.

All boaters must use a washable, reusable, toilet system that allows for sanitary transfer of waste to a sewage-treatment facility. A non-formaldehyde chemical is recommended.

Sponsoring Partners

WILD SHEEP   AMERICA OUTDOORS

Activity Codes

 - geologic viewing, sightseeing

The San Juan River's sinuous course through Utah's high-desert country offers visitors satisfying whitewater in a remote wilderness environment. *(Photo by Jerry Sintz, Utah State Office)*

Westwater Canyon

Location
70 miles northeast of Moab, Utah

Description
The Westwater Canyon area provides a stretch of renowned whitewater opportunities for both rafters and kayakers. The black, uplifted rocks in the canyon represent the oldest exposed formations in eastern Utah. Many species of wildlife inhabit the canyon. There are also several historic sites along the river corridor. Heading west, this is the first canyon along the Colorado River within Utah.

Mailing Address
BLM - Moab District Office
82 East Dogwood
Moab, UT 84532

Phone Numbers
(801) 259-6111 (Moab District)
(801) 259-2196 (River Permit Office)

Fax Number
(801) 259-2106

Directions
From Interstate 70 in the area of Moab, take exit 225, Westwater. Turn east and travel on the paved road approximately 6 miles. Then at the main intersection, turn left and proceed another 2 miles to the Westwater ranger station.

Visitor Activities
River running, kayaking, wildlife viewing, camping, hiking, and exploring geologic, natural, and historic features.

Permits, Fees, Limitations
Because of the heavy demand for launches, permits and advance reservations are required for both commercial outfitters and private boaters to run this section of the river. The fee season is April 1 through November 1, with fees charged per person. Contact BLM for details. The permit application period is December 1 through January 31. Call the River Permit Office for more information.

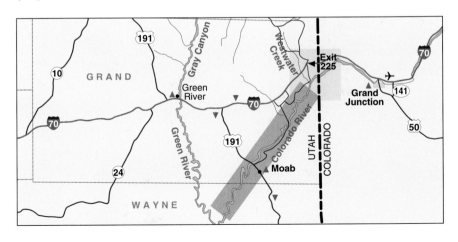

Whitewater rafters hurtle past Westwater Canyon's ancient black walls, home to a great variety of wildlife. *(Photo by Brad Frank, Moab District Office)*

Accessibility

Toilet facilities at the launch and take-out are not wheelchair-accessible. Many commercial outfitters are equipped to provide trips for those requiring special accommodations. SPLORE, a local outfitter, can accommodate visitors with severe disabilities and can be reached at (801) 484-4128 for further information.

Camping and Lodging

There are 10 campsites in Westwater Canyon, which are assigned at the ranger station at launch time. Camping is limited to 1 night, not to exceed a party size of 25. Camp assignments are made at the ranger station at time of check-in. Minimum-impact camping techniques are required; all solid waste must be packed out, and river-runner's toilets are mandatory. First-aid and repair kits are required, as well as an extra oar, air pump, fire pan, and personal flotation devices. Commercial lodging is available in Moab.

Food and Supplies

Food and supplies are available in Moab.

First Aid

There is no first aid on-site. The nearest hospital is in Grand Junction, Colorado, about 40 miles east on Interstate 70.

Additional Information

Only experienced boaters should pilot rafts through the canyon. Life jackets must be worn, as required under Utah State Law. The river is not suitable for open canoes. As a general rule, the river peaks at about 20,000 cubic feet per second (cfs) in late May or early June, and recedes throughout the summer and autumn months to reach a low of less than 3,000 cfs. The character of the river varies with each change in river flow. Some rapids are most challenging at high water, while others require greater skill at low water. Within Westwater Canyon, there are 11 rapids that range in difficulty from 1 to 9, on a scale where the most dangerous rapids have a rating of 10. The rapids of note are Funnel Falls, Skull, and Sock-It-To-Me. From the ranger station, it is approximately 17 river miles to the first available take-out point at Cisco Landing. In this distance, the river drops 125 feet.

Sponsoring Partner

Activity Codes

-kayaking, geologic interpretation

Woolsey Ranch Rio Grande Turkey Viewing Area

Location
10 miles west of Cedar City, Utah

Description
This viewing area comprises privately owned fields surrounded by BLM public lands. The BLM lands are primarily piñon-juniper hillsides with scattered patches of Gambel's oak. A small willow-lined stream bisects the area.

Turkeys are present in this area year-round, but are most commonly observed during the winter, when they spend much of their time feeding in the private fields along the highway. This area is within the East Pine Valley Turkey Unit, a spring gobbler unit.

Mailing Address
BLM - Cedar City Field Office
176 East D.L. Sargent Drive
Cedar City, UT 84720

Phone Number   **Fax Number**
(801) 586-2401   (801) 865-3058

Directions
From Cedar City, travel west on State Highway 56 (200 North in Cedar City) for approximately 10 miles. The turkey viewing area is on both sides of the highway.

Visitor Activities
Wildlife viewing and hunting.

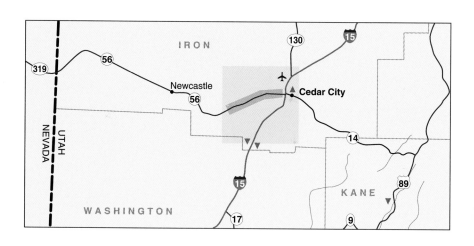

Permits, Fees, Limitations

No permits or fees are required to enter the area. Hunters are required to have a permit to hunt turkeys in this and all other units in Utah. Check with the Utah Division of Wildlife Resources for current hunting license requirements (Tel.: (801) 538-4700). Private lands may be posted: either view the turkeys from the roadside, or obtain permission from private landowners before entering their lands. Failure to respect the rights of private landowners could result in loss of public access.

Accessibility

None

Camping and Lodging

There are no developed facilities in the viewing area, but private camping is available in Cedar City at the KOA campground and at Country Aire Recreation Vehicle Park. There are also several motels in Cedar City.

Food and Supplies

Food and supplies can be obtained in Cedar City.

First Aid

First aid and the nearest hospital are in Cedar City.

Additional Information

Highway 56 is maintained year-round, but off-highway travel is often restricted by heavy snow in the winter.

Sponsoring Partner

Activity Codes

Wyoming's Split Rock Interpretive Site provides visitors a spectacular view of the Sweetwater Mountains, which appear today much as they did to 19th-century travelers on the Oregon Trail.
(Courtesy BLM)

Wyoming

High desert plains, sand dunes, badlands, and rugged mountains characterize the 18.4 million acres of public lands in Wyoming. Representing about 20 percent of the State, these public lands are concentrated in the western two-thirds of Wyoming, with small, scattered parcels throughout the state.

As they say in Wyoming, the state is "like no place on earth." The public lands managed by BLM offer exceptional recreational activities away from the crowd. Remote and primitive open spaces provide blue-ribbon trout fishing, world-class hunting, primitive camping, and exceptional caving, hiking, and snowmobiling. Although public lands offer mostly primitive recreational experiences, there are a number of developed sites with easy access.

Visitors to Wyoming's vast high plains and deserts stand a good chance of seeing pronghorn antelope, wild horses, and golden eagles. And the Whiskey Mountain Bighorn Sheep Area hosts the largest wintering herd of Rocky Mountain bighorn sheep in North America.

Wyoming's public lands help tell the story of the West through several interpretive sites. Some of the nation's most significant paleontological discoveries have been made on Wyoming's public lands, including the first fully articulated allosaurus, now in the Museum of the Rockies in Bozeman, Montana. Visitors will also enjoy historic sites, including Native American petroglyphs, emigrant etchings, as well as portions of trails used by settlers moving westward. Original wagon ruts along National Historic Trails, such as the Oregon Trail, can still be seen. Gold Rush buffs appreciate a visit to the South Pass Historic Mining District, which includes the ghost town of Miner's Delight.

With Wyoming's diverse geography and rich history, a visit to the Cowboy State will only confirm that the public lands, like Wyoming itself, are truly "like no place on earth."

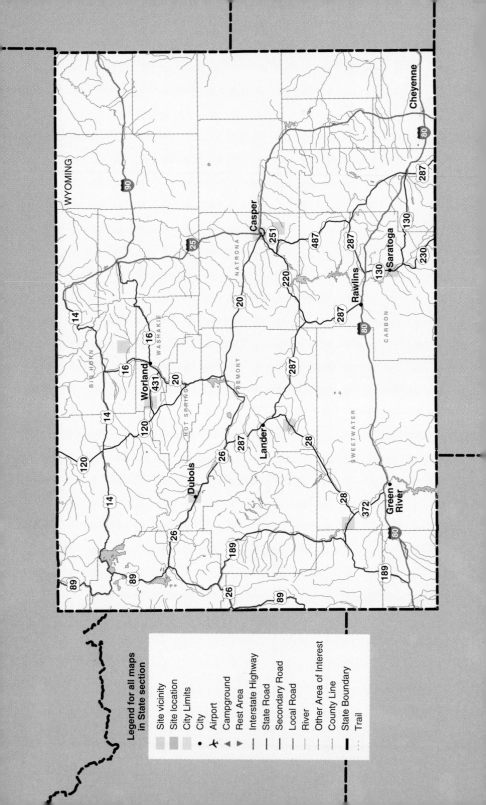

WYOMING

Cheyenne

Casper

Worland

Dubois

Lander

Rawlins

Saratoga

Green River

BIG HORN

WASHAKIE

HOT SPRINGS

FREMONT

NATRONA

CARBON

SWEETWATER

Legend for all maps in State section

Site vicinity
Site location
City Limits
City
Airport
Campground
Rest Area
Interstate Highway
State Road
Secondary Road
Local Road
River
Other Area of Interest
County Line
State Boundary
Trail

Gooseberry Scenic Interpretive Site and Hiking Trail

Location
30 miles southwest of Worland, Wyoming

Phone Number
(307) 347-5100

Fax Number
(307) 347-6195

Description
The Gooseberry Scenic Interpretive Site and Hiking Trail have been described as a miniaturized cross between the Painted Desert and the Grand Canyon of Arizona. Colorful and fabulously-formed rock formations inspire the imagination of visitors from around the world. Rock cairns mark the trail, and a BLM information sheet guides visitors. The information sheet has a trail map and information about each cairn location, and includes a plant and animal identification guide. The trail length is approximately 1.5 miles. There are ample photographic opportunities; early mornings and late afternoons provide the best pictures.

Mailing Address
BLM - Worland District Office
101 South 23rd
Worland, WY 82401

Directions
From Worland, travel south on U.S. Highway 20 for 7 miles. Turn west onto State Highway 431 (Gooseberry Highway) for about 23 miles. The turnout/parking areas are marked about 0.5 mile from either side of the site.

Visitor Activities
Photography, hiking, sightseeing, geologic sightseeing, rockhounding, and wildlife viewing.

Permits, Fees, Limitations
No fees. No motorized vehicles or bicycles are permitted.

Accessibility
The turnout and overlook are wheelchair-accessible. Trail development has been minimized to protect fragile resources; the overlook rim trail is dirt and of moderate difficulty for wheelchairs. The lower hik-

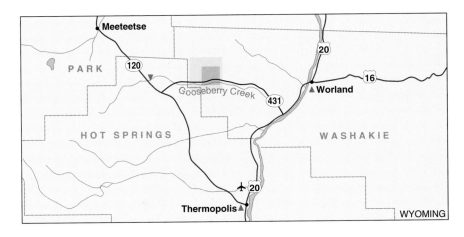

ing trail is accessible, but has the highest challenge level.

Camping and Lodging
Camping and motels are available in Thermopolis (39 miles west on Highway 431 and south on Highway 120), Worland, and Meeteetse (25 miles west on Highway 431 and north on Highway 120).

Food and Supplies
Food and supplies are available in Worland, Thermopolis, and Meeteetse.

First Aid
Worland and Thermopolis both have hospitals. There is no first aid available any closer.

Additional Information
This site provides a primitive recreational experience. The parking area provides parking for tour buses and other large vehicles. There are currently no facilities at this site. Rockhounds interested in fossils are only allowed to collect invertebrates. For more detailed information, contact BLM.

Sponsor

Activity Codes

 - photography, rockhounding, sightseeing

Green River

Location
Southwest Wyoming, near the towns of LaBarge, Fontenelle, Green River, and Kemmerer

Description
Although much of western Wyoming is sagebrush desert, the Green River provides other important habitats for a variety of wildlife, as well as excellent fishing for rainbow trout, brown trout, and kokanee salmon. Portions of the river flow through a broad, steep-sided valley with prominent rock formations along either side. The Green River in Wyoming is approximately 180 miles long, not all on BLM land.

Mailing Address
BLM - Rock Springs District
Highway 191 North
Rock Springs, WY 82902

Phone Number
(307) 352-0311

Fax Number
(307) 352-0329

Directions
From Green River, take State Highway 372 to the town of Fontenelle. There are 3 campgrounds there. To get to the Fontenelle Creek Campground, take State Highway 189 and travel approximately 4 miles to Fontenelle Creek.

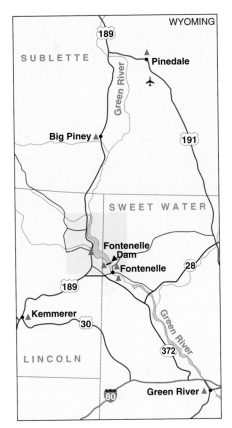

Visitor Activities

Hunting, hiking, wildlife viewing, bird-watching, plant viewing, boating, rafting, swimming, fishing, and picnicking.

Permits, Fees, Limitations

Fees are charged at the Fontenelle Creek Campground. The other campgrounds are free. Licenses are required for hunting and fishing, and are available at the Fontenelle camp store.

Accessibility

The following campgrounds are wheelchair-accessible: Fontenelle Creek, Weeping Rock, Tailrace, and Slate Creek.

Camping and Lodging

Camping is available at Fontenelle Creek, Upper Green River (north of Fontenelle Reservoir), and Flaming Gorge. There are motels available in Big Piney, Green River, Pinedale, Kemmerer, and LaBarge.

Food and Supplies

Food and supplies are available in Rock Springs, Green River, Kemmerer, Pinedale, and LaBarge.

First Aid

Hospitals are located in Rock Springs and Kemmerer. A first-aid clinic is located in Big Piney.

Additional Information

Visitors should be prepared for all kinds of weather.

Sponsoring Partner

Activity Codes

 - swimming, picnicking

Muddy Mountain
Environmental Education Area

Location
18 miles south of Casper, Wyoming

Description
The 1,260-acre Muddy Mountain Environmental Education Area (EEA) has 2 developed campgrounds and an interpretive trail system, as well as several miles of trails and roads that can be used for hiking, biking or equestrian activities.

Mailing Address
BLM - Casper District Office
1701 East "E" Street
Casper, WY 82601

Phone Number
(307) 261-7600

Fax Number
(307) 261-1525

Directions
From Casper, drive south approximately 9 miles on State Highway 251 to the top of Casper Mountain, where the state road ends and County Road 505 begins. Continue on this paved road for approximately 3 miles, where it turns into a maintained dirt road. Follow this road for 3 miles to its intersection with Circle Drive. A BLM gravel road begins here; a sign indicates that it is 4 more miles to the EEA.

Visitor Activities
Picnicking, hiking, mountain biking, and interpretive trail.

Permits, Fees, Limitations
There is a nightly camping fee from June to September.

Accessibility
The area within the campground loop road has approximately 2 miles of hard-surfaced, wheelchair-accessible interpretive trail for hiking. The main loop-road area has 2 developed campgrounds; Lodgepole Campground has 14 sites that have been upgraded with handicap-accessible picnic tables and concrete pad fire pits. Two vault toilets are located in this campground, but only 1 is wheelchair-accessible.

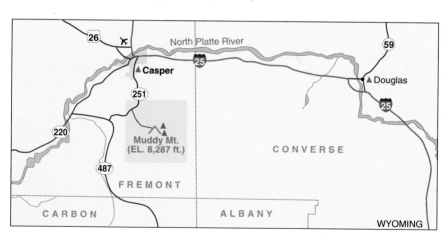

Camping and Lodging

There are 2 campgrounds, with a total of 20 camp sites. The Rim Campground is on the north end, and the Lodgepole Campground is on the south. Rim Campground has 6 campsites and 2 day-use sites, which may be used by large groups or families. A vault toilet is located within the Rim Campground. There is no potable water at this site. Both campgrounds sites are first-come, first-served. No reservations are taken.

Food and Supplies

Food and supplies are available in Casper.

First Aid

There is no first aid available on-site. The nearest hospital is in Casper.

Additional Information

Visitors should be prepared for all types of weather.

With extensive hiking trails, Muddy Mountain is a popular recreational and educational retreat for local residents and tourists alike. *(Courtesy BLM)*

Sponsor

Activity Codes

 - mountain biking, horseback riding, picnicking, interpretive trail

National Bighorn Sheep Interpretive Center and Whiskey Mountain Bighorn Sheep Area

Location

76 miles northwest of Lander, Wyoming

Description

The Interpretive Center provides an educational wildlife experience that highlights the local Rocky Mountain bighorn sheep herd, the largest wintering Rocky Mountain bighorn sheep herd in North America.

Mailing Address

BLM - Lander Resource Area
P.O. Box 589
1335 Main Street
Lander, WY 82520

Phone Number

(307) 332-8400

Fax Number

(307) 332-8447

Guarded by his off-camera mother, a young Rocky Mountain bighorn sheep grazes contentedly at Whiskey Mountain. *(Courtesy National Bighorn Sheep Interpretive Center)*

Directions
From Lander, take U.S. Highway 287 north 76 miles to the town of Dubois. The Center is located on Highway 287. Whiskey Mountain is located 5 miles southwest of Dubois.

Visitor Activities
Interpretive center, wildlife viewing, bird-watching, and plant viewing.

Permits, Fees, Limitations
There is a fee for admission to the Interpretive Center.

Accessibility
The Interpretive Center has wheelchair-accessible parking, restrooms, and interpretive exhibits.

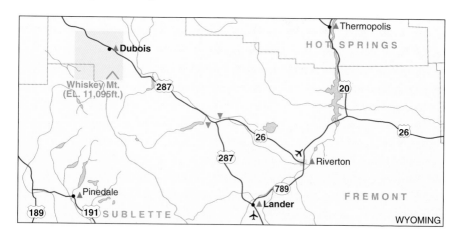

Camping and Lodging

Commercial campgrounds and motels are available in Dubois. Several private campground facilities are available at Ring Lake and Trail Lake, 8 miles southeast of Dubois.

Food and Supplies

Restaurants, groceries, and sporting goods stores are located in Dubois.

First Aid

There is a medical clinic in Dubois. Ambulance service and 911 emergency service are also available.

Additional Information

Warm days and cool nights are the norm for summer. Thunderstorms are common. In the spring and fall, snowstorms may occur. Winter storms can be severe. Winds are common throughout the year. The elevation of Dubois is 6,917 feet; the Whiskey Mountain area is 8,000-9,000 feet above sea level. From mid-November through March, privately-run tours to the Whiskey Mountain Bighorn Sheep Area are available from the Center (P.O. Box 1435, Dubois, WY 82513; Tel.: (307) 455-3429).

Sponsor

Activity Codes

 – interpretive center

North Platte River and Seminoe Reservoir

Location

Begins at the Colorado border, 27 miles southeast of Riverside, Wyoming and runs 122.5 miles north to Seminoe Reservoir

Description

The North Platte River is a popular fishery that traverses various terrains. The upper 20 miles run through rugged forest. The next 40 miles alternates between agricultural meadows and rugged sagebrush/ juniper communities. The rest of the river to Seminoe Reservoir is primarily rolling sagebrush hills and juniper breaks.

The North Platte River is a blue-ribbon "wild" trout fishery from the border all the way to the Pick Bridge access north of Saratoga, about 65 river miles. Seminoe Reservoir, 57 river miles north of Pick Bridge, is popular for its trout and walleye fishing, as well as boating opportunities.

All of this section of the North Platte River is floatable, but there are several rapids in the 13 miles just north of the border. The first 5 miles can be floated by raft or kayak only.

Mailing Address

BLM - Great Divide Resource Area
1300 North 3rd Street
Rawlins, WY 82301

Phone Number   Fax Number
(307) 328-4200   (307) 328-4224

Directions

The uppermost access point, nearest the border, is Six Mile Gap (on U.S. Forest Service lands): From Interstate 80, take State Highways 130 and 230 south 38 miles to Riverside, then go 23 miles southeast on State Highway 230 to the Six Mile Gap Access Road.

Other river access points are signed along the highways on the way to Six Mile Gap. As you head south on State Highway 130 from Interstate 80, look for access points at Pick Bridge, Foote, Saratoga, Treasure Island, Bennett Peak, and Corral Creek. Bennett Creek and Corral Creek are BLM river access points with campgrounds.

River access is also available at Fort Steele, 13 miles east of Rawlins on Interstate 80. Take the Fort Steele exit south to the east frontage road. Follow this to the dirt road that runs south along the river.

To access Seminoe Reservoir and the North Platte River north of Interstate 80, take the Sinclair exit west and follow County Road 351 north. It's about 8 miles to BLM's Dugway Recreation Site on the river and about 23 miles to Seminoe Reservoir.

The Miracle Mile, managed by the Bureau of Reclamation, is downstream of Seminoe Reservoir. It is a very popular fishery, which is about 5 miles long. To get there, continue on County Road 351 another 12 miles. These last 12 miles are extremely steep, and are not recommended for motor homes or vehicles that are towing trailers. The road is gravel and there is often no snow removal. Four-wheel-drive vehicles and chains may be required in winter.

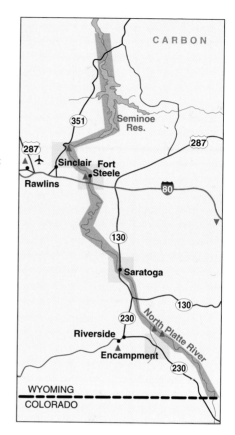

Visitor Activities

Fishing, rafting, wildlife viewing, plant viewing, birdwatching, picnicking, sightseeing, scenic drives, and hunting.

Permits, Fees, Limitations

No day-use fees. There are camping fees at Bennett Peak Campground. State hunting and fishing licenses are required.

Accessibility

Bennett Peak Campground has restrooms and campsites that are accessible to persons with disabilities.

Camping and Lodging

No hookups are available at public campgrounds. To get to camping facilities at Bennett Peak and Corral Creek, travel 4

Anglers come from miles around to try their luck on the North Platte River, famous for its blue-ribbon trout. *(Courtesy BLM)*

miles east of Riverside on State Highway 230, then travel 12 miles east on graveled County Road 660, then take BLM Road #3404 for another 6 miles to the river and campgrounds. Camping is also available at Dugway Recreation Site and various Wyoming Game and Fish and U.S. Forest Service sites. Lodging is available in the towns of Rawlins, Saratoga, and Riverside/Encampment.

Food and Supplies

Grocery stores and sporting goods are available at Rawlins, Saratoga, and Riverside/Encampment.

First Aid

No first aid is available at the river access sites. There is a hospital in Rawlins and a clinic in Saratoga.

Additional Information

Camping is best from June through September. Weather may be extreme at any time of year. Roads may be muddy and rough. County Road 351 between Seminoe Reservoir and the Miracle Mile is graveled and very steep in places, so it is not recommended for motor homes or trailers.

Sponsor

Activity Codes

 –sightseeing, picnicking

Oregon National Historic Trail Corridor Sites

Location
Throughout central Wyoming

Description
The Oregon Trail Corridor includes the Oregon, Mormon Pioneer, California, and Pony Express Trails. This corridor of overland routes was created by more than 350,000 emigrants as they traveled west. The year 1843 is recognized as the start of the Oregon Trail from Independence, Missouri; the trail is marked with hundreds of sites emblematic of the courage and hope of the people who traveled it. The Oregon Trail crosses what are now the states of Kansas, Nebraska, Wyoming, and Idaho, and ends in Oregon City, Oregon. Wyoming contains the middle span of the 2,000-mile-long trail. The Mormon Pioneer Trail in 1847, and the California Trail in 1848, generally followed the Oregon Trail, with some deviations through Wyoming, to their respective

endpoints in the Great Salt Valley, Utah, and Sacramento, California. The short-lived operation of the Pony Express followed this same corridor through Wyoming in 1860 and 1861. The trail corridor in Wyoming crosses a mixture of federal, state and private lands. Several of the important historic trail sites are located on BLM-administered public lands.

Mailing Addresses
BLM - Casper District Office
1701 East "E" Street
Casper, WY 82601

BLM - Lander Resource Area
1335 Main Street
P.O. Box 589
Lander, WY 82520

BLM - Rock Springs District Office
Highway 191 North
P.O. Box 1869
Rock Springs, WY 82903-1869

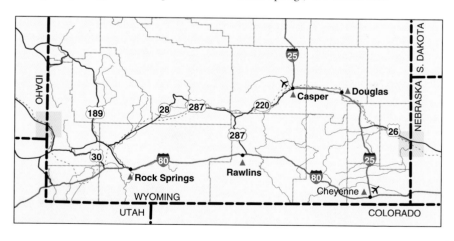

As Devil's Gate looms in the background, modern-day pioneers form a wagon train in celebration of the Oregon Trail's sesquicentennial anniversary. *(Courtesy BLM)*

Telephone Numbers
Casper District Office: (307) 261-7600
Lander Resource Area: (307) 332-8400
Rock Springs District Office:
(307) 352-0256

Fax Numbers
Casper District Office: (307) 234-1525
Lander Resource Area: (307) 332-8447
Rock Springs District Office:
(307) 352-0329

Directions
Contact BLM for detailed descriptions of, and directions to, historic sites within the corridor.

Visitor Activities
Historic interpretive sites, hiking, picnicking, photography, and scenic drives.

Permits, Fees, Limitations
Restrictions may exist for vehicle use along some trails. Check with BLM for details.

Accessibility
Devil's Gate, Split Rock, and South Pass interpretive sites have wheelchair-accessible paths. Devil's Gate and Split Rock also have accessible vault toilets.

Camping and Lodging
Camping and lodging are available in Casper, Glenrock, Douglas, Torrington, Lander, Rawlins, Rock Springs, and Green River. Most of these cities are located on Interstate 25 and Interstate 80.

Food and Supplies
Gas and groceries are available in Alcova, Muddy Gap, Sweetwater Station, and Lander, located on State Highways 220 and 287.

First Aid
Emergency services are available through local law enforcement. Hospitals are located in Casper, Rawlins, Lander, and Rock Springs.

Additional Information

The historic trails share a corridor and setting that appear much as they did 150 years ago. Federal, state, and private lands are intermingled along the various trail routes. Public access to sites along the corridor may be limited. Visitors are encouraged to contact BLM for detailed information prior to traveling the historic trail corridor.

Sponsoring Partner

 SOCIETY *for* HISTORICAL ARCHAEOLOGY

Activity Codes

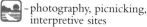 – photography, picnicking, interpretive sites

Red Gulch/Alkali Back Country Byway

Location

4 miles west of Shell, Wyoming

Description

This BLM-administered Byway runs alongside the western slopes of the majestic Bighorn Mountains. In traveling the 32-mile Red Gulch/Alkali Back Country Byway, you'll witness spectacular views of the area's unique geologic features and abundant wildlife, and you may catch a glimpse of its rich history. Information

kiosks at both Byway entrances highlight this back country road as an early transportation route.

Mailing Address
BLM - Worland District Office
101 South 23rd
Worland, WY 82401

Phone Number   Fax Number
(307) 347-5100   (307) 347-6195

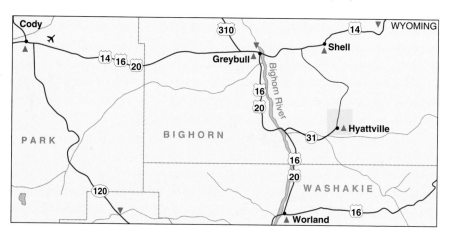

A rainbow of colors paints
the sky, mountains, and
vegetation at Red Gulch.
(Courtesy BLM)

Directions

From Shell, travel 4 miles west on U.S. Highway 14 to the northern end of the Byway. This Byway winds south for 32 miles and joins State Highway 31 just north of Hyattville.

Visitor Activities

Sightseeing, scenic drives, geologic sightseeing, birdwatching, and wildlife viewing.

Permits, Fees, Limitations

None

Accessibility

None

Camping and Lodging

Lodging is available in Worland (38 miles west on Highway 31 and south on State Highway 16/20).

Food and Supplies

Food and supplies are available in Worland and Greybull (8 miles west of the north end of the Byway on Highway 14).

First Aid

Cody and Worland have hospitals. Cody is 53 miles west of Greybull on Highway 14/16/20. There is an emergency care facility in Greybull.

Additional Information

The road may not be traveled by regular passenger vehicles. High-clearance vehicles are needed.

Sponsor

Activity Codes

 - sightseeing, geologic sightseeing

South Pass Historic Mining District

Location

25 miles southwest of Lander, Wyoming

Description

This 30-square-mile area was a focal point for the discovery of gold in 1842 and the resultant 1867 gold rush that settled this part of Wyoming. By 1868, about 1,500 people lived in the District towns of South Pass and Atlantic City, but by 1872 the boom was over and the area was all but abandoned. BLM maintains 2 campgrounds and the ghost town of Miner's Delight in the area. Other attractions in the vicinity are the South Pass City State Historic site, the Wild Iris world-class rock-climbing site, remnants of five National Historic Trails (the Continental Divide, Oregon, Mormon Pioneer, California, and Pony Express Trails), and a Volksmarch Trail.

Mailing Address

BLM - Lander Resource Area
P.O. Box 589
1335 Main Street
Lander, WY 82520

Phone Number

(307) 332-8400

Fax Number

(307) 332-8447

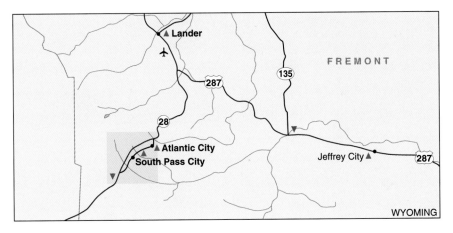

Directions
From Lander, take U.S. Highway 287 south for 8 miles. Take U.S. Highway 28 west for another 19 miles. Turn left on the Atlantic City Road (Fremont County Road 516) and proceed 2 miles to the townsite of Atlantic City. Other sites within the district can be accessed from here.

Visitor Activities
Picnicking, hiking, historic sites, fishing, hunting, wildlife viewing, scenic drives, mountain biking, and cross-country skiing.

Permits, Fees, Limitations
A nightly fee is charged at the 2 BLM campgrounds (Big Atlantic Gulch and Atlantic City). Licenses are required for hunting and fishing, and are available from licensing agents in Lander.

Accessibility
The BLM campgrounds have wheelchair-accessible sites and vault toilets.

Camping and Lodging
The BLM campgrounds are open from June 1 to October 15. Private accommodations are available in Lander and Atlantic City, and at the Rock Shop located 32 miles from Lander on U.S. Highway 28.

Food and Supplies
Groceries may be obtained in Lander. Restaurants are available in Lander, Atlantic City, and at Rock Shop.

First Aid
Emergency first aid is available from local law enforcement. A hospital is located in Lander.

Additional Information
Elevations in the area average 8,000 feet. Weather conditions in the summer generally produce warm days and cool nights, with the chance of thunderstorms. Snow showers can occur in the spring and fall. Winds are often present throughout the year. Winter storms can be severe.

Sponsor

Activity Codes

 - cross country skiing, mountain biking, picnicking

Century-old saguaros and craggy rock spires tower above Aravaipa Creek, a wilderness waterway that contrasts sharply with the surrounding Sonoran Desert. *(Photo by Diane Drobka © , Safford Field Office)*

Appendix A
Names and Addresses of BLM State and Headquarters Offices

Washington Office
(Headquarters)
Bureau of Land Management
Office of Public Affairs
1849 C Street, NW, LS-406
Washington, DC 20240
Telephone: (202) 452-5125
FAX: (202) 452-5124
http://www.blm.gov

Alaska State Office
222 West 7th Avenue, #13
Anchorage, AK 99513-7599
Telephone: (907) 271-5555
FAX: (907) 272-3430
http://www.ak.blm.gov

Arizona State Office
222 N. Central Avenue
Phoenix, AZ 85004-3208
Mailing Address:
P.O. Box 555
Phoenix, AZ 85001-0555
Telephone: (602) 417-9504
FAX: (602) 417-9424
http://www.az.blm.gov

California State Office
2135 Butano Drive
Sacramento, CA 95825-0451
Telephone: (916) 978-4610
FAX: (916) 978-4620
http://www.ca.blm.gov

Western Alaska's seldom-traveled Squirrel River offers visitors a Class I river float as well as superb fishing for Arctic grayling, northern pike and pink salmon. *(Courtesy BLM Northern District Office)*

Colorado State Office
2850 Youngfield Street
Lakewood, CO 80215-7093
Telephone: (303) 239-3670
FAX: (303) 239-3934
http://www.co.blm.gov

Eastern States Office
7450 Boston Boulevard
Springfield, VA 22153
Telephone: (703) 440-1713
FAX: (703) 440-1701
http://www.blm.gov/eso

Idaho State Office
1387 S. Vinnell Way
Boise, ID 83709-1657
Telephone: (208) 373-4013
FAX: (208) 373-4019
http://www.id.blm.gov

Montana State Office
222 N. 32nd Street
Billings, MT 59101
Mailing Address:
P.O. Box 36800
Billings, MT 59107-6800
Telephone: (406) 255-2913
FAX: (406) 255-2898
http://www.mt.blm.gov

Nevada State Office
1340 Financial Blvd.
Reno, NV 89520
Mailing Address:
P.O. Box 12000
Reno, NV 89520-0006
Telephone: (702) 861-6586
TDD Telephone:
(702) 861-6760
FAX: (702) 861-6602
http://www.nv.blm.gov

New Mexico State Office
1474 Rodeo Road
Santa Fe, NM 87505
Mailing Address:
P.O. Box 27115
Santa Fe, NM 87502-0115
Telephone:(505) 438-7514
FAX: (505) 438-7684
Public Lands Information Center (PLIC)
Telephone: (505) 438-7542
http://www.nm.blm.gov

Oregon State Office
1515 S.W. 5th Ave.
Portland, OR 97201
Mailing Address:
P.O. Box 2965
Portland, OR 97208
Telephone: (503) 952-6027
TDD Telephone: (503) 952-6372
FAX: (503) 952-6333
http://www.or.blm.gov

Utah State Office
324 South State Street, Suite 301
Salt Lake City, UT 84145
Mailing Address:
P.O. Box 45155
Salt Lake City, UT 84145-0155
Telephone: (801) 539-4021
FAX: (801) 539-4013
http://www.blm.gov/utah

Wyoming State Office
5353 Yellowstone Road
Cheyenne, WY 82003
Mailing Address:
P.O. Box 1828
Telephone: (307) 775-6011
FAX: (307) 775-6003
http://www.wy.blm.gov

Appendix B
Names and Addresses of Organizations that Selected Attractions for This Guide

America Outdoors
P.O. Box 10847
Knoxville, TN 37939
Telephone: (423) 558-3595
FAX: (423) 558-3598
http://www.americaoutdoors.org

American Bird Conservancy
1250 24th Street, N.W., Suite 400
Washington, D.C. 20037
Telephone: (202) 778-9666
FAX: (202) 778-9778
e-mail: abc@abcbirds.org

American Hiking Society
1422 Fenwick Lane
Sliver Spring, MD 20910
Telephone: (301) 565-6704
FAX: (301) 565-6714
http://www.outdoorlink.com/ahs

American Motorcyclist Association
33 Collegeview Road
Westerville, OH 43081-1484
Telephone: (614) 891-2425
FAX: (614) 891-5012
http://www.ama-cycle.org

American Rivers
1025 Vermont Avenue, N.W., Suite 720
Washington, D.C. 20005
Telephone: (202) 547-6900
FAX: (202) 347-9240
http://www.amrivers.org

California Association of
Four Wheel Drive Clubs, Inc.
3104 O Street, #313
Sacramento, CA 95816
Telephone: 1-800-494-3866
FAX: (916) 332-1730
http://www.cal4wheel.com

Ducks Unlimited
1 Waterfowl Way
Memphis, TN 38120
Telephone: 1-800-453-8257
FAX: (901) 758-3850
http://www.ducks.org

Foundation for
North American Wild Sheep
720 Allen Avenue
Cody, WY 82414
Telephone: (307) 527-6261
FAX: (307) 527-7117
http://www.iigi.com/os/non/fnaws/convent.htm

The Garden Club of America
14 East 60th Street
New York, NY 10022
Telephone: (212) 753-8287
FAX: (212) 753-0134
http://www.gcamerica.org

International Mountain
Bicycling Association
P.O. Box 7578
Boulder, CO 80306
Telephone: (303) 545-9011
FAX: (303) 545-9026
http://www.imba.com

The Izaak Walton League of America
707 Conservation Lane
Gaithersburg, MD 20878
Telephone: (301) 548-0150
FAX: (301) 548-0149
http://www.iwla.org/iwla

National Audubon Society
700 Broadway
New York, NY 10003
Telephone: (212) 979-3000
FAX: (212) 979-3188
http://www.audubon.org

National Geographic Society
1145 17th Street, N.W.
Washington, D.C. 20036
Telephone: (202) 857-7215
FAX: (202) 828-5460
http://www.nationalgeographic.com

National Wild Turkey Federation
P.O. Box 530
Edgefield, SC 29824
Telephone: (803) 637-3106
FAX: (803) 637-0034
http://www.hooks.com/nwtf/home.html

The Nature Conservancy
1815 N. Lynn Street
Arlington, VA 22209
Telephone: 1-800-628-6860
FAX: (703) 841-1283
http://www.tnc.org

Pheasants Forever
1783 Buerkle Circle
St. Paul, MN 55110
Telephone: (612) 773-2000
FAX: (612) 773-5500
http://www.pheasantsforever.org

Quail Unlimited
P.O. Box 610
Edgefield, SC 29824
Telephone: (803) 637-5731
FAX: (803) 637-0037
http://www.qu.org

Rocky Mountain Elk Foundation
P.O. Box 8249
Missoula, MT 59807
Telephone: (406) 523-4500
FAX: (406) 523-4550
http://www.rmef.org

Scenic America
21 Dupont Circle, N.W.
Washington, D.C. 20036
Telephone: (202) 833-4300
FAX: (202) 833-4304
http://www.transact.org/sa/scenic.htm

Society for American Archaeology
900 2nd Street, N.W.
Suite 12
Washington, D.C. 20002
Telephone: (202) 789-8200
FAX: (202) 789-0284
http://www.saa.org

The Society for Historical Archaeology
P.O. Box 30446
Tucson, AZ 85751
Telephone: (520) 886-8006
FAX: (520) 886-0182
http://www.sha.org

Trout Unlimited
1500 Wilson Blvd
Suite 310
Arlington, VA 22209-2404
Telephone: (703) 522-0200
FAX: (703) 284-9400
http://www.tu.org

Site Index

A BLM specialist gives a young student a hands-on
lesson about one of Utah's many wild plant species.
(Courtesy BLM)